GITĀ & BEYOND

A SPIRITUAL JOURNEY INTO HINDU PHILOSOPHY

PART I

Sarang Tilak

Clever Fox®
PUBLISHING
Chennai • Bangalore

CLEVER FOX PUBLISHING
Chennai, India

Published by CLEVER FOX PUBLISHING 2025

ISBN: 978-93-6707-744-3

Preface

by Dr. Deepak Tilak

Dr. Deepak Tilak is the great grandson of Lokmanya Bal Gangadhar Tilak and serves as the Chancellor of Tilak Maharashtra Vidyapeeth.

This book serves not only as an elucidation of the profound teachings of the Geetārahasya, or Karmayoga Shāstra by B. G. Tilak but also as a guide for understanding the path to self-realization and personal transformation. Following are some of my views and observations:

Geetārahasya, written by Lokmanya Tilak as the science of action; is a monument in Indian Moral philosophy. Philosophers and critiques like Shri Ādi Shankarāchārya, Madhvāchārya, and Vallabhāchārya commented on and interpreted Shrimad Bhagavad Gitā as a philosophy of detachment or withdrawal from action (Nivrutti or Sanyās). Lokmanya Tilak however, emphasized that on the battlefield of Kurukshetra, Arjun was demoralized to see his kith and kin among the enemy-warriors and was thus in extreme agony. He expressed his desire to withdraw and lay down his weapons and requested Lord Krishna to guide him in such a critical situation. He expressed his repentance in achieving the kingdom of Indraprastha for Swarājya.

Lord Krishna did not give consent to Arjun's request to withdraw from action as a warrior. Instead, Lord Krishna stopped Arjun from refraining from action and asked him to go to war, which was his social and ethical duty (Dharma) as a warrior.

It was believed that, like most Upanishads, Bhagavad Gitā also advocated resignation from action. Lokmanya Tilak did not agree with this interpretation because Gitā emerged in Mahābhārat times where the social system and family institutions were highly stable. In that period, concepts like Dharma (ethical action) and Adharma (unethical action), Good and Bad, Worthy and Unworthy etc. got deeply blended into the social fabric. Lord Krishna at the juncture of battle deliberated on the importance of performing action (karma).

Arjun by nature is knowledge itself. However, he raises several questions, which later have been answered by Lord Krishna. Gitā is in the form of a colloquy of knowledge, which applies not only to Arjun but also to people belonging to all religions and castes. Bhagavad Gitā after remaining inconspicuous for five thousand years re-emerged for making human beings action-oriented. Therefore, it provided an impetus to Lokmanya Tilak to write his commentary on Karmayog Shāstra, an action-oriented path towards attainment of oneness (Yog) with God.

Life is impossible without action. Even when a person remains silent, breathing continues. Bhagavad Gitā does not promulgate any particular religion but propounds the action-oriented society and following of Dharma to the world. It is the crux of Vedic Literature. It belongs to the entire human race. Lokmanya Tilak wrote his commentary on Gitā in Marathi Language so that it could percolate to the downtrodden sections and the masses of the society for their use. Other writings by Lokmanya are in the English language - except Geetārahasya. Lokmanya Tilak told all the Indian citizens to act instead of following inaction or Sanyās.

Human existence without Karma (action, function) cannot be imagined. Even in sleep, the function of breathing continues endlessly. Karma includes all types of actions – even remembrance (smaran), listening (shruti), routine Karma and occasional Karma. In the Karmayog Shāstra or Geetārahasya by Lokmanya Tilak, 'Yog' implies appropriate deployment of Karma wherein skill or proficiency is the best. Lord Krishna says to Arjun - "Arjun, employ your skill with maximum proficiency and diligence in executing the war-deed". Even the scholars, who preached inaction or Sanyās worked or acted to spread their thoughts in the society. In Bhagavad Gitā, the word Yog does not mean Pātanjal Yog, but it means performance of action.

However, the purity, righteousness or piousness of Karmayog has to be judged by the soul with its discriminating faculty. The method of this discrimination is the vital question posed to the entire human race.

In this preface, I encourage readers to explore the layers of meaning within Geetārahsya or Karmayog Shāstra by B.G. Tilak with patience and reverence. This book is not merely a word-for-word translation but a gist, which is written, in a clear and accessible language suitable for today's generation. This book helps you to translate complex philosophies into accessible concepts and has brought the ancient text of the Gitā into the modern consciousness with clarity and reverence. I wish the book and its author Shri. Sarang Tilak all the success in getting the recognition they deserve.

Dr. Deepak Tilak
Chancellor, Tilak Maharashtra Vidyapeeth
Editor & Trustee, Daily Kesari
Great Grandson of Lokmanya Tilak

Foreword by
Dr. Geetali Tilak

Dr. Geetali Tilak, who is the great, great granddaughter of Lokmanya Bal Gangadhar Tilak, serves as the **Vice-Chancellor of Tilak Maharashtra Vidyapeeth**, continuing the legacy of academic excellence and cultural preservation established by her family. Their efforts in preserving heritage and promoting progressive ideas have made an indelible mark on Indian society.

Gitā & Beyond: A Spiritual Journey into Hindu Philosophy, penned by Sarang Manohar Tilak, is a profound exploration of the timeless wisdom of the Bhagavad Gitā, presented with remarkable depth and clarity. Drawing inspiration from Lokmanya Tilak's seminal work *Shrimad Bhagavad Gitā Rahasya*, the book does justice to its core message by examining deeply into the philosophy of Karmayog, or the path of selfless action, as a guide for leading a purposeful and balanced life. Tilak expertly navigates the diverse interpretations of the Gitā by renowned scholars like Adi Shankarāchārya and Rāmānujāchārya, offering a comparative analysis that highlights the rich diversity of Hindu thought.

The book stands out for its meticulous verse-by-verse translation, enriched with detailed footnotes that make the ancient text accessible to modern readers. Tilak's engaging narrative seamlessly connects the spiritual teachings of the Gitā with contemporary dilemmas, demonstrating its relevance in today's complex world. By emphasizing the practical application of Gitā's principles, the author encourages readers to embrace their duties with detachment and equanimity, making this work a valuable resource for both spiritual seekers and those interested in Hindu philosophy. With its blend of scholarly rigour and relatable insights, Gitā & Beyond is an essential read for anyone looking to deepen their understanding of Gitā's enduring message.

Gitā & Beyond

A Spiritual Journey into Hindu Philosophy

Shree Ganeshāya Namah.

Om Tat Sat.

Shrimad Bhagavad Gitā, or simply *Gitā* as it's more popularly known worldwide, is one of the most important scriptures of Hindu philosophy. It forms one part of the *Prasthānatrayi* or Three texts to go through (consisting of *Upanishads, Vedānta Sutras/Brahma Sutras* and *Gitā*) which are unanimously established as the three pillars of Vedic Hindu philosophy. It has since become mandatory for any sect or any religious/philosophical branch of Hinduism to prove that the opinion held by their sect finds unanimous agreement with all three of these pillars. Any opinion not finding agreement with these was considered trivial or unacceptable by the Vedic followers of the time. Till date, there have been numerous interpretations, critiques, commentaries, studies and summaries of Gitā done by various authors, ranging from the 8th century great Ādya Shankarāchārya to 13th century Maharashtrian Sant (Saint) Dnyāneshwar. There have been many others before that as well but due to unavailability of any written evidence, most efforts to find them have been inconclusive. Likewise, there have been many more subsequently. However, they're more or less just adaptations or blends of the already made commentaries.

Although all these commentaries are written by great scholars of unparalleled knowledge and intelligence, they're mainly written to prove how their respective sect/community is the one proposed in the Prasthānatrayi and hence end up being communalistic and partial, to some or great extent. Bāl Gangādhar Tilak, or Lokmānya Tilak as he's most popularly known, read all these commentaries with his tremendous command over multiple languages and still found inadequacies or disagreements with them and wanted to understand the true essence of Gitā himself. He, with his own analysis of Gitā and with almost every other document available in Sanskrit, Marathi or English globally about Gitā, philosophy, religion or ethics, has written this magnificent manuscript called Geetārahasya athavā Karmayogshāstra which is one of the most (if not *the* most) comprehensive and pragmatic commentary on Shrimad Bhagavad Gitā written in Marathi language. Reading this gem of a book made me meditate greatly over this book again and again and made me dive deep into Hindu philosophy and do a comparative study. It also made me delve into the profound spiritual inquiry through the context of Gitā and Geetārahasya.

Let us understand the context of the Gitā first. The epic Mahābhārat (originally called Jaya meaning victory, later Bhārat and finally Mahābhārat) is the longest epic poem in the world consisting of 100,000 shlokas or verses, if we go by its most widely accepted current version. It entails the story of Kuru dynasty. The story of the 'Great War' forms the heart of the epic and the entire history of the dynasty forms the backdrop and side stories. There are 18 parvas or books of the epic and Gitā is found in the Bheeshma Parva (sixth). Gitā (literal: a song) was sung by Bhagwān Sri Krishna to Arjun before the start of the great war, Mahābhārat. Sanjay, an assistant of the blind king Dhrutarāshtra, was lent divine powers by the great sage Vyās to see/hear the proceedings of the war and paraphrase the same to the king as he couldn't witness them by himself. The Gitā that we follow currently (and has been so since the last 1500 years at least) is the retelling of the conversations between Shri Krishna and Arjun by Sanjay to Dhrutarāshtra. It consists of 700 shlokas or verses divided among 18 Adhyāyas or sections. Of these, 1 shloka is from Dhrutarāshtra, 40 from Sanjay, 84 from Arjun and 575 from Bhagwān Shri Krishna.

Before the beginning of the war, Arjun is perplexed by the thought of fighting his own teachers, kith and kin. He says that his limbs give up, mouth dries up, his body starts trembling and he gets goosebumps by just thinking about the imminent slaughter of his close ones he'd end up doing if he chooses to participate in the war. If the path of winning the war and reclaiming the kingdom is riddled with such violence and sins, he doesn't want it at all. He wants to renounce everything and go live away in a forest. It is then that he seeks advice from Shri Krishna to solve his dilemma. Shri Krishna then elaborately imparts the great knowledge to him and it's very well known how Arjun gets ready for the war after listening to his words of wisdom. None of the existing commentaries conclusively explain why this convincing of Arjun for the war involves discussion about Moksha (liberation) through knowledge or devotion. Reading the Gitā and countless other books/epics directly or indirectly related to it over and over again helped Lokmanya Tilak, and through him me, to arrive at the conclusion which is narrated through this entire book. For a person who has extreme attention to detail, the experience of reading this book would be rewarding due to its meticulousness and the range of concepts covered in it. I would go to the extent of saying that if you read this book carefully with patience and rapt attention, you don't need any other book to grasp the entire Hindu philosophy and you'd even learn a word or two about everything in history of the world related to ethics, philosophy and life in general.

I thought of writing a treatise which shall try to capture the essence of Gitā and Geetārahasya. It is obvious that a writer of minor talent like me wouldn't be able to do justice to the gems that both these pieces of literature are, and I make no claims of trying to grapple with their greatness. However, I started writing this because I would love more and more people to get a glimpse of these great works of literature through my book and get inspired. With people's attention spans fast approaching the flapping time of a hummingbird, reading such huge books seems like a thing of the past. To top it, the literature is in Marathi and Sanskrit. It is filled with many difficult jargons which were very difficult to comprehend even for me, despite having a decent background in reading such literature since childhood. With almost all caring parents getting their kids admitted in an English medium school, the potential readers for the original texts are sadly becoming few and far in between. This motivated me to write this book in English and I have made full efforts to make sure that the book is comprehensible for a person without much knowledge of Marathi or Sanskrit. I have also tried to capture as much as possible from the original texts and added a few things with my little understanding of these concepts. I hope this book finds resonance with the readers of today and even if a small percentage of them understand what Lokmānya Tilak and essentially Bhagwān Shri Krishna wanted to convey, I'd consider myself privileged. I also thoroughly loved the essence of Gitā as captured and restated by Mr. Tilak and that's one of the major reasons why I felt like retelling his version of it in my words.

The book is in two parts: The first part has an in-depth analysis of Gitā and many other texts of Hindu philosophy as well as global literature on this and other related topics from the point of view of arriving at the conclusive essence of Bhagavad Gitā. The second part is a verse-by-verse translation of the entire 700 shlokas (verses) with many footnotes to elaborate on the meaning. While the readers can independently read both parts separately, I'd insist on reading the book through the flow for a more rewarding experience.

I'd like to state here that the copy of the original book (Geetārahasya) that I read (an eighth edition printed in 1963) originally belonged to my Great Grandfather Mr. Damodar Hari Tilak and was preserved by my grandfather and father till date. I'm forever indebted to them for enabling me to read the book. I chose to begin reading and then just couldn't stop, although finding quality time to sit quietly and read this meticulously written book needed patience and a lot of efforts.

I'd love to thank my lovely wife Shirin, without whose urge and encouragement, writing this book wouldn't have been possible. She's the reason I could survive the long process of writing, editing and proofreading. I'd like to thank my father, Manohar Tilak, for reading the first draft and suggesting valuable changes wherever necessary. I'd also like to express my thanks to the 'Bhagavad Gitā Commentary by Swāmi Mukundānanda' which helped me while capturing the meaning of many words during verse-by-verse translation. I humbly bow down to my spiritual Guru, Āchārya Mahendranāth, who has influenced my life in more ways than imaginable. Finally, I'd like to thank you readers for blessing me by taking up to read this puny effort at writing by an amateur author like me.

Om!

Sarang Tilak

7th March 2022

Table of Contents

Chapter 1. Vishayapravesh (Prologue) ... 1
Chapter 2. Karmajidnyāsa (Passion for Knowing Karma Or Action) ... 12
Chapter 3. Karmayogshāstra (the Doctrine of Action-Oriented Yog) ... 19
Chapter 4. Adhibhautik Sukhvāda (Corporeal Hedonism) ... 31
Chapter 5. Sukhadukkhavivek (Comparative Scrutiny of Happiness and Sorrow) ... 39
Chapter 6. Adhidaivatpaksha Va Kshetrakshetradnyavichār (Theology/Institutionist School and Discussion of Body and Soul) ... 51
Chapter 7. Kāpilsānkhyashāstra Kinva Ksharāksharvichār (Kāpilsānkhya Philosophy and Discussion of Impermanent and Permanent) ... 64
Chapter 8. Vishwāchi Ubhārni Va Sanhārni (Birth and Death of the Universe) ... 76
Chapter 9. Adhyātma (Spirituality) ... 90
Chapter 10. Karmavipāk and Ātmaswātantrya (Fruition of Karma and Freedom of Soul) ... 120
Chapter 11. Sanyās and Karmayog (Asceticism and Action-Oriented Yog) ... 137
Chapter 12. Siddhāvasthā Va Vyavahār (Enlightened State and Way of Life) ... 163
Chapter 13. Bhaktimārg ... 176
Chapter 14. Geetādhyāyasangati (Sequential Account of Gitā) ... 192
Chapter 15. Upasanhār (Epilogue) ... 206
Chapter 16. Appendix Chapter: Geeteche Bahirangpareekshan (Peripheral analysis of Gitā) ... 220

CHAPTER 1

Vishayapravesh (Prologue)

Shrimad Bhagavad Gitā is one of the most radiant and pure diamonds that our sacred Hindu texts are. It's unique in its way of explaining the deepest and most mysterious of principles in a clear and concise way, thereby calming a confused mind that might have strayed away from the path of righteousness with many confusions and apparent contradictions. It also distinctively unites the paths of devotion and knowledge and collectively links it to practical aspects of life. It almost creates a roadmap for a conscious human being to follow. It's no surprise then that it has been translated in almost all Indian languages and major global languages including Greek, Latin, German, French and English. It captures the essence of all Upanishads. In fact, the full name of Gitā is 'Shrimad Bhagavad Gitā Upanishat' which indicates the link very clearly. At the end of every Adhyāya or section, there's a line – "Iti Shrimadbhagvadgeetāsu Upanishatsu Brahmavidyāyā Yogashastre Shrikrishnārjun Samvāde". Although this line isn't there in Mahābhārat, it's there in every copy of Gitā ever found which means it must've been added whenever Gitā was separated from Mahābhārat for individual learning and recitals. The meaning and importance of the entire line shall be covered in subsequent chapters later. Now, we just need to note the 2nd and 3rd word. Although the word Upanishat belongs to the neuter gender in Marathi, it is feminine in Sanskrit. This is the reason why even the shorter version of Shrimad Bhagavad Gitā became Bhagavad Gitā or Gitā for short and not Geetam as it would have if it weren't for the word Upanishatsu next to it. The two words mean the Upanishat sung by Shrimad Bhagwān. As indicated by the connection, Gitā aptly captures the core of all Upanishads and unifies the message in a clearer and more comprehensible form.

As you may know, the Bhagavad Gitā which most of us know isn't the only one with the name Gitā attached to it. There have been several imitations, summaries or versions with little or no difference from the original. Most notable is the Anugitā which comes in a subsequent Parva of Mahābhārat itself. After the war, while sitting and chatting with Shri Krishna, Arjun says that he has forgotten the knowledge that Shri Krishna gave him before the war and he wants to listen to it all over again. At this juncture, Bhagwān Shri Krishna who's the incarnation of the almighty himself says he can't repeat the same knowledge exactly as it was done at that time with a lot of immersion. This goes to show what importance it carried even in the eyes of Bhagwān Shri Krishna. Other than this, there are many small sub-chapters in Shānti Parva of Mahābhārat with names such as Pingal Gitā, Hāreet Gitā, Vrutra Gitā, etc. There are also a few more such as Avdhoot Gitā, Ganesh Gitā, Brahma Gitā, Yama Gitā, Rām Gitā, Shiva Gitā, Soorya Gitā etc. which are famous. Some of these are separate treatises while some are part of some Purānas (vast genre of Indian literature covering legends and traditional lore). Anyway, all these versions upon analysis point to the same thing that they've been composed well after the original Bhagavad Gitā became famous. Some are not worthy of noting while some others are praiseworthy. Even among these, nothing unique or new appears to have been communicated which the original Gitā has not covered. Thus, they end up enhancing the significance of the original even more. As the original Gitā shone through these auxiliary versions, pundits from Vedic community considered it their primary responsibility to understand, interpret and explain its meaning to others.

Analysis of any book is mainly of two types: Peripheral and Central. Studying the semantics of a book with focus on details such as who's written it, where was it written, how poetic does it sound, which meter is it tied up in, is it grammatically correct, which references it has through which we can decide its period, whether it's an original or it has been inspired from some other book etc. form the peripheral analysis. Central analysis, on the other hand, covers going through the entire book to decipher the secret, core idea, implication or any hypothesis that the book is aimed at making. Most ancient analysts have focused on covering the central part as doing a peripheral analysis of Gitā would be like counting the petals of a beautiful flower or counting the lines of an intricately beautiful carving. It's not that these details aren't important. They may be important from botanical or archaeological point of view and hence our book also covers a brief peripheral analysis of Bhagavad Gitā in a separate chapter at the end.

While seeking guidance regarding how to decipher the true meaning or the central idea of Gitā, we must turn to the great pundits and gurus who have delved deep into this ocean of knowledge. The first and foremost among them are the authors of Mahābhārat. We could call them the authors of the contemporary Gitā in a way; as they have weaved the whole epic together, not just the Gitā. Let's first see briefly what they have to say about Gitā.

Words like Bhagavad Gitā or the song sung by Bhagwān sufficiently point to the fact that Gitā is considered to belong to the Bhāgwat tradition because Shri Krishna has been called Shri Bhagwān often in the Bhāgwat tradition. While Gitā says: "This preaching isn't new; it's been given by Bhagwān to Vivaswān, through to Manu and to Ikshvāku" (Gitā 14.1-3); Bhāgwat or Nārāyaneeya tradition (described in detail in Shānti Parva of Mahābhārat) also says that this Bhāgwat institution has been communicated in the Vivaswān-Manu-Ikshvāku lineage. As these two lineages agree exactly between Gitā and Bhāgwat tradition, along with the fact that same lineage wouldn't be communicating different institutions, it's pretty clear that the institution of Gitā and that of Bhāgwat tradition are one and the same. Not just this but there are several other anecdotes which clearly say that this Bhāgwat tradition has been described with rituals in the Bhagavad Gitā. This description also states: "This Nārāyaneeya sect avoids reincarnations and is a giver of Moksha (liberation) and it's action-oriented as well". Thus, it is clear that the teaching given to Arjun is considered action-oriented by Mahābhārat authors. Vaishampāyan also tells Janamejay "I've similarly described to you the renunciative sect of the ascetics in the Bhagavad Gitā". However, Manu-Ikshvāku lineage in the Gitā doesn't match the renunciative sect of the ascetics at all. It finds agreement with the Bhāgwat sect, however. Thus, it's clear that Mahābhārat authors mainly consider Gitā to be action-oriented and not renunciative.

We saw what the take of Mahābhārat authors is. Now let's see what the critics and commentators of Gitā have to say about it. It's important to note the difference between a Critique and a Commentary. The two words are often used interchangeably, although they're not the same. A critique is mainly a decoding of the words in the book/poem with a simplification of the crypts in it whereas a commentary doesn't stop at that but does a complete analysis of the whole book and comments their own views on the moral or essence of the book. The Shānkarbhāshya or Commentary by Shankar, written by Ādi Shankarāchārya is considered one of the ancient manuscripts today. This is mainly because the commentaries on Gitā before Shānkarbhāshya and after Mahābhārat are not available and the efforts to find them have yielded no result. However, Shankarāchārya himself states in his own book that the commentaries before him interpret the meaning of Gitā as Action-oriented and as Dnyān-Karma-samucchayātmak, a blend of Knowledge and Action. Before understanding how Shankarāchārya interpreted Gitā, it is important to note the historical accounts. Vedic Dharma (loosely translated as Vedic Religion although Dharma is different from the traditional meaning of religion) is not just ritualistic. A lot of thought had been given to understand the true philosophy of Dharma in Upanishads.

However, Upanishads are numerous and written by various rishis (sages) over a long period of time and appear contradictory at times as well, when read in isolation. To eliminate these contradictions and unify all the Upanishads, Bādarāyanāchārya authored Vedānta Sutras. These Vedānta Sutras (or Brahma Sutras/Shāreerak Sutras as they are alternatively called) are considered gospel as much as the Upanishads. However, the Vedic philosophy wasn't complete yet as like Upanishads the Vedānta Sutras are renunciative and don't cover the action-oriented aspect. Therefore, when Bhagavad Gitā completed this gap, it became as significant as the other two and finally Upanishads, Vedānta Sutras and Bhagavad Gitā came to be called as Prasthānatrayi which form the ultimate trio of Vedānta.

Shrimad Ādya Shankarāchārya (born Shaka 710 or 788 A.D.) was a great scholar and guru originally from southern India who was instrumental in challenging and successfully defeating the Buddhist and Jain philosophies' dominance throughout the Indian subcontinent. He famously founded 4 Maths or Institutes in four cardinal directions of the land and reinstated the Vedic sect in the Kali Yug. Any sect has two main parts; one of philosophy and the other of behavior. While the first part of his sect deals with knowledge of the self and the universe, deliberation about the ultimate and what Moksha or liberation is; the second part deals with how to achieve Moksha and what should a person's behavior on a day-to-day basis be, so as to succeed on this path. There are mainly 3 principles of the sect which are Advaiti or monistic: (1) I, You, the visible universe or the varied substances are not real while a single pure and permanent Parabrahma or Absolute spans the entire universe. (2) Human Ātmā (self) resembles the absolute and (3) Complete and experiential knowledge of the unity between self and absolute is the only way to attain Moksha. This is called Advaita vāda (Monist or Non-dualist school). In order to attain this Moksha, Shānkar sect in addition to Advaita Vedānta philosophy also proposes asceticism as the important characteristic. It says that even if one follows the 4 Ashrams or stages of life as proposed in the Smruti (literally that which is remembered), Moksha isn't achievable unless one renounces every action. It says that as Action and Knowledge are like night and day, one cannot achieve knowledge of the absolute without renouncing desire and action. It also gives provisional references from Gitā to support its preaching, viz. "Dnyānāgnih Sarva Karmāni Bhasmasātkurute" (Gitā 4.37) – Fire of Knowledge reduces all action to ashes or "Sarva Karmākhilam Pārth Dnyāne Parisamapyate" (Gitā 4.33) – All action ends in knowledge. Shankarāchārya said that the action-knowledge blend claimed to be in Gitā is ancillary and is simply means to an end, which is knowledge. The entire Shānkarbhāshya is written to prove that Gitā was told to Arjun for emphasizing the importance of renunciation as the only means of attaining Moksha. His successors such as Madhusudan were mainly inspired by his work. Some weirdly proposed that one of the gospels of Advaita Vedānta – Tat-Tvam-Asi, which means You (Shwetaketu) Are That (Absolute), is the one proposed through the 18 Adhyāyas but the sequence is not as in Tat-Tvam-Asi but rearranged as Tvam-Tat-Asi and each is described in 6 Adhyāyas each. Then there are some misunderstood commentaries such as Paishāch Bhāshya. It is believed to have been written by Hanumān himself but is actually written by a certain Hanumān Pandit much after Shānkarbhāshya and even borrows from it.

Once started, this tradition of interpreting Gitā and the others from Prasthānatrayi became a norm with some notable ones being as follows:

1. Shri Rāmānujāchārya (born Shaka 938 or 1016 A.D.) – Vishishtādvaita or Specific Advaita which denied the Advaita philosophy proposed by Shankarāchārya and said that while Jeev (self), Jagat (Universe) and Ishwar/Parabrahma (Almighty/Absolute) are different, self and the universe both belong to the body of Ishwar. It claims that the gross innumerable selves and the gross universe have evolved from the subtle self and subtle universe and that this is what is proposed in the Prasthānatrayi. In fact, he was the reason for introducing Vishishtādvaita to Bhāgwat tradition. Being from the Bhāgwat tradition, ideally, he should've seen the action-oriented nature of Gitā. However, as the original Karma Yog (Yog of action) in Bhāgwat sect had vanished before his time and it had become predominantly devotional, he couldn't see the Dnyān-Karma-Bhakti (Knowledge-Action-Devotion) triumvirate actually proposed in Gitā. He thus ended up claiming that devotion is the central route proposed in Gitā while Karma Yog (Yog of Action) is ancillary to Dnyān Yog (Yog of Knowledge) and not separate. It ended up proposing ultimate devotion to Vasudev as the only thing to do (in place of renunciation) thus rendering any other Karma (action) meaningless and thus being indirectly renunciative. While his opposition to Māyāmithyavāda (considering the whole world as unreal) had some merit, treating the Absolute and the Self as

same in some aspects while different in others, is contradictory and proved to be self-defeating.

2. Shri Madhvāchārya (Shaka 1119 or 1197 A.D. – Shaka 1198 or 1276 A.D.) – Dvaiti Sect which considers the Absolute and the Self as different. It says that although Nishkām Karma Yog (Action without desire) is proposed in Gitā, that is a means to an end which is ultimate devotion and thus Bhakti (devotion) supersedes everything as the ultimate tool for Moksha.
3. Shri Vallabhāchārya (born Shaka 1401 or 1479 A.D.) – Shuddhādvaita which although disagrees with Vishishtādvaita and Dvaita sects in considering Parabrahma (Absolute) and Jeev (self) as the same, it treats Māyā (Universe) not as unreal but a power separated from the Absolute by the will of the Absolute. It claims that the Self is to Absolute what thousands of sparks are to the fire. As Jeev (self) dependent on Māyā needs knowledge which is unattainable without devotion, devotion is the ultimate tool for Moksha.
4. Nimbārka (circa Shaka 1084 or 1162 A.D.) – Dvaitādvaiti Sect which although considers Jeev (Self), Jagat (Universe) and Ishwar (Almighty) as different, considers the interaction between Jeev and Jagat as wished by Ishwar and says that Ishwar has the minute principles of Jeev and Jagat ingrained in it.
5. Sant (Saint) Dnyāneshwar (Shaka 1197-1218 or 1275-1296 A.D.) – One doesn't need to reject Advaita and Māyā vāda to explain Bhakti (Devotion). This is proven by the saints and sages of Maharashtra who have existed from before Shankarāchārya's time. Sant Tukārām and Shridhar Swāmi have been some notable greats who've chosen and propagated the path of devotion, finding agreement in Gitā. However, the best treatise on Bhagavad Gitā from this sect has to be Dnyāneshwari, an exposition written in Marathi language. Sant Dnyāneshwar has written that he wrote this commentary 'while seeking directions from the commentators (mainly Shankarāchārya)'. However, the art of explaining the essence of Gitā through various eloquent examples, propagation of 'Bhakti' path and to some extent Nishkām Karma (Action without desire) makes Dnyāneshwari a uniquely independent commentary on Gitā.

Sant Dnyāneshwar was a yogi and thus emphasizes on Pātanjalyog (mentioned in the 6th Adhyāya of Gitā) and declares it the king of paths to attain Moksha.

All these communalistic commentaries declare the Action-oriented path proposed in Gitā as auxiliary and claim that paths proposed by their respective (ultimately renunciative) sects as the central idea of Gitā. They claim that theirs is the principal and final path preached by Bhagwān Shri Krishna to Arjun. Looking at all these different commentaries, it is natural for a reader to ask a question: How is it possible that so many different conclusions can be drawn from the same ancient poem? Even if possible and considered correct, what could be the intention behind it? Gitā isn't some riddle or a mystery that people can draw separate meanings from it. It was told by Shri Krishna to Arjun for clearing his confusion and indecision, not to increase it. It has a very clear and definite advice given to Arjun (Gitā 5.1,2) and it has had the desired impact on Arjun. Why then is it that there is so much confusion? The answer is seemingly difficult, but actually isn't. Consider this: Looking at a sweet and appetizing dessert, one might say it's made from flour, other from butter or another from sugar. All are correct as per their taste and still different from each other. We still don't know what the dessert is. There are many different desserts we can make using these same ingredients and even by debating whether it's made from flour, butter or sugar we don't get the answer to the question of what the dessert is. Just as one might get a thousand different things from the ocean, none of them truly describe the actual nature of the ocean. Such is the case of different commentators of this gem called Bhagavad Gitā. Barring the interrelationship between Jeev (Self), Jagat (Universe) and Ishwar (Almighty), most other concepts are identical across these different sects. They also decipher 90 out of 100 shlokas the same way. Difference lies in the remaining 10% and if we take straightforward meaning then it wouldn't be favorable to most sects. Owing to this, each sect treats shlokas favorable to them as principal and others as auxiliary or smartly twists the meaning of shlokas disapproving their beliefs.

If we treat this communalistic method of analysis as wrong, we must provide an alternate and apt way. Mimāmsaks (Followers of 'Mimāmsā' or Critical Investigation school of Hinduism) are considered the masters of interpreting any book, epic or poem and they describe seven tools of interpreting any literature. They are as follows:

1. Upakram (Beginning)
2. Upasanhār (End): Anyone begins writing a book with a particular intention in mind and ends it after achieving the motive. Just like in geometry a straight line is defined as the line that travels from one point to the other without bending anywhere, we should accept that interpretation which sits perfectly between the beginning and the end. All others should be considered non-straight or incorrect.
3. Abhyās (Literally study but contextually means Recurrence): After deciding the direction, we must see what idea has been recurring throughout the book. Author often reestablishes their intended idea by proving it definitely through different anecdotes.
4. Apoorvatā (Uniqueness): No author began writing a book unless they had something unique to propose or put forward (at least before the invention of printing). One must identify this unique feature of the book while drawing interpretation from it.
5. Phal (Intended Result): Generally, an author or a poet writes something with some intended result in mind and thus looking at the results of a literature we could strengthen our argument about its interpretation.
6. Arthavāda (Supplements): Arthavāda is a Mimāmsak jargon. Although having firmly decided what to communicate, author writes supplementary things during the flow of explanation to show similarity or differences, putting forward a point, as a figure of speech, to show connection, for some other reason or sometimes even without one. They could further be classified as factual (anuvāda), opposite (gunavāda) and miscellaneous (bhootārthavāda). One should often learn to ignore or take with a pinch of salt these supplementary inserts.
7. Upapatti (Proof): To prove a point, one puts forth a systematic sequence of statements for and against the argument. This proof,

similar to the one we use in theorems or theories, comes in handy while drawing interpretation of any literature.

Using these 7 tools of Mimāmsaks we can interpret any literature. To this, one could argue whether the great Gurus and Āchāryas were unaware of this Mimāmsak method. While one might know the method, when the intention of a commentator is to prove the relevance of their own sect through the interpretation; they tend to bend these checkpoints blinded by the need to establish congruence between the two philosophies. This observation is not limited to Gitā or just Hinduism but for commentaries on all books across the world, religious, philosophical, legal or otherwise.

If we objectively look at the Gitā without a communalistic view, we see that it is told by Shri Krishna to Arjun on the eve of the battle when he was perplexed by conflicting thoughts and to dissuade him from his decision to renounce and walk away from the righteous war he was supposed to fight and win. Looking at the imminent annihilation of own and rival army, both of which contained his kith and kin, brothers and cousins, uncles and gurus, friends and relatives he desisted from the duty-bound decision of war and was plagued by indecision. In this baffled state of mind, he turned to his charioteer, friend and adviser Bhagwān Shri Krishna who then solved his dilemma through the teaching of Gitā and brought him back to his senses. Subsequently, Arjun fought and won the war. If we are to interpret Gitā as it is, it should follow the beginning, the end and the intended result. Neither did Krishna want to teach Arjun the path of attaining Moksha through Bhakti (Devotion), Dnyān (Knowledge) or Pātanjalyog through renunciation; nor did he want to make Arjun go to the mountains following asceticism or to replace his bow and arrow with musical instruments to dance his way through the battlefield in devotion. There are many places in Gitā where Krishna uses words such as "Hence, go to war", "Thus, get up and ready yourself for war", "Therefore, quit desire and do your duty" or "Remember me and fight". Even in the concluding Adhyāya, Shri Krishna most definitively says "One must perform all these actions" and extracts a reply from Arjun confirming that he's come out of his indecision. Not only through words but also through action, Arjun proves this by fighting the war and killing Gurus and relatives by following his Dharma.

Even after this, there are weak arguments still refusing to agree that Nishkām Karma (action without desire) and Karma Yog (Action-oriented path) as tools to attain Moksha are proposed in Bhagavad Gitā. There are also many Eastern or Western authors who, through their commentaries, agree with this central idea. However, none of them have analyzed it through the point of view of Karma or action and explained in detail how all arguments and Adhyāyas fall in place with justification. This book aims to do so. However, before doing so, we shall understand the contradictory thoughts and moral ambiguity without which it is not possible to appreciate the true essence of Gitā. Situations with questions such as "To be or not to be" and how a person gets confounded in such situations is the topic of discussion in the forthcoming chapter.

CHAPTER 2

Karmajidnyāsa (Passion for Knowing Karma Or Action)

At the start of the Bhagavad Gitā, Arjun became perplexed with conflicting emotions. The situation that he represents isn't exactly new. It's different for people who renounce and live away in a forest or for those who tolerate everything happening to them. However, for those who want to live righteously and diligently while performing their duties, such experiences are plentiful. Similar indecision plagued Yudhisthir, the eldest brother of Arjun, after the Great War while cremating his relatives. Many poets and playwrights have also drafted many exquisite works of art picking up such incidents from the past or conceptualizing them. Hamlet is one such famous example in which the Danish prince faces the legendary dilemma of "To be or not to be". How in absence of a philosopher guide like Shri Krishna he almost goes mad and dies a sad death is at the heart of this world-famous play written by the legendary playwright William Shakespeare. Coriolanus is another play by Shakespeare which explores similar indecision faced by an exiled Roman soldier when he faces his own mother and wife when he joins the enemy and attacks Rome. Our ancient and modern history is dotted with countless such examples as well. Why go far, Mahābhārat itself is a treasure-trove of such incidents. Vyās, the sage credited with authorship of Mahābhārat himself says this with pride about the epic: "Yadihasti tadanyatra yannehasti na tatkwachit" – That which is here is elsewhere while that which isn't here is nowhere else. It encompasses Dharma Shāstra, Artha Shāstra and Moksha Shāstra; the treatises related to Righteousness or law, wealth or economics and

Moksha or liberation. [The word Shāstra in Sanskrit can be equated to the word doctrine or –logy in English e.g. Biology is Jeevashāstra, Chemistry is Rasayanshāstra]. It narrates, through medium of storytelling, the behavior of great individuals during times of moral dilemmas and conflicts. Otherwise, we didn't need 100,000 shlokas to describe the war story.

One may argue why we need to delve so deep in matters of philosophy. Our ancestors have laid out through classical literature the golden rules of how to live an ideal life. Isn't it enough? Follow non-violence, respect the elders, don't steal, never lie etc. are the moral guidelines given by most religions and following them is enough. Counterargument to this is that unless everyone in the world starts living by this code, it's always a conflict whether to live by the code and get duped by the sly selfish people or to counter them by following tit-for-tat principle. Further, even if we follow all the ideal codes of conduct, we often come across situations where two or more such codes are found applicable simultaneously and also conflicting each other. Then we find ourselves at crossroads and in a baffled state mulling over which action to take.

Manu, through his famous Sanātan Neetidharmas (eternal morals) has given five codes common for all, irrespective of which class you belong to. They are: Ahimsā (Non-violence), Satya (Truthfulness), Asteya (Non-stealing), Shucham (Purity of body-speech-mind) and Indriyanigraha (Control over the senses). Let us take the first one, non-violence. It is unanimously considered a major value across religions. Non-violence isn't just about not killing someone but it means not hurting or harming any living being. It is unarguably a great virtue. However, shall one be sticking to non-violence if faced by a life-threatening attack, a rapist trying to rape their spouse, someone trying to burn your house down or to steal everything you possess? Should one be non-violent or should they punish the attacker? Even Manu has indicated that one must kill such person irrespective of who they are. As pointed out by Arjun in Shānti Parva of Mahābhārat, even blinking one's eye might mean killing of microorganisms. What then is the point of crying out non-violence? This is justified by the

Brāhman-Vyādh samvāda (dialogue between a Brāhman and a butcher) where the butcher tells the Brāhman how every living being depends on another for food and how that kind of violence is inevitable. Further, if there are no protective warriors or police to enforce law and order, anyone could attack and steal from anyone. Similar is the case with mercy, peace and forgiveness. One must maintain a balance of rage and forgiveness. However, it's critical to know when to be angry and when to be forgiving and the essence of how to choose.

Another unanimously chosen virtue is of truthfulness. It's said that before there was Mother Nature, there was Rutam and Satyam (the cosmic law and the ultimate truth). All the five elements and the universe as we know it, came from this Truth. Such is the supremacy of Truth described in the sacred texts. Truth is said to singlehandedly beat a thousand displays of might and power. However, even truthfulness faces a dilemma in certain situations. If you see a group of peasants hiding in a bush to escape the bandits and you're asked by the following bandits of their whereabouts, do you stick to truthfulness or lie to the bandits in order to save the innocent? Saving innocents from persecution is said to carry equal weightage as truth in philosophy. Manu says: "Don't say anything unless asked for. If someone's asking through injustice, don't answer. Even if you know, just keep nodding and save the day. Isn't nodding along the same as lying in a way? About such incidents of coercive unjust interrogation, Bhagwān Shri Krishna tells Arjun in Karna Parva and later tells Yudhisthir in Shānti Parva: "If you can save yourself by not speaking then don't open your mouth at all. If silence would be doubted and you must speak, then in such incidents lying is more appropriate than being truthful". "Saying the truth is appropriate, however universal welfare shall prevail over truth", says Nārad to Shuka. This is because truthfulness isn't just literal. The behavior which is for the universal welfare is superlative and utterance of truth shall not be the deal breaker. That truth which damages the welfare of all is neither true nor non-violent. Hearing the phrase 'Universal welfare' one might say it's inspired from Western materialism so let me state here that it's used multiple times in Mahābhārat and the dating of Mahābhārat is undeniably way before the origin of Western materialism. Even in case of the famous phrase "Naro wā kunjaro wā" (I don't know if it was the man or the elephant) which Yudhisthir said at a critical point during the war where he forced Drona into a predicament; it was the same logic of lying for the greater good. Our Dharma doesn't ask us to lie in order to protect the wicked. British author Green, in his famous book 'Prolegomena to ethics' on moral philosophy says all ethics stays mum in incidents like this. Manu and Yādnyavalkya call these incidents as 'exceptions to the truth'. However, they still treat it as a mistake and suggest penance. Some British who aren't amused by exceptions to non-violence have tried to denigrate our moral code. However, there are countless examples from British literature and religious texts where it's considered pardonable to lie when it's for the spread of religion. New Testament has Paul saying "If my lies help the spread of truth (translated as spread of Christianity), how can it be considered sinful"? Many priests follow this, according to Millman, a historian of Christianity. No religion would pardon lies said in order to deceive but they'd also agree that truthfulness isn't without exceptions. Henry Sidgwick, whose 'Methods of ethics' is often considered a modern guide to ethics, also says under the utilitarian method (promoting everyone's well-being) that it is ok to lie to a child, mad, ill (if truth shall damage their health), enemies, thieves, unjust and by advocates while practicing law. John Stuart Mills, Leslie Stephen, Bain, Whewell etc. have similarly described exceptions to truthfulness under different such circumstances. Our scriptures have said, "Jokingly, with women, at your wedding, to save your life and to save your wealth are the five times it is not sinful to lie". This doesn't mean our scriptures encourage lying to women but it's said for exceptional circumstances. However, British authors who have done away with spirituality and transcendence have gone one step ahead and rendered lying for profit pardonable. Moreover, our scriptures advise reparations even for such accepted lies. This is because even though justifiable, lying is considered partly sinful. E.g. After the "Naro wā kunjaro wā" incident, Yudhisthir, whose chariot was said to hover over the ground, had it grounded as a consequence of this lie and had to spend a brief time in hell as well. There are more such incidents mentioned across Indian literature.

However, identification of such incidents when a lie trumps truth is very minute and difficult to decide.

Asteya (non-stealing) is another such code or rule which finds such rare incidents where it's considered pardonable. E.g. If a person is starving to death and can't get food by straightforward means, it is believed to be justifiable to steal in order to survive. Contrary to this, death is considered inevitable and great pride has been shown in sacrificing life for patriotism, righteousness, glory, to save someone's life etc. For a common man, it might become confusing to make a choice in the situation they face as the history seems to be full of (apparent) contradictions. To answer such questions, spirituality is inevitable.

Deifying of mother, father and teachers is yet another principle. It's a commonly known expression: "Matru Devo Bhava, Pitru Devo Bhava, Āchārya Devo Bhava" which means Mother is God, Father is God and Teacher is God". While it is widely accepted and followed religiously, there are incidents where exceptions are found. E.g. If you're a king and even if your father is found to be guilty of a sin, you are expected to punish him. Here, duty to your kingdom is considered superior over duty to your father. In cases where a child attains a higher stage of knowledge, they are considered fit to teach even their elders including father. Even Gautama Buddha accepts this as correct, saying maturity just by age isn't worthy enough as much as a maturity by knowledge, truthfulness and non-violence. Buddha considers a new monk worthy of sitting on a pedestal and preach knowledge to elder or senior monks if he's mature and worthy. At the same time, someone insulting their guru, elder or father except under such circumstances is strongly condemned. A warrior who kills someone for their vile, unjust and condemnable acts is considered righteous even if the person is their guru.

Indriyanigraha (Control over senses) is yet another virtue. Kāma (Lust), Krodha (Anger), Lobha (Greed) are considered enemies of humans by all scriptures and even Gitā states so. However, in another verse Shri Krishna calls himself the Kāma that is in line with the Dharma. The answer to this is like this, Kāma (lust) requisite for procreation is essential and all living beings on the earth would cease to exist without it and there would be no reincarnations of Ishwar ever. The key is to pursue these in moderation. E.g. Bhāgwat states: "You don't need to preach someone towards intercourse, alcohol or eating flesh. However, in order to moderate these, there are marriage, Somayāg (A particular sacred fire) and Sautramani (another sacred fire). Similarly, righteous anger is justified and so is greed as even an ascetic is greedy for Moksha.

Similar to such contradictions, sages have advised sensibility of time and space to be applicable to these virtues as well. E.g. Bravery is a virtue fit for adversities, forgiveness in the hands of a capable leader, eloquence in an assembly and bravery in battles. Even though generousness is a virtue, a donor who doesn't look at the need of the receiver and donates indiscriminately isn't considered wise. In addition to this, era or epoch is also considered critically relevant to display of certain attributes. So, Dharma changes its guise as per the times we live in. Some social restrictions were absent in ancient times which are moderated now. Thus, we shall assess Dharma as per the period in which it was practiced and not identically across times.

Anyway, if we attempt to solve all such perplexities, we'd have to write another epic as big as Mahābhārat. The intention of this chapter was to show how Arjun's situation wasn't exceptional or unusual. Many greats have been plagued by indecisiveness or predicaments time and again; sometimes between non-violence and self-defense, sometimes truth and universal well-being and some other time between survival and glory. Common codes or rules don't work or show the right way always. Even greatest of human beings face difficulty in deciding which action to take. There are, however, minute differences between when exceptions shall be made and when rules shall be followed. Some incidents such as life-threatening events are where choice is relatively clear. However, many incidents don't have such clear distinction between the two options where both choices justify separate virtues or codes where precise judgment is critical. Some choices could be made using past examples while some have no answers in history. More we think, more become the contradictions and more difficult is the choice. If you consider, the discussion of decision making between right and wrong or just and unjust is a separate discipline in itself and is more complex than grammar or law. There are numerous questions about many acts of historic personalities which are difficult to judge. How did five Pāndav marry a single lady, Draupadi? Why did greats like Bheeshma and Drona sit idle while Draupadi was being undressed? Why did they not quit their post rather than serving Duryodhan's side? The answers to this are very tough as views are highly subjective. Not only "Sookshma Gatirhi Dharmasya" (Principles of Dharma are minute) but "Bahushākha Hyanantika" (branches of it are numerous as well). Mahābhārat authors were well-versed with this Dharma Shāstra (here as principles of ethics) and they've written Mahābhārat to illustrate to us all these examples as it was vital to describe the essence of it in the epic. This essence is described by Vyās in the form of 'Bhagavad Gitā' in Mahābhārat and thus Gitā has become the jewel in the crown and Mahābhārat has become the elaborate description of Gitā with numerous examples. To the critics who claim Gitā to have been interleaved in Mahābhārat as an afterthought, we strongly advise paying attention to this aspect. Although there are many other texts on attainment of Moksha, there's hardly any other document in history which is as apt and precise as Gitā, which solves such predicaments using complex philosophies from Vedānta. Thus, there are many before and many after but Bhagavad Gitā is magnificently unique!

CHAPTER 3

Karmayogshāstra (the Doctrine of Action-Oriented Yog)

If one doesn't have a longing to know something, they're unfit for gaining the corresponding knowledge. Trying to impart that knowledge to them is like watering a fallow land. While the recipient doesn't learn anything, the guru unnecessarily wastes time and effort. "Athāto Brahmajidnyāsa" (Let's now begin the quest of Brahman) or "Athāto Dharmajidnyāsa" (Let's now begin the quest of Dharma) are sentences that thus aptly appear at the start of Vedānta Sutra and Jaiminiya Sutra respectively. The deeper meaning of this is, after you've proven your passion to gain the knowledge (of Brahman or Dharma), now let's begin the quest of it. Similarly, only someone who has Karmajidnyāsa (or passion for knowing Karma) should begin the quest of Karmayogshāstra. While we did Athāto (softly opening the topic) in the first chapter, we covered Karmajidnyāsa in the second by explaining the importance of Karmayogshāstra. Only someone who's faced a difficulty understands the importance of tricks to get out of difficult situations. Arjun faced a predicament whether to kill his own kith and kin or not. Taunting him with the threat of losing a place in heaven or calling him weak didn't provoke him for war. This is when Shri Krishna sarcastically said to him, "You grieve about those unworthy of grieving and go on and on (incorrectly) about Brahmadnyān (Knowledge of Brahman)", and then he taught him the knowledge of Karma. Many greats have faced similar situations like Arjun. In such cases, it is not correct to quit Karma altogether just because it creates so many predicaments. It's prudent to behave in such a way that you perform the duties yet don't get bound by the results or sins of it. "One must acquire this Yog (meaning 'tact' here) and you too shall acquire it" is what Shri Krishna has told Arjun. This Yog is the Karmayogshāstra. To understand this discipline, one should understand the relevant terms and their meaning. Otherwise, many misunderstandings or confusions are possible. Let us examine a few key words and their meaning before we delve into the finer aspects.

The first word is Karma. Karma has been derived from the Sanskrit verb Kru and means 'doing or action', and this basic meaning is the one intended in Bhagavad Gitā as well. The point of clarifying this is not to get confused with the meaning of this word according to Mimāmsak or like in a few other instances where it has a limited, specific meaning. All religions have suggested various rituals to connect with God and ancient Vedic religion prescribes Yadnya-Yāg (ritualistic fire) as this act. There are a lot of instructions in Vedas about how to carry out these rituals. To unify these scattered and sometimes contradictory statements, an erudite Rishi (sage) called Jaimini compiled them all and wrote Poorvamimāmsā (there's another part called Uttaramimāmsā). According to him, performing these Vedic (from Vedas) or Shrauta (from Shrutis) rituals is the primary and ancient Dharma or duty. Whatever a man does is for Yadnya, may it be earning money or hoarding food. Doing these things for Yadnya, as ordered by Vedas themselves, isn't independently binding. It forms part of whatever is the aim behind performing the Yadnya.

[Let's understand the concept of this bondage. Every Karma or action is supposed to have an impact on one's being and it affects one's lives, the current one as well as the afterlives. Hinduism considers one's journey post death to be governed by their actions in their past and current life. We shall discuss all this later in detail. For now, just understand that due to these implications of Karma, every Karma is considered as 'binding' and a human being gets bound more and more as they perform actions. This is the root cause of asceticism being favored, in order to reduce or end this bondage.]

Although these actions may not be independently binding, the Yadnya itself assures entry to heaven (in a way a pleasure, according to Mimāmsaks) and a person performs Yadnya willingly for it. Thus, Yadnya is 'Purushārtha' Karma. Whatever a person likes and yearns achieving it is called 'Purushārtha'. On the other hand, the actions performed as a part of performing the Yadnya are 'Yadnyārtha' or 'Kratvārtha' meaning 'for the Yadnya' (Kratu is another word for Yadnya). Thus, there are two types of Karma – Yadnyārtha/Kratvārtha, which are independently non-binding and Purushārtha, which are beneficial and binding. Samhitā and Brāhmanas (parts of Vedas) entirely describe Yadnya-Yāg. According to orthodox Mimāmsaks, one gets heaven by performing Vedic Yadnyas (rituals), otherwise not; be it knowingly or unknowingly. Although Upanishads recognize Yadnyas, they regard them as inferior to Brahmadnyān (knowledge of Brahman). Thus, they're considered enough for achieving Swarga (heaven) but not Moksha (liberation). Gitā mentions the binding/non-binding nature of these Karmas briefly, paraphrasing Mimāmsaks. Other than these ritualistic Shrauta Karmas, there are other essential Smārta Karmas (called so as they appear mainly in Smrutis or remembered texts) which are as per the societal structure – War for warriors, Trade for traders etc. There are others like fasting, pilgrimage etc. which are classified as 'Paurānic' as they are mainly described in Purānas (mythology).

All Karmas can also be classified as: Nitya, Naimittik and Kāmya. Karmas which must be performed periodically (like bath, worship etc.) are called Nitya (periodic) Karmas which don't yield anything but non-performance is considered inappropriate. Naimittik Karmas are causal and not necessary without the cause (repentance, corrective rituals etc.). All the Karmas that we perform, desiring a particular goal in mind are Kāmya (desirous) Karmas. In addition to these three, there are Nishiddha (prohibited) Karmas (drinking alcohol, adultery etc.) Shāstra (doctrine) has categorically decided which Karmas are Nitya, Naimittik, Kāmya or Nishiddha. A by-the-book follower of the doctrine would declare a Karma as good or bad simply by classifying it as per the definitions given. View of Gitā is broader or more advanced than this. A Karma may be otherwise taboo yet recommended in certain situations while some other may be correct according to doctrine but not advisable. We've discussed these situations in the last chapter. What to do in such situations is the subject of Gitā and it doesn't need the help of the classification stated above. Gitā does consider in its 18th Adhyāya these categorical Karmas given by Mimāmsaks to do a comparative analysis of Karmayog in Gitā vis-à-vis that purported by Mimāmsaks. However, the core subject of Gitā is much more comprehensive and thus the meaning of Karma isn't limited to Shrauta or Smārta Karmas but is wider. To summarize, everything that we do – eating, drinking, standing, sitting, playing, breathing, laughing, crying, smelling, seeing, listening, touching, tasting, giving, taking, thinking, trading, desiring, imagining, deciding etc. are classified as Karma by Gitā; may it be physical, verbal or psychological. Even living or dying is Karma and it may be a choice to live or die in a certain situation. This is about human action. Even every exchange happening in the entire universe between living and/or non-living thing is considered Karma. However, this shall be covered later in 'Karmavipāk' (effect or fruition of Karma) chapter.

A word even more confusing or befuddling than Karma is Yog. The modern Yog or Yoga predominantly refers to the physical and breathing exercises or a group of activities covered in Pātanjalyog (condensed by the great ancient sage Patanjali). However, one should remember that Gitā doesn't refer to this narrow meaning of Yog. Yog has been derived from the Sanskrit verb Yuj (meaning 'joining or uniting') and means union or merger and later also used as 'A tool, remedy or means to achieve this union'. Yog in astrology is a certain combination of events which have a certain meaning while the word Yogakshem uses Yog as 'earning something we don't have'. There are around 80 occurrences of the word Yog or its derivative in Gitā. However, except for a maximum of 4-5 instances, Pātanjalyog isn't intended. Tool, method, idea, skill or remedy is the approximate anticipated meaning with a few exceptions. It could be one of the most all-encompassing words in Gitā. "Yogah Karmasu kaushalam" (Gitā 2.50) or 'Yog is the skill, idea, ability or way of performing an action' is one place in Gitā where you find this word clearly defined. If you delve deeper, there might be many ways of performing an action but the best or most appropriate one is intended by Yog.

Actually, this definition should leave no room for doubt or debate about use of the word Yog in Gitā. However, ignoring this definition given by Bhagwān Shri Krishna himself, many commentators have twisted the meaning of this word to interpret Gitā differently. Thus, it's important to clear the air around it. Gitā uses the word Yog for the first time in 2nd Adhyāya and defines it well there. After explaining with the help of 'Sānkhya' doctrine why Arjun should go to war, Shri Krishna says, "Now let me explain to you using Yog" (Gitā 2.39). Then after asking Arjun not to quit action altogether but to abandon desire from actions, Krishna says, "Be Yogastha (immersed in Yog) and act" (Gitā 2.48) and mentions for the first time the meaning – Yog means indifference about achievement or non-achievement and then the definition of Yog – "Yogah Karmasu kaushalam" (Yog is the skill, idea, ability or way of performing an action) (Gitā 2.50). This clarifies that Yog means 'the skill or ability to perform actions being indifferent about the outcomes and thus staying unbound by Karma'. The same is then cross-referenced in 6th Adhyāya (Gitā 6.33). There have been two paths of life for an enlightened human being, from way before Shankarāchārya – One, to give up all Karma after being enlightened and second, to continue doing the same Karmas in such a way that would avoid getting bound by its effects. These two paths are called Sanyās and Karmayog (Gitā 5.2). Sanyās means 'leaving' while Yog means 'union'. Thus, these are two separate paths with respect to Karma. The same are termed as 'Sānkhya' and 'Yog' subsequently (Gitā 5.4). Even though the 6th Adhyāya describes Pātanjalyog and methods to stabilize intellect, it is to inculcate equanimity in a Karmayogi. Gitā reiterates this in 3rd Adhyāya and later in 4th as well. Similar to Gitā, Mahābhārat also mentions – "Pravruttilakshano yogah Dnyānam Sanyāslakshanam" or "Yog means action-oriented path while Sanyās means renunciative path" in Anugeetā. With these and many more examples, the meaning of words Karma and Yog in Gitā are clear.

As stated earlier, there is a line at the end of every Adhyāya – "Iti Shrimadbhagvadgeetāsu Upanishatsu Brahmavidyāyā Yogashāstre ..." where Brahmavidyāyā Yogashastre means the following – Brahmavidyā means Brahmadnyān or knowledge of Brahman. Post acquiring

Brahmadnyān, two paths (stated earlier) are open to a Brahmadnyāni (enlightened being). Of these, Sānkhya, Sanyās Nishthā or Dnyān Nishthā as it is also called, is described in Upanishads by various rishis and authors. However, detailed deliberation of the path of Karmayog or Yog is available only in Bhagavad Gitā and nowhere else. This is the reason of introducing these two words 'Brahmavidyāyā Yogashāstre' in this line by the authors. It is our great fortune that Bhagwān Shri Krishna himself was a proponent and practitioner of this Yog and explained all its secrets to Arjun via Bhagavad Gitā. Although Karmayog and Karmayogshāstra are longer words compared to the short Yog and Yogashāstra, we have deliberately given the name Karmayogshāstra to this chapter in order to avoid any further misgivings.

There are different ways, ideas or means of performing the same action. The science or doctrine that decides by deliberating on questions like – which path is pure and righteous, whether we'd be able to regularly follow it or not, if yes what are the exceptions, why a particular path is good or bad, how to decide whether it's good or bad and what's the essence behind this decision making – is **Karmayogshāstra** or **Yogashāstra**.

Terms such as good and bad, holy and unholy, favorable and unfavorable, righteous and non-righteous, just and unjust etc. are loosely and interchangeably used; as the meaning is derived subjectively by different people. Accordingly, there are different sects formed through analysis of Karmayogshāstra. In any doctrine, there are 3 bases of discussing its topics:

1. All the things in this universe are just as perceived by our senses – there's nothing beyond it. The thought process and the analysis based on this assumption is the first discipline and is called **Adhibhautik** or positive/corporeal. It would not consider Sun as God but an aggregation of the five elements and would only assess its physical properties like heat, light, weight etc. If you take an example of a tree, Adhibhautik discipline wouldn't try to gauge what makes it bud or blossom but would accept that once you plant the seed it would germinate and grow into a tree full of branches,

leaves and flowers and study its external properties. Modern science with Physics, Chemistry, Biology etc. are all of this discipline and for them knowing the physical properties of any substance and assessing its behavior is the limit. They consider it futile to think about anything beyond it.

2. Leaving aside the objects perceivable by senses, trying to perceive what's beyond the physical properties of all objects requires going beyond Adhibhautik or corporeal discipline. E.g. considering that beyond the combination of five elements, there's a deity or higher power operational within the sun that's operating its functions. This is called **Adhidaivik** or theological discipline. Similarly, it believes that everything – from trees, water, air etc. have deities within them that control their functions.
3. Instead of believing there are thousands of separate deities (one in each separate entity), the discipline that considers that there is a single universal principle and power governing everything – is called **Adhyātmik** or spiritual discipline. E.g. a sun's shining, movement of the leaves of a tree etc. are all through the activities of this universal power and they're not separate deities according to Adhyātmik discipline.

These three paths or disciplines of discussing any topic are ancient and found in Upanishads as well. Similarly, French philosopher August Comte, a great pundit, also concluded the same three paths as Theological (Adhidaivik), Metaphysical (Adhyātmik) and Positive (Adhibhautik) and termed this as the law of three stages. It wasn't an original thought to name these stages but the sequence of these stages of growth in human mind was a novel concept. According to him the Positive (Adhibhautik) is the most advanced/superior stage. He said that humans first took things like moving clouds, volcanoes, trees as deities. Soon afterwards they thought there must be a soul in every substance. However, when despite thinking on these lines science couldn't progress, humans ultimately focused only on visible/perceptible properties and thus achieved a lot of progress in technology. He thus declared the Positive stage as the most superior. Based on this, he also says sociology and Karmayogshāstra shall be studied with Adhibhautik discipline. He proposes that every human shall love whole humanity and strive for the betterment of it. We could say British authors like Mills, Spencer etc. are proponents of similar philosophy whereas German philosophers Kant, Hegel and Schopenhauer deemed this method inadequate for studying ethics and started a thought process in Europe based on our Vedic Adhyātmik principles.

If an Adhibhautik pundit had to solve Arjun's dilemma, he would've simply seen the impacts of the war on his own good and that of the society as a whole and suggested the correct way to Arjun as they wouldn't see any other impact as valid. However, Arjun's dilemma wouldn't have been solved by this as he was interested in knowing not just the Material impacts but also the ethereal or extramundane impacts and how it would affect his soul. He wasn't concerned with whether killing Bheeshma and Drona would yield him the kingdom or whether his rule would be better for the general public than that of Duryodhan. He wanted to see if what he does would be dhārmic or adhārmic, good or sin and Gitā is also written addressing this predicament. It is important now to discuss what Dharma is and what Adharma is as their meaning is very broad and their usage can, at times, be confusing. Let us know which meaning is mainly used in Karmayogshāstra.

Dharma is mainly used as 'path taken to attain ethereal pleasure'. When we ask, "What's your Dharma?" we mean to ask which path you take for otherworldly achievement – Vedic, Buddhist, Jain, Christian, Muslim, Parsi etc. In other words, it is used synonymously with the English word 'Religion'. However, the true meaning of Dharma isn't so limited. In words like Rājdharma, Prajādharma, Deshdharma etc. the word Dharma is used as duty (respectively duty as king, duty as subjects, duty towards nation etc.) towards worldly things as well. If we want to split these two meanings of the word, otherworldly Dharma could be called 'Mokshadharma' or 'Moksha' while worldly duties or ethics could be termed as simply 'Dharma'. E.g. In case of Chaturvidha Purushārtha (Four objectives of human life) defined as Dharma-Artha-Kāma-Moksha, first word Dharma means the worldly duties as Moksha is mentioned as a separate objective. Neeti (ethics) and Dharma are not distinguished from each other clearly throughout

Sanskrit literature and are used interchangeably and even we have used the word Dharma generally as duty, ethical responsibility or objective. Wherever Moksha is discussed, we've used separate jargons. Ancient manuals such as Manusmriti classified all humans as Brāhman, Kshatriya, Vaishya and Shudra (priest, warrior, trader and servant) and mentions Kshātradharma (Dharma of Kshatriyas) as warrior's duties.

The word Dharma has been derived from the verb 'Dhru' meaning to hold or to support. That because of which everyone is supported or held together is Dharma. Thus, once Dharma breaks, the society would fall apart. It is thus a law or a code of conduct affixed for everyone so that all the happenings within a society run smoothly. Sage Vyās says, "I am shouting aloud with my hands in the air, why doesn't anyone listen? Dharma yields Artha and Dharma yields Kāma too. Why don't you follow such Dharma?" – Artha covers wealth, career and making a living while Kāma includes desire, passion, sensory pleasures and love. Living by Dharma thus leads you to achieve both Artha and Kāma according to Vyās.

Looking at this analysis of Dharma and Adharma, one may argue that if Social stability and Universal welfare is agreed by you, how is your discipline different from Adhibhautik? We shall discuss this in detail in subsequent chapters. For now, we'd just say that although social stability is the superficial benefit of Dharma, the unique feature of our discipline is that we never lose sight of Moksha as the ultimate goal. Just as Āyurveda (medicinal science included in Vedas) considers medical science worth following as it helps Moksha by protecting the body; it's impossible that our doctrine would regard Karmayogshāstra irrelevant to Moksha. Thus, whatever is conducive to attainment of Moksha is good, dhārmic or holy Karma and that unfavorable to it is sin, adhārmic or unholy according to us. The rationale behind use of the ambiguous words Dharma and Adharma rather than using responsibility and irresponsibility or action and inaction is this: Even if external action or exchange is discussed explicitly, we're constantly checking if these actions are favorable or unfavorable to the welfare of our soul. Adhibhautik would justify a selfless act by simply calling it innate human nature. Our thinkers' vision is much broader and they've used this broad Adhyātmik view of Karmayogshāstra in Mahābhārat. Gitā discusses Vedānta for this very reason. Aristotle has said: 'Ultimate well-being of humanity' or 'extreme goodness' should be set as the ultimate goal and then one should discuss ethics based on that policy' and he says in his book on ethics that welfare of soul covers all these topics. Our thinkers had gone one step ahead and made welfare of soul or spiritual accomplishment as the ultimate goal of humans. While discussing ethics, they regarded this as the primary wellbeing, before anything else. Some modern western philosophers have accepted this method. E.g. Immanuel Kant has written a spiritual essay 'Critique of pure reason' and its supplement 'Critique of practical reason'. Green, in his book 'Prolegomena to ethics', starts with consciousness at the root of the universe.

Another definition of Dharma given by Mimāmsaks should also be discussed here. "Chodanālakshanortho dharmah" (That which has the characteristics of an inspiration or commandment is Dharma), they say. Unless someone with a higher authority allows or prohibits something, everyone is free to do whatever they please. The thought behind it is that Dharma was originally invented because of restrictions. Barbaric humans learnt slowly the shortcomings of unrestrained behavior and created restrictions which were beneficial for all and humans started following such restrictions, created by etiquettes or otherwise, as a law. Once these restrictions became plentiful it became a code or a doctrine (Shāstra). Even if we consider Dharma as inspired or commanded, it was imagined by someone who understood its importance. To eat, drink and enjoy one doesn't need anyone's advice, it comes naturally. "Food, sleep, fear and copulation comes naturally to all animals. Dharma (limiting it with ethical guidelines) is what differentiates humans from animals. Without this, a human is but an animal" – says Mahābhārat and Gitā has a similar shloka (verse). Our senses are pulling us towards indulgence and our consciousness towards the other. One who burns the sensory urges in the sacrificial fire is truly remarkable.

Call it behavioral, supportive or inspiring; none of the definitions of ethics or Dharma are any good when faced with a perplexity. First tells its origin, second tells its practical use while the third tells us that the limit of Dharma was proposed by someone. However, while behaviors are different and same action has different implications, commandments given by different rishis are so different that in situations of dilemma, the decision of dhārmic action needs to be taken by some other way. Yudhisthir in answer to a Yaksha's (spirit) question says – "Reason is unstable, dependent on one's intellect and inconclusive. Shrutis (Vedic commandments) are varied. If you look at Smrutis there's no rishi whose doctrine is superior to everyone else. If you resort to (behavioral) Dharma, its root is hidden in obscurity and incomprehensible to a common man's intellect. In such cases, 'Mahājano yena gatah sa panthah' (the path which the majority/greats have taken is the dhārmic one)". If we take meaning of Mahājan as majority (which is one of the two meanings), it doesn't make sense as majority's decision may not necessarily be well-thought. If we go by the other meaning of Mahājan i.e. great personalities (which is most likely the implication of Yudhisthir), almost all such exceptional human beings have been found to be inconsistent – Shri Rām abandoned his wife for respecting people's opinion, in spite of her proven trial by fire! Parshuram killed his own mother! Pāndav had one wife among five of them! Even gods have been known to resort to various sins like adultery, deceit etc. If you look at biblical stories, more often than not it is the angels who've duped the devils. Thus, while following the behavior of greats is easy and helpful in many situations, it isn't foolproof. A thoughtful person must dive deep in the waters of Ātmadnyān (spiritual knowledge) and find out the underlying principle of these greats. You are advised not to follow anyone blindly for this very reason.

Another trick given by some is to avoid anything in excess. Aristotle has proved with examples how every virtue in excess is bad. Again, there's no standard definition of 'excess'. Excess for someone may not be as much for someone else. Deliberation cannot be resorted to either, as different experts may deliberate differently and give opposing verdicts.

In conclusion, to deal with this predicament, we must check if there are any tools to arrive at the perfect conclusion. If yes, check what they are and decide which the perfect tool is. This is the application of

Shāstra. Shāstra is known for imparting knowledge to clear the doubts generated by ignorance, for envisioning the invisible and educate us about the future. Still, before clearing the doubts, one must know what the doubts are. Ancient and modern authors have been known to point out and analyze other answers in order to show their limitations before revealing the ultimate answer. Likewise, we shall discuss a few major ideas proposed by various pundits before arriving at the perfect idea given by Bhagavad Gitā to solve this predicament.

CHAPTER 4

Adhibhautik Sukhvāda (Corporeal Hedonism)

We have learned in the last chapter that, like in any scientific analysis, there are three bases of discussing the topic of Karmayog – Adhibhautik (Corporeal or Utilitarian), Adhidaivik (theological) & Adhyātmik (spiritual). We also learned the differences between them. According to our thinkers, Adhyātmik is the greatest. However, to understand its significance, it's necessary to study the other two disciplines. We have chosen to first discuss the principles of Adhibhautik discipline in this chapter. As this path mainly focuses on the external or perceptible aspects, the pundits of this discipline develop a habit of thinking only about the external impact and don't give importance to Adhyātmik or otherworldly, intangible or invisible aspects. However, as ethics or laws are necessary for smooth functioning of the society, there has been a lot of deliberation about whether Adhibhautik or corporeal methods are enough for resolution of the dilemma about what is good Karma and what is bad Karma. In this deliberation, modern western philosophers have decided that spirituality is not at all necessary to discuss ethics. We can and should decide the nature of an action by its evident/apparent impacts. This is because whatever a person does is either to achieve happiness or to reduce sadness. Rather, 'well-being of all humanity' is the ultimate worldly goal. As the final visible impact of any action is certain, the correct way of ethics is deciding the morality of all actions by comparing how happy or less sad the action makes us. As this simple and scientific way is available, it's futile to delve into spiritual thoughts. We termed this approach as 'Corporeal hedonism' as the discussion involved is entirely pertaining to external or sensory pleasures or displeasures. It's developed by many philosophers with a corporeal approach. It's impossible to discuss it in detail as we'd have to write another book just to summarize the opinions of all the different authors. We've covered in brief the broad description, just enough for us to understand the appearance and importance of Karmayogshāstra from Bhagavad Gitā. Even though these corporeal philosophers are indifferent about otherworldly or spiritual thoughts, it doesn't mean all of them are selfish, greedy or unethical. There are many like Kant, Mills, Spencer etc. who've tried, not through spiritual view, but through broadening of worldly view to propose that working for betterment of the world is our duty; and their treatises are worth reading. As long as it's aimed at betterment of the world, whatever be the path, it's praiseworthy. Let's now briefly and sequentially see, what different subtypes of Adhibhautiks there can be and how apt or incorrect they are.

First one is that of self-centered hedonists. They believe that all otherworldly and charitable metaphysical approaches are false and all spiritual philosophies are made up by a few cunning people to have their way. Selfishness is the only truth and whatever ways help achieve it and all the physical pleasures are the justified and correct ones. This was proposed by Chārvāk in ancient India. Body is nothing but a combination of five elements and the arrangement ends at the time of death. Hence, there's no point in wasting time in spiritual pursuits. Rather, one should indulge in every way possible while alive. This is the view put forth by the Chārvāks. As long as one's alive, they must enjoy everything that they see and satiate their carnal desires as the world ends for them once they're dead. If one practices austerity, donations or any such act it's for fame and to enhance their importance – "I am the Ishwar, I'm the consumer. I am the almighty and the one appeased (through sacrifices) as well!" (Gitā 16.14) This is how Gitā describes such kind of people. An advisor of this kind would've slapped Arjun for even being in such dilemma and would've told him to win the war, enjoy all the kingly pleasures and satisfy all his possible desires. Arjun, however, clarifies right at the start to Krishna he doesn't want to win the war even for all such pleasures and that he would rather die than killing his own for this empire. Thus, a mere mention of this sect or school of thought is enough to discard it. As it's condemned by all philosophers and even general public, it's not worth discussing this any further; so let's move on to the second category of Adhibhautiks.

Unembellished and open selfishness wouldn't work as although everyone wants physical pleasure, it is opposed whenever it crosses paths with or is against the pleasure of someone else. Many Adhibhautiks thus feel that one should also look at others' happiness in order to ensure own happiness as only then you'd get your way. Nascent ethics begin here, as this second category of people, unlike Chārvāks, have tried to propose with justification, why everyone should follow ethics. They believe people feared they'd be killed if they kill others and then they'd lose their happiness. This fear arising out of self-interest is the root of non-violence, they say. They claim that all other laws or values – charity, generosity, mercy, love, gratitude, humility etc. – have also arisen out of such thoughts of self-interest and nothing else. One donates hoping he'd get the same help from others when needed. At least, they seek praise or respect from others against it. These people thus agree with having foresight and doing things that would benefit others, albeit for their own good. They still continue the opinion held by Chārvāks that a person is purely concerned with self-interest. Hobbes and Helvetius are philosophers who proposed this discipline. However, it doesn't garner much following today. Many philosophers like Butler contradicted this theory by proving that humans are not purely self-obsessed but possess other innate qualities such as love, gratitude etc. Thus, it is necessary to look at both innate human qualities - self-interest and selflessness – while discussing any behavior or action from ethical point of view. This is the third category of Adhibhautiks. While they think about ethical values from both angles; they still maintain that, self or others, humans only look at worldly happiness and nothing else. Largely, the self-interest and selflessness don't clash with each other; and hence this view holds well in many circumstances. These people suggest it is our duty doing selfless activities, albeit without ignoring our self-interest. It is when there is a conflict between self and others' interest that this theory falters. As this sect recommends weighing the comparative importance of self-interest and selflessness through one's own intellect, there's a risk of people tilting towards self-interest when faced with a dilemma between the two. They might praise someone else sacrificing their life for others but when in such a situation themselves, it's most likely that they'd choose self-interest. History tells us that those putting interest of others over their own are worthy of true greatness and not those ensuring selflessness while retaining self-interest. These people claim that even though selflessness is philosophically superior, they're simply recommending behavior in common situations and not proposing epitome of ethics. However, we don't see any merit in this as variation in practical weighing balances doesn't justify errors in model or standard weights. Ethics is in existence to decide the pure, complete and permanent form of Dharma and if it's not up to the mark with the ideals then there's no use of ethics.

We discussed Pure, Foresighted and Smart-selfish or Utilitarian Adhibhautiks and saw what the shortcomings are. However, there's another version which is the best among all Adhibhautik sects – those who don't look at a single human's interest but the interest of entire human race to decide the ethical correctness. They are called Sāttvic Adhibhautik (Righteous utilitarian). They say, no deed causes happiness to all. Something is delightful for some while being painful for others. However, something not being beneficial for a small minority doesn't make it useless for all. Thus, 'Everyone's happiness' can be interpreted as 'Majority's Happiness'. They state – "That thing which causes happiness to majority of people shall be considered ethically fair and acceptable". Adhyātmik sect agrees with this principle; rather this principle was discovered by them anciently. Sāttvic utilitarian have simply used this in a specific way. Even Bhagavad Gitā describes an ideal person having a characteristic of 'Sarvabhootahite ratah' or 'Working towards the interest of all'. However, our philosophers describe that it's one thing to treat this as the external characteristic of an ideal person, using it as a broad guideline and an entirely different thing to make this as the exclusive principle of morality and build the entire doctrine of ethics on this. Adhibhautik pundits assume the second way and discard Adhyātma as irrelevant to ethics.

'One's happiness' and 'One's interest' are a lot different. Let's keep it aside for time being and consider 'Everyone's interest' as 'Majority's happiness'. Still there are a lot of snags in considering this way of Adhibhautik in making decisions about right and wrong. Consider the Great War in Mahābhārat for example – Pāndav had 7 battalions against 11 of Kaurav. If we go by the principle of 'Majority's happiness', Kaurav winning the war would've caused happiness to more people and thus the victory of Pāndav in the war should be termed unjust. Is it correct? Even in common parlance, we consider that deed as good which makes one good person happy, rather than one that makes a thousand evil people glad. This makes the principle of 'Majority's Happiness' fall short. Thus, numbers or majority have no impact on ethics. Now let's understand that something that appears pleasurable to common people may be gauged as detrimental by the foresighted. E.g. Both Socrates and Jesus Christ had preached for the betterment of people but their contemporaries proved them 'enemies of society' and had them killed. These acts, performed from the point of view of 'Majority's happiness' by the erstwhile leaders, however, aren't considered justified or correct today. Even if one accepts for a moment that 'Majority's happiness' is the basis for ethics, there arises a question of who's the right person to decide what's in the best interest of millions of people. In times of crisis, letting an unfit person take this decision means risking everyone's future. Both these discussions point to the fact that 'Majority's happiness' can't be considered a base for ethics and that it isn't sufficient for deciding right and wrong.

There are other objections that can be raised against this method of 'Majority's happiness'. For one, we can't decide whether a deed is just or unjust only by looking at its apparent effects. While all good people work towards betterment of society, the converse may not be true. Not everyone apparently working for betterment of people is necessarily a sage. Unknowingly if one commits a crime, it is considered pardonable in the eyes of law. This is because, a decision about the deed being right or wrong, ethical or unethical shouldn't be decided just by looking at the apparent effect or whether it's causing 'Majority's happiness'. The thought or intention of the doer should also be considered. Although charity is considered a good deed, it's one thing to donate selflessly and another to donate with an ulterior motive. While the apparent effect is the same for the recipient, the evaluation of deeds is different in both cases. Gitā classifies charity under three categories, depending on the intention – A donation by someone considering it as their Dharma (duty in this case) is considered Sāttvic, one done with an ulterior motive is considered Rājas while one done without thinking whether or not is it being done to a deserving person is called Tāmas. A poor donating a penny for a noble cause is considered equally good as a billionaire donating a million when it comes to judging morally or ethically. If judged from the 'Majority's happiness' point of view, the two charities wouldn't be considered equal. The main flaw in that approach is this: it doesn't take into account the intention or thought process of the doer. The moment you try to consider it, it goes against the basic principle of 'Majority's happiness' as the sole basis. We are not saying that this principle isn't useful. In fact, when only external impact is to be judged there isn't a better principle. However, when it comes to deciding fairness or unfairness of a deed, one must consider other factors than this. Thus, when discussing ethics, we need to come up with another principle which is certain and flawless. Gitā says – "Buddhi is superior to Karma" (Intent is superior to action) (Gitā 2.49) and states this very point. [While Buddhi means Intellect, it is a broader term similar to Dharma. We shall discuss this later.]

There's another argument against the principle of 'Majority's happiness'. The statement 'Selflessness is better than self-interest' is taken as gospel in this approach. If both these intents have been there in humans right since inception, why should one consider selflessness as superior? There's no explanation or answer given to this basic question. Like we discussed earlier, this question isn't faced in all situations as displaying either of these values are often mutually exclusive. However, when it comes to a situation where it is self-interest against that of the others, there's no explanation as to why one should put others' interest before their own. One utilitarian scholar understood this difficulty and proposed a theory – As it is evident by observation that propagation and protection of one's own kind is a quality displayed universally, right from the smallest insect to the humans where it is at its highest, it is the basis of behavior for entire living world. Even a unicellular organism splits itself into two to propagate. It thus foregoes its own body to ensure propagation of its own kind. Similarly, higher organisms display similar qualities of selflessness for propagation of their kind. This quality gets magnified in humans to the point that they not only fight for their propagation but readily help others of their own kind. Thus, human beings, the epitome of all living beings, must strive to end this conflict between selflessness and self-interest. This viewpoint is well taken. Increasing knowledge of the universe through science has led to the Adhibhautik arriving at this viewpoint. Spiritual philosophers have been saying this since the ancient times. Another point that arises now is whether philanthropy is the only such virtue magnified in human beings or are there more – Justice, mercy, wisdom, foresight, philosophy, reason, bravery, valor, forgiveness, restraint etc. Once you see this, we'd understand that all qualities have been magnified in humans. Let's call this gamut of virtues as 'humanity'. With Humanity proven to be broader and better than philanthropy, it becomes imperative that we evaluate the ethical correctness of any deed with humanity at the core, rather than only philanthropy as suggested by the Adhibhautik/Corporeal/Utilitarian. Philanthropic assessment thus becomes a subset of the humanitarian view and not the sole assessment. Once you start pursuing the origin of humanity, the quest for existence of soul becomes natural.

One can see from the analysis how Adhibhautik have to graduate from the most inferior stage of self-centered hedonism to philanthropy and finally humanity. However, Adhibhautik still only consider corporeal happiness while considering humanity and thus this highest level of corporeal hedonism is still not considered flawless by the Adhyātmik as it misses out on internal purity or bliss. While it is accepted that every human strives for gaining happiness and escaping sorrow, we can't accept any Adhibhautik sect till the true nature of everlasting bliss is not identified. Even Adhibhautik agree the superiority of psychological pleasure over physical. Surely, nobody would accept the life of an animal even if they're granted all the pleasures that an animal can experience. Scholarly would agree that the kind of peaceful bliss one experiences through deep philosophical thoughts is far better than any other physical pleasure available. Even Arjun's question wasn't about how happy he would become by winning the war but was – "What should I do in the best interest of my soul?" (Gitā 2.7, 3.2) Interest of the soul is in the soul's everlasting peace. In the story of Nachiketā and Death; although Death offered him descendants, animals, grains and wealth, Nachiketā flatly said: "I want Knowledge of the soul, I don't want wealth". Kathopanishad further explains the difference between 'Preya' and 'Shreya' as: When presented with Preya (Temporary physical pleasure) and Shreya (True and everlasting happiness), a sane person would choose Shreya over Preya and a demented would choose otherwise" (Kath 1.2.2).

While spiritual bliss is better than physical pleasure, physical pleasure is also fleeting. Dharma isn't so. Virtues like truth & non-violence are timeless and independent of physical properties. There's no Adhibhautik explanation for this permanence as all physical pleasures are short-lived and any theory based on such weak base is equally weak. Virtues like truth even in the eyes of death can't thus be explained by the theory of 'Majority's happiness'. While one may argue that even great people quit truth in the eyes of death, even those great people agree the permanent superiority of truth.

In summary, as Vyās says in Mahābhārat – Happiness and sorrow are transient while Dharma is eternal; so never quit Dharma even for pleasure, fear and greed or in the eyes of death. Jeev (soul) is eternal while the intentions (physical pleasure) are temporary. So, Jeev should always be tied to Dharma. To test how true Vyās' sermon is, we must now look at the nature of happiness and sorrow and what eternal bliss is.

CHAPTER 5

Sukhadukkhavivek (Comparative Scrutiny of Happiness and Sorrow)

Our philosophers agree that every person in this world strives for achieving and enhancing happiness while also trying to avoid or minimize sorrow. They feel that, while being oblivious to the whereabouts of one's true happiness, they bide time in this never-ending pursuit or in the hope of achieving it; and die with a sudden blow from death. And yet, the others don't learn. They repeat the same mistakes. No one seeks the eternal bliss. Although happiness, interest, betterment or blessing are different from each other, let's for a moment consider happiness includes everything. However, one can't call whatever's appropriate for us as Happiness and whatever we dislike as sorrow; because appropriate might mean an object and then we'd have to call an object happiness. However, it isn't so. The sensory satisfaction that one gets from the object is happiness. A person likes this sensory pleasure but that doesn't mean whatever one likes means happiness. Naiyāyik (Philosophers from Nyāya School of philosophy) have then defined happiness and sorrow as follows: That sensation which is favorable to us is happiness while that which is unfavorable is sorrow. These sensations are inborn and experiential. There couldn't be a better definition of happiness and sorrow. This sensory happiness or sorrow may not necessarily be born of human actions. Sometimes it may be a result of divine intervention. Vedānta divides happiness and sorrow into three categories: Adhidaivik, Adhibhautik and Adhyātmik. Happiness or sorrow arising from divine blessing or curse are Adhidaivik or theological, those caused by the interaction of five elements with our senses are Adhibhautik or corporeal or physical and all those other than such external interactions are called Adhyātmik or Spiritual. If you accept this method of classification then those internal ailments such as acidity, fever etc. would need to be categorized as Adhyātmik as despite originating from the five elements they're not external and hence can't always be termed as physical. Then there's a need to classify Adhyātmik sensations as Physical and psychological. Instead, if you classify all of them as either Physical or Psychological, there's no need to have a third type. We've thus not referred to the classification as per Vedānta but have used a simpler system of classifying all sensations as either Adhibhautik/Physical or Adhyātmik/psychological in this book. We request the readers to remember this jargon in the subsequent study.

Both Vedānta and Sānkhya say that it is every person's goal to completely end all sorrows and attain utter and eternal happiness. It thus becomes imperative to discuss topics such as: What is utter, true and eternal happiness? Is it possible to achieve or not? If yes, how and when? etc. Naturally the next question that arises is: Whether happiness and sorrow are separate sensations as proposed by Naiyāyik or is absence of one sensation the other?

Bhartruhari, who's one of those who believed in the second logic, says: "Just like we satiate the sorrow of thirst by drinking water, sorrow of hunger by eating food and sorrow of lust by engaging in sexual intercourse; people mistakenly call the overcoming of any sorrow as happiness". Beyond overcoming of sorrow, there's no separate entity called happiness. Even when doing an act of philanthropy, it's the sympathy which makes us uneasy and to overcome it we perform the act of philanthropy. If we accept this sect, we've to consider all human tendencies as desires or cravings and until we forgo all the worldly actions the cravings wouldn't stop; and until we stop all the cravings, we wouldn't gain true and eternal happiness. Whoever wants utter happiness or Moksha must renounce all worldly ties and live an ascetic life. This is the final hypothesis of this sect. The Sanyās path suggested in Smruti and proposed in Kaliyug by Shri Shankarāchārya is this same path of renunciation. This Vedic path of Sanyās was further adopted by Buddhism and Jainism.

It's not that Gitā doesn't accept the ill effects of these cravings. However, as it says it's not appropriate to renounce all action to avoid these effects, it is important to minutely discuss the above stated explanation of happiness and sorrow. Firstly, we can't accept the premise that all happiness is achieved from eliminating sorrows alone. The phenomenon of wanting an object which we've experienced before is called desire or want (Vāsanā or Ichhā). When we don't get the desired object and this desire gets intensified or if the obtained object is not enough, this intensified desire is then called a craving (Trushnā). However, if the desire is satisfied before it becomes a craving, the happiness we experience can't be called as one experienced through elimination of craving. E.g. If we get daily meal on time, we don't experience sorrow before every meal. We'd get uneasy with hunger if the meal is delayed, otherwise not. Even if we consider desire and craving as identical, we can't say all happiness is through elimination of sorrow. E.g. If you put a candy in a kid's mouth, the happiness that the kid experiences isn't because of elimination of any previous sorrow. Thus, we have to let go of the renunciative definition of happiness. Senses have an innate ability of enjoying various objects and while doing this, the favorable or unfavorable events, in presence or absence of any desire or craving, cause happiness or sorrow. Assuming this definition, Gitā says we experience happiness or sorrow through interaction of external objects with our senses; and this is the idea in Karmayogshāstra. We don't know why we dislike harsh sounds or love pleasant smells. As the nature of physical happiness is sensory, we often experience happiness by continued indulgence in such sensory interactions. We often continue doing pleasurable actions. Thus, we can't consider happiness as sourced only from elimination of sorrow and must call innate sensory pleasure or displeasure as happiness or sorrow. Shri Krishna says – "Instead of foregoing all tendencies of senses or mind, it is imperative to keep senses and mind in control and use these tendencies to your advantage". This is far different from advocating complete annihilation of cravings and all feelings associated with it. Gitā doesn't demand extinction of all action or valor from the world. In fact, it says in the 18th Adhyāya that a person must have determination and enthusiasm along with equanimity. But let's not get ahead of ourselves. We'll discuss that in a later chapter. For now, we can understand from the above example what Gitā says about happiness and sorrow and that it doesn't take one to just be the absence of other. In fact, Gitā describes happiness as indicative of Sattva while craving as indicative of Raja, thus describing Sattva and Raja as separate virtues. The fact that Gitā says – "Abstinence of a task because it gives sorrow doesn't yield the fruit of charity, as attribute of self-restraint is Rājas" – goes to show that it is against the notion that all happiness comes by abstinence of cravings.

Even if we accept that happiness and sorrow are separate feelings, these two emotions are opposite to each other. Thus, there arises a question now – If a person doesn't have any experience of sorrow, would he be able to experience happiness? Many believe it's impossible to feel happiness without sorrow. On the contrary, if we look at the concept of heaven, we see that lasting happiness is possible despite sorrow. Just as one can experience a sweet taste despite having tasted any other tastes, one can experience happiness of different degree and kind without having experienced sorrow. However, this argument becomes invalid in practical world. Even gods have been told to have faced difficulties in stories from Purānas and even heavenly bliss has been described as non-perpetual. So, this example of heaven becomes ineffective. The world appears to have both happiness and sorrow and no one seems to have either everlasting happiness or everlasting sorrow but a mixture of both. Thus, whether the purpose of sorrow is to enhance the pleasure of happiness or it's something else, it seems certain that one can't expect all sorrow to become extinct and experience perpetual happiness in this material world.

If the world has a mixture of happiness and sorrow, the third question that arises is whether happiness exceeds sorrow or vice versa. Most western Adhibhautik pundits argue that the fact that majority of people don't commit suicide out of frustration, it seems certain that happiness is in majority as compared to sorrow and one must consider happiness as the ultimate goal and grade ethics in relation with this measure. However, this correlation of suicide with happiness is absurd. Even if someone does commit suicide, it's considered as an aberration or exception and thus an independent act. Darwin in his book 'Naturalist's voyage round the world' mentions tribes from southernmost parts living in one of the coldest climates without clothes, spending many days without food as they don't store food like we do. Just because these tribal people don't commit suicide doesn't mean they're eternally happy. It appears, for many humans, the fact that they're humans and not animals; is reason enough to continue with their lives. Even animals are not found to commit suicide but that doesn't mean they're always happy. As is written in our scriptures, "Living are superior to non-living, among them the ones with brain, among them humans, among them Brāhmans, among them the well-cultured, among them the doers and among them the ones that seek enlightenment" – being human is a blessing in itself and hence suicide is regarded as madness or sin. As is evident that not committing suicide can't be considered reason enough for dominance of happiness in the world, we must consider the worldly things to decide whether there's more happiness or sorrow. It now becomes necessary to see how many of the contemporary desires of an individual are fulfilled. The reason behind saying 'contemporary' is that once certain things become accessible to almost everyone, we stop being happy for them. The new wants or desires and their fulfilment starts deciding whether we're happy or sad. It's vastly different what was accessible to us a 100 years ago and what is today. A hundred years ago, we were happy to be able to send a letter to someone far away. Now we become irritated if we don't see someone's video clearly on a video call. Once we see this and find out what our wants are, we realize that there's no end to it, ever. One should note the difference between the two statements – 'All happiness is achieved through elimination of cravings' and 'A human is not satisfied despite getting all happiness'. It is one thing to point out that happiness and sorrow are different sensations and another to ignore all happiness achieved and remain discontented. First discusses the objectifying of happiness while another questions whether or not a happiness causes complete satisfaction. As sensory desires are ever increasing, even if we don't get new ways to get happy, we feel like enjoying the same happiness again and again and the greed of the mind can't be reined in. All historical accounts show examples of such insatiable hunger of the mind for happiness.

Gitā and Upanishads depict human birth as impermanent and home of sorrow. Schopenhauer also proves the same point by using a peculiar anecdote. He says – We decide people's happiness by looking at how many desires for happiness they successfully fulfilled out of the total they had. If fulfilment falls short of desires, we consider a person to be sad. Looking at this example mathematically, fulfilment is the numerator while desires are the denominator. How much ever you increase the numerator, the denominator keeps increasing by a higher degree. Thus, complete happiness is an illusion. Looking at the aforesaid scrutiny, an ascetic might say – As happiness is not an object, there's no peace till we rid ourselves of all Karma related to desire. Even if you don't accept this, you agree that desire leads to discontentment and discontentment leads to sorrow. Then at least to get rid of this discontentment, why shouldn't one abstain from all cravings and other worldly Karmas (whether selfish or selfless) to have lasting contentment? Counterargument to this is, do we cut off the tongue because it says bad words sometimes? Do we entirely abstain from using fire, even for cooking, just because it occasionally burns down houses? Even potentially catastrophic electricity, when contained properly, proves to be brilliant. It's possible to moderate and rein in desire or discontentment similarly and use it in our daily lives. Discontentment isn't always bad. The discontentment that prevents people from continuing with their plight and makes them improve on it with a calm mind and as per their capabilities is a favorable one. Thus, discontentment about knowledge, space, wealth etc. leads to exploration, discoveries and progress. Spiritually speaking, this discontentment is the seed for potential Moksha as well. If we give up such discontentment, we'd not survive, either on earth or anywhere else. Just as excess discontentment or greed are bad and they destroy Sāttvic tendencies from our mind, complete abstinence from all desire and Karma isn't Sāttvic either. One must choose the middle path between the two extremes and this tact of quitting desires leading to sorrow and following Karma according to one's Dharma is called Yog or Karmayog (Gitā 2.50). Let's now look at which desires Gitā classifies as those leading to sorrow.

We listen through ears, touch through skin, see through eyes, taste through tongue and smell through our nose. If these sensory exchanges are conducive to our natural preferences, we experience happiness; otherwise, we experience sadness. Aforementioned are the objective characteristics. However, the thought about happiness or sorrow isn't complete through this. Although sensory exchange is primarily needed for happiness or sadness, the experience is ultimately felt through mind. Often you miss an event if your mind is somewhere else. Spiritual happiness or sadness are, in turn, completely psychological. We can thus infer that all experience ultimately depends on mind. If this is true, we could also control feeling happy or sad through psychological resolve. Manu beautifully defines happiness and sorrow as – All that's controlled by external things is sorrow and all that's controlled by our mind is happiness. If you consider Naiyāyik definition, it considers both external and internal sensations while Manu considers internal feelings towards the experience of happiness or sadness. Once the dependence on external sensory inputs is overcome, not thinking about the sorrow becomes the perfect remedy for overcoming sadness. Once we quit the 'desire' part of anything we do using mental resolve, and maintain equanimity towards happiness or sorrow, there's no possibility of sorrow. This is what Gitā says. It doesn't mean sacrificing the fruit upon fruition or desiring that no one gets that fruit. A desire or a simple wish to perform an action is different from an action performed with a premeditated intention of achieving something. First one is just for the sake of the action. If this wish or desire is lost, all action would stop. Moreover, one must also have the knowledge that every action would have a consequence or a fruit and every action must be planned keeping in mind the fruit or the consequence. Otherwise, all actions would be rendered meaningless. Gitā doesn't ask us to rid ourselves of these wishes, intentions or plans. It goes far ahead and asks us to let go of the feeling that 'I'm performing this action with the sole purpose that I MUST get the fruit'. It tells us to forego this self-seeking attachment, greed, ego and stubbornness that our mind gets preoccupied with.

Once there's a barrier to achieve the fruit, sorrow begins. If this barrier is unavoidable or fate-induced, we're merely disappointed. If, however, this barrier is human, it leads to anger and even hatred. This hatred leads to wrongdoing and this wrongdoing leads to ruin. This attachment to the consequence of an action is termed desire, craving, ego or lust. This marks the true beginning of sorrow. Gitā says in 2nd Adhyāya to establish this – Attachment to fruit causes lust, lust leads to anger, anger leads to delusion and delusion ultimately leads to destruction of a human being. Once it's thus established that actions themselves don't lead to sorrow; but the lust, desire or attachment to its fruit leads to it – it's clear that it is sufficient to let go of only this attachment. There's no need to let go of the action itself as claimed by the ascetics. Gitā says that one who accepts the achieved fruits without attachment or lust is the true Sthitapradnya (firm in wisdom).

The nature doesn't stop. Even if we're not here, nature would follow its course as per the properties of matter. Nature doesn't have happiness or sorrow about the outcomes. Humans vainly give themselves importance and get attached to the happenings and become happy or sad. Once we know that all happenings are simply following nature or virtues of the respective subjects and objects, there doesn't remain any cause of sorrow. Many duties in life need to be performed despite experiencing sorrow while performing them. They reiterate the importance of this lesson that we must continue to perform actions without being perturbed by their outcomes. Whatever the Karma, when one performs it without leaving the wish or the action and while staying away from being attached to the fruit and being indifferent about happiness or sorrow that it may lead to; it avoids the ill effects of the inevitability of desire or discontentment while also avoiding destruction of the world through complete annihilation of Karma along with desire. It makes the emotions pure and benevolent. It is certain that this requires Vairagya (internal dispassionate state of mind) to achieve restraint of senses and mind. It is one thing to control senses, give up selfishness and give up desire through Vairagya while continuing to perform all tasks for well-being of the world. It is entirely another to exterminate all desire through abstinence from all actions of the senses through asceticism. Gitā advises the Vairagya of the 1st kind and not the 2nd. This leads us to the ever-famous verse from the 2nd Adhyāya of Gitā:

Karmanyevādhikaraste mā faleshu kadāchan |

Mā Karmafalaheturbhurmā te sangostvakarmani || (Gitā 2.47)

(As you're born in the Karmabhoomi or the land of Karma,) "You only have the right to perform Karma". The word 'Only' indicates clearly that one doesn't have the right to fruit of the Karma. However, not leaving this to interpretation, second half says clearly – "You never have the right to the fruit of the Karma". This is because, getting or not getting the fruit of Karma isn't in your hands but a consequence of overall scheme of things and a universal system of causality. Expecting something beyond our control to behave as if under our control is nothing but foolishness. However, not even leaving this to interpretation, first half of the second verse says – "Hence, you shouldn't perform any Karma having the greed for its fruit". Overall, as a result of universal causality whatever fruition is to happen would happen. You expecting a certain outcome would only lead to possible disappointment. This is the interpretation of this half. However, one (especially the ascetics) may infer that instead of indulging in this tedious manner of performing the action without anticipating the fruits, isn't it better to forego Karma altogether? To clarify this, Bhagwān Shri Krishna has said in the second half – "Yet, don't be insistent on foregoing Karma". Through this definitive statement, he has clarified that one must, without expecting the fruits, continue to perform Karma. From the point of view of Karmayog, this verse is so significant, we may safely call this the essence of Gitā Dharma.

If we consider only physical pleasures, it may be safely inferred that it's pointless to pursue true happiness if we've established that happiness and sorrow are incidental and that sorrow exceeds happiness. However, physical happiness isn't the only type and thus albeit ridden with difficulties, one may find the path to absolute and eternal happiness. Once we classify happiness as physical and psychological, the latter wins hands down against the former as we saw how even physical pleasure is ultimately felt psychologically. Mill agrees with this principle in his book 'Utilitarianism'. Although animals experience sensory pleasures much like humans and if we believed in only this kind of pleasure, we'd have been happily willing to be reborn as animals. However, the fact that no one aspires to be born as even an ever-happy animal proves that there's something special about being born a human. Once we delve into this, we're forced to think about the soul that perceives the self and the outer world. Once we pursue this further, we conclude that the psychological and spiritual pleasure of humans is the greatest and the absolute. These pleasures are personal, internal (without need of any external stimulus and without depriving anyone of their pleasure) and achievable through one's own efforts. As we go up this ladder, they keep becoming purer and unadulterated. Even if we keep Moksha or liberation aside, we can infer that psychological pleasures outweigh the physical pleasures. Gitā classifies pleasures as Sāttvic, Rājas and Tāmas and says – "The soulful spiritual pleasure (achieved through the knowledge that we're all part of the same Brahman) is the best or Sāttvic. Physical sensory pleasures come next and are called Rājas while those that lure our mind and are derived from slumber or sloth are the lowest and called Tāmas. Once someone experiences the ultimate pleasure, no future sorrow would be able to shake the person. Even heaven doesn't promise this level of happiness which is attainable only through a blissful state of mind. If one ignores this bliss and runs after physical pleasures, they're bound to experience momentary pleasures. Moreover, what pleases the senses today may not do so some other time. E.g. Cold water that pleases you during summer appears harsh on your throat during winter. Apparent or superficial pleasure (Preya) and True or everlasting pleasure (Shreya) as elucidated by Nachiketā (briefly discussed in last chapter) are the two types of pleasure. Our scriptures have regarded Shreya or spiritual pleasure as ultimate.

While it is now firmly established that this spiritual pleasure is ultimate, some degree of physical pleasure, albeit just enough for sustenance, is necessary for survival. Just as other metals are also required even though gold is undoubtedly the best metal, or just as food must have all tastes even though sweet taste is the most pleasurable, one needs some degree of physical happiness. This is why our scriptures have included peace, prosperity and (spiritual) bliss in blessings. This is precisely why Nachiketā in his encounter with death himself asked for these three blessings in succession and didn't directly ask for spiritual bliss. Summarily, all the requisites of a perfect person can be boiled down to two things – prosperity and knowledge. Prosperity covers success, power and wealth. Knowledge covers Dharma and Vairagya. Bhagwān Shri Krishna is a model of achievement of these two aspects. Karmayog thus emphasizes on both these factors while Sanyās (path of asceticism) rejects Samsāra or Karma altogether and trivializes prosperity. We shall discuss the futility of this ascetic approach in the 9th and 10th chapter from Moksha and Karma point of view, like we saw it from pleasure point of view here.

To summarize, we saw how Happiness and Sorrow are two separate entities. Desire can't be satiated through pleasure and hence we see the world with more of sorrow than happiness. To avoid sorrow, however, it's not advisable to give up desire, discontentment and Karma altogether but to only let go of the expectations of its fruit. Physical pleasure is impermanent, insatiable and animalistic. A human must aim for a superior, permanent pleasure which is achievable through spiritual bliss. To live in this world, however, one also needs to pay attention to physical aspects and hence should perform all Karma without keeping expectation for its fruits.

It's thus amply clear that it's pointless to evaluate an action through its apparent consequences and the sensory happiness or sorrow it leads to. It's also wrong to consider physical pleasure as ultimate and decide ethical validity of an action through that. We also come to the debate about what 'Majority's happiness' would actually mean and many intellectuals have changed it to 'Majority's interest'. Even then, there's no emphasis on the doer's mindset. The moment we give importance to the psychological aspect of happiness, it contradicts the Adhibhautik approach of evaluating a Karma based on its apparent outcomes and indirectly validates acceptance of Adhyātmik approach. If Adhyātmik approach is thus inevitable, what's the point of half-accepting it? Hence, Karmayogshāstra treats Adhibhautik criteria like majority's happiness, everyone's well-being, humanity's ultimate progress etc. as inferior and declares spiritual eternal bliss and the associated pure intent of the doer as the appropriate criteria for evaluating the correctness of Karma. Unfortunately, most commentaries on Gitā follow the biased approach of asceticism and don't give the Karmayog based explanation clearly, declaring Sanyās as the only correct path to knowledge. As a matter of fact, Karmayog has been equally ancient in Vedic Dharma as the path of Sanyās.

It's pleasing to see that the approach of evaluating Karma through the Adhyātmik way is finding more and more ground worldwide with Green from England and Kant from Germany commenting on similar lines. No matter how much we discuss about the visible world, the discussion about the ultimate goal of a human would remain inconclusive unless we understand who does things and who sees this visible world. If it is benevolence that we find at the root of the visible world, the relevance of Adhyātmik approach is reaffirmed and the philosophy of universal soul being present in us all is reiterated. Adhibhautik people can't go beyond the limitations set by themselves but we can't help them there. Our scriptures have gone beyond them and have explained Karmayogshāstra through Adhyātmik approach. Before discussing this explanation, however, it's important to evaluate another discipline which we shall now discuss in the next chapter.

CHAPTER 6

Adhidaivatpaksha Va Kshetrakshetradnyavichār (Theology/ Institutionist School and Discussion of Body and Soul)

In addition to Adhibhautik (corporeal) discipline, there's another discipline that studies and discusses ethics. It's called Adhidaivik (theological) discipline. People from this sect say that when humans take a decision regarding ethics, neither do they look at who would be happier or gloomier nor do they indulge in thoughts about the soul. Many are clueless on this matter. Rather, not every action is taken for pleasure. If we evaluate the mindset while deciding on an ethical dilemma, we'd find that natural emotions like compassion, empathy, benevolence etc. make people do certain things. E.g. Upon seeing a beggar, many help him automatically out of compassion, without thinking at all about what happiness it would yield them or how it would make the world or their soul better. Adhidaivik believe that such emotions are the real bases of Karmayogshāstra. These aren't given to us by anyone but occur naturally in a person, and are in a way, deities that arise on their own. A judge is inspired by the deity of justice and performs judicial duties. Similarly, compassion, empathy, benevolence, gratitude, duty, courage etc. are all deities and we all inherently know the purest forms of them. However, through greed, jealousy or such vices we don't follow our instincts and perform a bad deed. Often, we're faced with a conflict between these deities in our mind and we need to resort to the deity of our mind to decide rather than resorting to spirituality or utilitarianism. Mind accurately tells us in such instances which deity to follow and thus it proves to be the supreme deity. This broad deity is named 'Conscience' and it's observed that it is the most reliable in all situations. A member of this sect has tried to list and rank different virtues according to the conscience. He's put humility at the epitome, followed by compassion, gratitude, philanthropy, affection etc. in the descending order. He believes in following the deity based on its rank in the event of a conflict between them. They believe that as much farsighted we may become, we can't be authoritatively definitive in terms of asking someone what to do. Rather, depending on this God-given deity of conscience is the most sensible thing to do. We often see phrases such as – 'My conscience told me to…' or 'My conscience doesn't permit me to…' According to these people, there's no other explanation than existence of this deity for us feeling the guilt of a wrongdoing. What we saw above is a summary by Western Institutionist schools, predominantly proposed by Christian philosophers and they seem to prefer this over the Adhibhautik or Corporeal approach while deciding on ethics. Although, there wasn't such a separate school in Indian subcontinent historically, we see many anecdotes mentioning various deities such as Dharma, Truth, Character etc. sporadically in the scriptures. There are many verses calling mind as a deity and asking one to listen to it while making any decision. Controlling mind & its compulsions, and focusing on a single topic is the teaching of Pātanjal Yog; and this school is prevalent in India since ancient times. Resorting to what your mind thinks is also apparently an easier way out. However, if we philosophically delve deeper into knowing what a pure mind is, we find that this easy way doesn't hold for long. This is why our scriptures didn't use this method to base the entire ethics on. We shall understand what the Adhidaivik School has to say but let's first understand how Adhibhautiks reject the philosophy.

Adhidaivik sect regards deity of mind as supreme. In doing so, they correct the flaw of Adhibhautiks that there's no consideration of doer's mindset in 'Majority's happiness' approach. Thus, they're sounder than Adhibhautiks in one aspect. However, once you start analyzing in detail about what they call a deity (conscience), several issues start surfacing.

It's beyond doubt that mind is the final decision maker (not the senses that gather the inputs) when it comes to deciding whether something's beneficial or not, doable or not, acceptable or not etc. You call this mind another organ or a deity. If that's all what Adhidaivik school is proposing, there's nothing wrong with it. However, they go one step ahead. They say that there are two different decision-making processes. One that decides what's right or wrong, just or unjust and righteous or non-righteous etc. There's another that decides what's heavy or light and what's white or black etc. Decisions of the second kind can be made by mind through logic or law. However, mind is incapable of making first kind of decisions and that's entirely done by the deity of conscience. Taking second type of decisions involves some calculation or deliberation. However, taking the first type of decision (e.g. opinion about someone murdering someone) is instantaneous. It doesn't take anyone even a moment to decide that murdering someone is bad. This is because the deity of conscience is equally active in everyone and is innate. Adhibhautiks counter this by saying that this is just a question of degree and not kind. If someone does a calculation faster, their decision making would be faster, but it doesn't make the decision-making deity different. Sometimes, some things become so habitual that someone can do them instantaneously while others take longer. No one claims existence of different deities there. Neither does anyone discount the scientific process of arriving at the decision. Moreover, if the deity of conscience was enabling instantaneous decisions, there would've never been a moral dilemma that Arjun faced and Gitā itself would've been unnecessary. Not only did Arjun face this dilemma, the opinions about what he should've done also differ from person to person. If conscience is an omnipresent deity, why this difference? This is because the degree of knowledge, maturity or culture is different between different individuals. Practices considered a taboo in one country or religion are common in another. Similar habits or manners are interpreted differently in different cultures. Having more than one wife is considered a crime in one country while it's permissible in another. If the deity is same everywhere, why are people having different opinion about this polarizing act? As humans developed culture, some things have become so habitual that making decisions about them has become natural and takes no time. Looking at an object near you and one away from you need different adjustments of the muscles of your eyes. However, the changes are so seamless that you don't realize it. Does anyone discount the efforts taken by the muscles because of this? No. Summarily, mind or intellect of human beings is homogeneous at all times and doesn't have different kinds that think about different topics. Someone's intelligence may be less, more, underdeveloped or highly developed. Moreover, being able to do something slower or faster is subjective and a result of practice and habit. Once you see this, there doesn't arise any need to postulate existence of any deity called conscience. This is how Adhibhautiks have rejected the Adhidaivik philosophy.

The final decision of our ancient philosophers about this is similar. They agree that one must take a decision using a calm and peaceful mind. However, even they discard the logic of separate entities making ethical and calculative decisions. Depending on the capability of mind, one makes good or bad decisions and hence one must strive hard to improve the capability. There are also ways advised to achieve this improvement; but like Adhibhautiks even they don't accept the existence of any separate deity other than mind or intellect. Ancient studies have analyzed in depth how we acquire knowledge and how our intellect operates. This study is called Kshetrakshetradnyavichār or the study of body and soul. Kshetra (literal – field) means body and Kshetradnya (literal – who knows the field) means soul. This thought is the foundation of Adhyātma (spirituality). Once we understand Kshetra and Kshetradnya in detail, no deity – conscience or any other – appears superior and we also find out how Adhidaivik (Institutionist) discipline falls short. Let's understand this Kshetrakshetradnyavichār which shall also elucidate to the readers the true essence of Gitā to a large extent.

A human body (Kshetra) is like a factory. Just as a factory intakes raw material, sorts and classifies them, decides what's useful and useless and then processes the raw materials to make a finished product and sends it out; there are many different processes going on in the human body constantly. Senses/organs are the first tools for us to gain knowledge of the five elements of nature. We'd never understand the true nature of these elements through our organs. Adhibhautiks consider that whatever we perceive of the world is the ultimate truth. However, if we develop a new sensory organ tomorrow through evolution, it's needless to say that the properties of matter would be interpreted differently from what they are today. Anyway, there are different types of organs. First type is Karmendriye (Action organs) and Second type is Dnyānendriye (Knowledge/sensory organs). Hands, Legs, Voice, Genitals and Anus are the five Action organs. Whatever actions we perform are through these five organs. Apart from these, Nose, Eyes, Ears, Tongue and Skin are the five Knowledge or sensory organs. We see through eyes, smell through nose, hear through ears, taste through tongue and sense touch through our skin. You take any object outside your body, whatever knowledge you develop of it is through these five sensory organs; beyond that we know nothing else. Take Gold for example – We see it as golden yellow, feel its weight, see that it gets elongated once struck etc. Whatever we perceive about gold through our senses is Gold for us. The factory has inward and outward doors. Similarly, five sensory organs are our inward doors and five action organs our outward doors. Whenever light reflects from an object, we see it; whenever minute particles from a substance enter our nose and touch the nerves, we smell it and so on. Once our sensory organs start operating, we gain knowledge of our surrounding. However, whatever inputs the sensory organs give, they themselves can't make any sense of it. Hence, they're called the doors and not knowers. Once the goods are in, sorting and processing of it is the work of mind. E.g. when the clock strikes twelve, ears don't understand what time it is. Hearing 12 strokes separately, mind sums it all up and tells us it's 12 o'clock. Scientifically speaking, animals may hear the same clock striking twelve. However, their mind isn't developed enough to understand that it's 12 o'clock. The meaning behind a verse from Gitā is this – 'Organs are better than the objects and Mind is better than the organs' (Gitā 3.42). While understanding the operations of this factory of our body, once we see the raw material being input by the Sensory organs and see the clerk called Mind processing it, we've to divide this Mind further into different sub-types to understand the further process. Let's now study the different names this mind adopts because of the different tasks it performs.

Once we receive the inputs from our sensory organs, they need to be enlisted, sorted into better and worse, acceptable and worth rejecting, beneficial and detrimental etc. Once done, we get ready to do the beneficial thing. E.g. If we go to a garden, using eyes and nose we analyze the different flowers and only after our soul processes this and decides which flower we want, we pluck it. Thus, there are 3 broad types of operations that our mind does – 1. Getting the input via the sensory organs and arranging them properly for evaluation; 2. Evaluating these arranged inputs to decide which one's beneficial and which one's not; and 3. After the decision is made, developing or making the wish to discard the unwanted thing and choosing to get the thing we want. It's not mandatory that these three things must happen sequentially. Even in case of liking a thing already known, we can't say any of these processes are unnecessary. Just as in a court, both sides present their pleas, judge evaluates both pleas and gives a decision which is then executed by the Nazir (executive). Thereby, mind which we've called the clerk till now, gets divided into sub-types based on its operations. The task of making the final decision that a particular thing is THIS and not THAT (the judge's task) is of Buddhi (Intellect). The part of our mind that does all other operations except the one stated above is termed Man (Mind) according to both Vedānta and Sānkhya philosophies. This mind, like an advocate, presents inputs as THIS and THAT to the intellect and hence it's called 'Sankalp-Vikalpātmak' or mere presenter of the choices. The word Sankalp indicates definitiveness in some cases but not in the case in point. However, it's not only the advocate's part the mind plays. After the intellect makes the decision, the task of the Nazir (executive) also needs to be performed by Man (Mind). Thus, Mind can also be defined in another way. The thought of how to implement the decision made by intellect is in a way elaborative. In Sanskrit it has another term – 'Vyākaran (Grammar) or to expand'. Tasks other than these are of the intellect. Mind doesn't do evaluative tasks. The task of evaluating the inputs and giving knowledge to the soul, making a definitive choice about certainty of a topic or deciding on an ethical problem etc. are the operations of Buddhi (intellect). In Sanskrit it's called 'Vyavasāy' or 'Adhyavasāy' (professional or businesslike). Hence, using this terminology to distinguish between Buddhi and Man, following verse is written in Mahābhārat –

Vyavasāyātmikā Buddhih Mano Vyākaranātmakam

"Buddhi (intellect) is professional (evaluative and decisive) and Man (mind) is grammatical (executive or doing expansion)". Intellect is like a sword. Its only virtue is to slice whatever it confronts. It doesn't have any other property. Will, desire, wish, memory, courage, reverence, enthusiasm, compassion, kindness, love, empathy, gratitude, lust, shame, joy, fear, anger, attachment, hatred, greed, pride, envy, fury etc. are all properties of Mind. As one or more of these emotions arise, one tends to tilt towards performing an action accordingly. E.g. Irrespective of how intelligent they are and however aware they may be of the plight of poor and destitute people; they wouldn't act on it unless they possess compassion or kindness. One won't fight even if they wish to unless they possess courage. Intellect only tells us the consequences of our actions. As it doesn't possess qualities such as kindness or courage, it can't inspire action organs to act. Conversely, if mind inspires organs to act without consulting intellect, the action may not turn out to be ethical. E.g. if kindness inspires one to do charity without the intellect getting to make a decision, such charity may result in a consequence that is detrimental. Thus, mind is blind without the intellect. One must have a discerning intellect, obedient mind and controlled action organs for a pure Karma. Other than Buddhi and Man, there are also Antahkaran and Chitta. Antahkaran literally means 'Inner organ' and thus includes Buddhi, Man, Chitta, Ahankār etc. When *Man* starts to think about outer things it becomes Chitta. However, in common parlance, all these words are used loosely and become confusing. Hence, Man and Buddhi are the only two words definitively used in scientific approach. As seen above, intellect naturally becomes the judge and mind its clerk or Nazir. Intellect is superior to mind (Gitā 3.42) means exactly this. However, mind has two tasks as envisaged – That of an advocate who presents the processed inputs to the judge and also that of a Nazir or executive who carries out operations as per the instructions of the intellect.

In a classic verse by great grammarian Pānini, the process of voice is beautifully explained as follows: Soul first analyzes through intellect and develops a desire in mind to speak. Mind then operates kāyāgni (neurons) which in turn modulates air. The air then enters the diaphragm to generate a sound. This sound finally travels through the larynx and vocal cords to come out as voice. Kāyāgni is called neurons by modern physiological science and like separate neurons bringing message in and sending out, there should be two minds according to western physiologists. However, our philosophers have considered mind as singular and having dual characteristics and acts as per requirement in case of action and sensory organs. Conclusively, both agree with each other in calling intellect the judge and mind the executive.

Although Buddhi (Intellect) is the discerning organ as seen above, it's for the minute scientific analysis. However, these scientific meanings are also retrospectively derived and hence, we must now discuss the practical meanings of Buddhi in common parlance. Just as the mango tree and the mango fruit are both denoted as simply 'mango', Buddhi is similarly used singularly for both professional intellect and executive or desirous mind. When someone calls someone with wrong intellect, they actually mean wrong mind. However, usage of Buddhi as both 'Discerning intellect' and 'Desirous mind' had been in use before coining of terms Buddhi and Man denoting different exclusive meanings. Hence, just like tree and fruit are added to mango to distinguish what we mean, adjectives Vyavasāyātmak (professional) and Vāsanātmak (desirous) are added to the noun Buddhi. Gitā uses the word Buddhi in both ways mentioned above (Gitā 2.41,44,49 and 3.42) and to understand the analysis of Karmayog, both the meanings of Buddhi need to kept in mind. Whenever someone is performing an action, they first decide on whether it's a good or a bad thing to do, doable or not etc. using professional Buddhi and then the desire is developed in his desirous Buddhi for performing that action. Once the professional Buddhi is in proper place, the desirous Buddhi doesn't waver. Hence, one must first purify and stabilize professional Buddhi. This is the first teaching of Gitā about Karmayog (Gitā 2.41). Even Kant distinguishes reason as 'pure reason' and 'practical reason' in his book. Honestly, stabilizing of Professional Buddhi is a topic of Pātanjal Yog and not Karmayog. However, Gitā emphasizes on knowing the desire of the doer before evaluating any Karma and once we start thinking about desire, we see that whoever's professional Buddhi isn't stable and pure, develops varied ripples of desire which may not be pure. Hence, it becomes relevant in Karmayogshāstra to see ways of stabilizing and purifying professional Buddhi. This is why sixth Adhyāya mentions Pātanjal Yog as a tool. However, some critiques have mistakenly inferred that Gitā expounds only Pātanjal Yog exclusively. It's clear how important it is to understand the correct meanings of Buddhi in Gitā to make perfect sense of it.

Let's now move to understand how concept of the deity of conscience goes for a toss once we separately consider Buddhi (intellect) and Man (mind). Deciding between right and wrong is the task of this deity and thus it can't be included in *Man*. As Buddhi is the single entity deliberating on all topics to give a decision, there's no scope for a separate deity called conscience. The decisions taken by this Buddhi may be different based on its maturity, evolutionary state, education or history which may have rendered it Sāttvic, Rājas or Tāmas. This may render opinions about one's decisions disagreeable to someone else. However, it's still the same Buddhi. This explains how a thief thinks differently from a saint which can't be explained by the concept of deity of conscience. It is the task of every human to make their Buddhi Sāttvic. If we do not, however, and it listens to the sensory organs to make its decisions, we can't call it pure. For this, we shall not let intellect listen to the body or the mind. It should be the other way round. This is the reason why Kathopanishad uses the famous allegory of a chariot to one's body where the charioteer (Buddhi) must use the reins (Man) to keep horses (senses) in check. This was so appropriate that even Plato, the famous Greek philosopher, used it in his book (Phaedrus) to depict restraint of senses. We've to make our intellect stable using either Pātanjal Yog (Samādhi), Bhakti (reverence), Dnyān (knowledge) or Dhyāna (Meditation) to know and imbibe on it that there's only one universal soul present in everyone. This is called Ātmanishtha Buddhi (Subjective Intellect). Once the professional intellect thus becomes subjective with mind and senses in its control, desire automatically gets purified and body naturally tends to tilt towards Sāttvic actions. This is the root of all good conduct according to Karmayogshāstra with a spiritual view. It's clear from the entire analysis we saw above why our philosophers didn't depict conscience as a separate deity. One may be tempted to call glorified intellect as a deity. However, even after in depth analysis we don't find a separate entity other than intellect or mind. It's only the degree of intellect that's different in different individuals – Sāttvic in saints and Tāmasi in thieves. Reiterating the emphasis on degree rather than kind defeats the concept of deities and the Institutionist school this way.

Once we see that Adhibhautik approach is insufficient and Adhidaivik approach incapable, we need a third approach to explain Karmayogshāstra. This approach is Adhyātmik (spiritual). Although intellect is better than actions, it's not a deity. It's necessary to then know how to purify this intellect, what a pure intellect is and how to keep it pure. This knowledge is impossible without entering the waters of spirituality. The intellect which doesn't yet have the true knowledge of the soul is not pure. This is the final proposition of spirituality. Gitā describes spirituality precisely to describe what a pure or Ātmanishtha (subjective) intellect is. However, some communalist critics have tried to depict Vedānta as the main subject of Gitā. We shall prove later how this depiction is wrong. For now, we shall only see how soul becomes relevant while describing pure intellect. There are two sides to this approach – 1. Watching the operations of our Kshetra (field) meaning body and mind to see how we arrive at Kshetradnya (knower of the field) meaning soul. This is called Kshetrakshetradnyavichār. This is why Vedānta Sutras are also called Shāreerak (pertaining to the body) Sutras. After studying body and mind, then 2. Comparative investigation of the principle/essence found in this study and the principle/essence found after studying the universe surrounding us and checking if they're the same or different is called Ksharāksharvichār or Vyaktāvyaktavichar (study of the impermanent and permanent or expressed and unexpressed). After reflecting on the two principles found through Kshetrakshetradnyavichār and Ksharāksharvichār the one principle we find beyond these two, from which they've arose, is called Parmātmā (Ultimate soul) or Purushottam (Supreme Being). Gitā tells us how knowledge of this absolute principle purifies our mind. The Ksharāksharvichār shall be discussed later in a separate chapter. Let's now see the Kshetrakshetradnyavichār.

We discussed the body made up of five elements, five action organs, five sensory organs, their five perceptions (taste, touch, smell, vision and hearing), executive mind and professional intellect. However, this doesn't conclude the study of a human being. If there's no life-force (which puts the word 'being' in human being), everything else becomes meaningless. This life-force is called 'Chetanā'. It's different from Chaitanya (consciousness) because of which life is infused in non-living things. Apart from Chetanā, there's one more virtue within us which makes us distinguish between 'mine' and 'someone else's'. It's called 'Ahankār' (ego). The five principles from which the five elements have evolved are different and are also part of a human being. The power that keeps all of it together is yet different and is called 'Dhruti' (determination). When we get all these together, we get a complete human being which is called 'Kshetra'. This terminology is according to Gitā and we shall follow that. Kshetra originally means a field. However, here it's used as living human body or human being. It's similar to the analogy of factory we gave earlier. Once we call this the field, the next logical question is whether or not there's an owner of the field. Often, the word soul is used loosely as mind or self. However, its true meaning is Kshetradnya or the owner of the field. Whatever activities a human does, be it physical or psychological, they're done by either action organs, sensory organs or internal organs like mind and intellect. Mind and intellect are the greatest among these. However, they're still part of the body or Kshetra (covered in detail in a later chapter). Intellect and mind perform a certain function and motivate the organs to perform an action, but for whom? Who collates all the different activities of these parts and decides the flow and direction? We can't say body does this; because once Chetanā (life force) exits from it the body is dead and can't do a thing. Additionally, the body mass is made up from the food we eat and is lost and renewed over time so we can't say the body is the constant. If we consider Chetanā as the owner, we don't feel the being of ourselves during sleep although Chetanā is active and performing the action of breathing, circulation etc. Ahankār decides 'Mine' and 'someone else's' yet it doesn't decide who 'I' am. If we consider 'I' as an illusion, it doesn't make sense and we don't get the answer of who gets everything collated. Many say there's no separate entity called 'I' but a group of Buddhi, Man, Body etc. However, just like a machine is not just the sum of its parts, all the parts of the body are not just senselessly put together but there's a definitive driving force behind its operations. What is that common thread that goes through them all? Some say just the aggregation of these parts generates a virtue in the body. However, it's not plausible that 'something' could come from 'nothing' as it's been proven so by numerous philosophers after thorough evaluation. Still, let's imagine this as a possibility for time being. Many physicists say, the matter and virtues/properties can't be separate entities, properties need a base and hence instead of the virtue, we consider the aggregation as the owner of the field. Why then, do we not call fire as wood, lightening as clouds or gravity as earth? Just because we don't know the base of the energy doesn't mean it doesn't exist, right? Just as one can't sit on one's own shoulders or knowledge of aggregation of components couldn't possibly be done by aggregation itself; it can be derived logically that 'that for whom' the aggregation of different body parts happens is different from the aggregation itself. This principle (different from the aggregation) being the knower of all things, is not perceivable to itself. Yet, its existence can't be denied. Dnyāta and Dnyeya ('knower' and 'to be known') are two categories of substances. If something doesn't fall in one category, it automatically falls in the other and its existence is proven equally. Rather, as this 'soul' (beyond the aggregation) is the knower; it's not surprising that it doesn't belong to the category 'to be known'. Thus, we must infer that, rising above physical organs, being separate from Prāna, Chetanā, Man and Buddhi, aggregating them all, assigning tasks to them and being witness to their actions; there's a bigger, all-encompassing and potent energy that lives in all living beings. Sānkhya and Vedānta both agree with this concept and Kant through his minute analysis of intellect has arrived at the same conclusion. Sānkhya call it 'Purush' and Vedānta calls it 'Kshetradnya' (knower of the field) or soul. The feeling of 'I'm there' which everyone has is a testimony to its presence. Even if someone says 'I'm not there', the subject of 'not there' is undeniable. Vedānta philosophy was conceived specifically to understand the pure and formless/abstract nature of the Soul or Kshetradnya, which is felt by itself inside the material body, as 'I'. However, this is not decided just by Kshetrakshetradnyavichār (discussion of body and soul). It also explores outer world or Brahmānd (the entire universe) which is called 'Ksharāksharvichār' (discussion of impermanent and permanent). Former tells us the fundamental principle in one's body while the latter finds the fundamental principle behind the universe. Once we separately establish these two, further study leads us to the conclusion that they're both the same. This is termed as – 'Je Pindi te Brahmāndi' (Whatever is the governing principle of the Pinda or Kshetra i.e. body is the same governing principle of the universe). This is the ultimate cosmic truth. Day by day, western philosophical studies are advancing and beginning to agree with Vedānta philosophy. Despite the advancement of science being way behind what we have today, the Vedānta philosophers proposed these concepts in those ancient times. We can't help but wonder and feel proud of their unparalleled wisdom.

CHAPTER 7

Kāpilsānkhyashāstra Kinva Ksharāksharvichār (Kāpilsānkhya Philosophy and Discussion of Impermanent and Permanent)

After studying body and soul, we are now delving into the study of the principle behind this universe which we're surrounded by. For this, we shall begin with Ksharāksharvichār (Discussion of impermanent and permanent). There are three philosophies engaging in this study. First is Nyāya philosophy and second is Sānkhya. Proving the theories of both these to be insufficient, Vedānta philosophy has proposed a third conclusive theory. Let us study these two like Bādarāyanāchārya has done in his Vedānta sutras (albeit briefly). Even though Naiyāyik principles are not accepted by any Vedānta scholars, many concepts of Sānkhya philosophy find acceptance in Manusmriti and Gitā and is thus worth studying. However, let me make it very clear right at the outset that the final positions taken by Sānkhya and Vedānta philosophies are very different. There can be a debate about which philosophy was proposed first. There are 3 options – Either both developed in parallel, writers of Upanishad might've improved upon original Sānkhya principles or sage Kapilāchārya might've drafted Sānkhya philosophy as per his take on ancient Upanishads. However, considering that Upanishads are more ancient (Shrauta or heard), third possibility seems most likely. Let us now probe into Nyāya and Sānkhya philosophies which are Smārta (remembered) and see what their take on the structure of the universe is.

Many believe that the only subject which Nyāya philosophy deals with is drawing inference logically from different assumptions or hypotheses and deciding which inferences are right or wrong and why. However, it's a misconception and that's only a branch of Nyāya philosophy. Classification of different substances in the universe, going deeper to see how many different elemental entities exist, defining their properties and to find out the origin of all substances from these elements are all parts of the study. Kanād and his disciples (called Kānād) postulate that Parmānu (indivisible atoms) are the ultimate building blocks of the universe. Kanād's definition matches that of the modern physicists. As these Parmānu aggregate, different properties arise due to their combinations and different substances come into existence. Mind and Body, too, have Parmānu and once they come together, Chaitanya (consciousness) is created. Pruthvi (Earth), Aap (Water), Tej (Fire) and Vāyu (Air) have naturally and uniquely different Parmānu. Earth elements have four properties (visibility, taste, smell and touch), Water elements have three, Fire elements have two and Air elements have one. The universe is full of these permanent Parmānu since beginning of time. There's no separate reason or purpose behind this universe. When these permanent and minute Parmānu interact with each other, different substances manifest. This is called Ārambhavāda (Origin theory). Some Naiyāyik never go beyond this. However, some consider Parameshwar (almighty) to be the reason behind aggregation of Parmānu to complete the question of creation. Vedānta Sutras prove both these approaches wrong in its second Adhyāya.

Looking at above mentioned Nyāya philosophy, one can't help but notice its similarity to Dalton's atomic theory, proposed in early 19th century. However, just as Dalton's theory was defeated by Darwin's theory of evolution, Sānkhya philosophy replaced Nyāya philosophy of Kanād. Kanād's theory can't explain how Parmānu got their initial stimulus. Not only that, it can't even explain other factors like how trees, animals and human developed as higher life forms. This clarification was done by Lamarck and Darwin in the 19th century and in ancient India by Kapil. Both approaches conclude that single original substance developed properties that ultimately resulted in formation of the whole universe as we know it. These theories resulted in debacle of Parmānu theory in ancient India and 19thcentury Europe. Modern physicists have also proved today that atom is not really indivisible. Ancient Indians like Kanād and Kapil didn't have the sophisticated machinery and equipped labs to experiment and evaluate. It's astounding to see what they proposed simply by observing what they could with what they had and how similar it is to modern physicists' theories proposed millennia later. Science has developed a great deal and many things can be proven in a better way through proofs, too. Additionally, science has made lives better practically as well. However, there's little that modern physicists can tell about the origin of the living-breathing universe from unexpressed Prakruti (matter) better than Sānkhya philosophy even today, and this we shall prove by comparing Sānkhya principles with Haeckel's principles. (Please note here that Geetārahasya being written in early 20th century benchmarks Haeckel as he was the contemporary modern scientist at that time). Haeckel declares that all his principles are not originally his but he's based his principles on previous scientists like Darwin, Spencer etc. However, he's compiled them well in his book 'Riddle of the universe' and hence we've chosen him as a benchmark in further discussions.

Before discussing Kāpilsānkhya philosophy, one must understand two different meanings of the word 'Sānkhya'. First meaning is the philosophy proposed by Kapilāchārya and it's been mentioned in Gitā once (18.13). However, other than this specific meaning, it's also used as a term for any type of philosophy in general, which also includes Vedānta philosophy. When someone says Sānkhya Nishthā or Sānkhya Yog, it's this general meaning intended. Further, a knowledgeable person is regarded as Sānkhya in Bhagavad Gitā (2.39, 3.3, 5.4, 5 and 13.14) where it doesn't mean Kāpilsānkhya but even a Vedānti (Vedānta follower) who's engulfed himself in knowledge and renounced all Karma. The word Sānkhya comes from *Sankhy*ā which means 'number' and Sānkhya literally means one who counts. Kāpilsānkhya philosophy enumerates only 25 total elements and hence originally received the Sānkhya name and the specific meaning first. Later, Sānkhya started to mean any philosophy in general and started having a broader meaning, according to etymologists. As Kāpilsānkhya monks were called Sānkhya, it appears that even Vedānti ascetics started being called Sānkhya later on. Whatever be the case, we gave this chapter a longer name 'Kāpilsānkhyashāstra' especially to make it clear what we mean. Like Kānād Nyāya Shāstra, Kāpilsānkhya Shāstra has sutras too. However, Gaudapāda or Shankarāchārya didn't include them as basis of their study, which indicate that they must've been developed later. Sānkhyakārika by Ishwarkrishna is considered to predate those. Gaudapāda (great Guru of Shankarāchārya) as well as Shankarāchārya have included verses from this Sānkhyakarika in their writings and Chinese translation is available from time older than 570 A.D. We've thus considered this one as the reference for Sānkhya philosophy.

Bhagwān Shri Krishna, while describing his great incarnations/ forms, says – "Siddhānām Kapilo Munih" (Among the realized beings, I am Kapil) (Gitā 10.26). This proves the greatness of Kapilāchārya. However, exact identification and chronology of rishi Kapil isn't clear. One account in Mahābhārat calls him one of the 7 sons of Brahma (the creator) who were born knowledgeable. Another says, Kapil's disciple was Āsuri and Āsuri's disciple Panchashikha taught Sānkhya philosophy to king Janak. Many other accounts regard Kāpilsānkhya as the source of knowledge and credit it with being the original knowledge bank just as all modern scientists credit the theory of evolution. We've described the background here in detail to apprise readers of the same because study of Kāpilsānkhya philosophy has not been prevalent in recent years.

Let's now understand the key principles of Kāpilsānkhya philosophy. First principle is – Not a single thing is originated in this world anew, because 'Zero' or 'Nothing' can't give rise to 'Something'. Whatever properties you observe in the thing that is formed (effect), are present in the thing that leads to this new thing (cause) in minute form. According to Buddhists and Kānād, one substance gets destroyed to form the other; e.g. Seed gets destroyed to form a sprout and this sprout gets destroyed to form a sapling and so on. However, Sānkhya and Vedānti don't agree with this. They say, the ingredients of the seed don't get destroyed but accumulate other nutrients from the soil and air to form a sprout. Similarly, when wood burns, it doesn't completely disappear but it gets transformed into ash, smoke etc. Wood doesn't disappear to form smoke. How can 'Nothing' give rise to 'Something'? Milk becomes curd, water doesn't. If we assume properties not a part of cause appearing independently in the effect, we don't get an answer of why curd can't be formed from water. If you take any effect, its current traces and properties must've been present in the cause in some form, according to Sānkhya. This is called 'Satkāryavāda' (Theory of Causality). Even modern scientists have today arrived at the conclusion that 'Total amount of Matter and Energy in the universe is always constant' (Even after Einstein's theory of special relativity, we still maintain that total sum of Mass and Energy, although interchangeable, is the same). Although Sānkhya and modern scientific principles appear similar, one must remember that the principle of modern physics is broader and more comprehensive – they're only similar to the extent of the 'Theory of Causality'. Anyway, not only can the effect not have any property which wasn't a part of its causes, the total mass-energy of the cause and effect are exactly identical. This has now been proven mathematically, too. This is the key feature of both these principles. Bhagavad Gitā says – "Nāsato Vidyate Bhāvo" (Gitā 2.16) – "What's not there can never come into existence". This principle is closer to the modern theories of Conservation of Energy and Momentum than it is simply to the Theory of causality. Vedānta agrees with the theory of causality but it doesn't apply beyond Saguna Srushti (Universe with form). How Nirguna (without form or attributes) becomes Saguna (with form or attributes) needs to be explained in a different way according to Advaita Vedānta. This shall however be discussed in a subsequent chapter called Adhyātma (Spirituality). For now, let's understand how Sānkhya have discussed Ksharākshar (Impermanent and permanent) based on Satkāryavāda (theory of causality).

Once we establish the theory of causality, the premise that 'the universe came into existence from zero or nothing' naturally falls flat. It also proves that properties of whatever we see today must've been in the substance that was there at the beginning of the universe. If we see today, we find plants, animals, humans, rocks, gold etc. which are all perceivable by our senses. They have different appearance and properties. However, this variety isn't permanent or original; there's only a single original element which is the basis of everything, according to Sānkhya. Even the elements of the periodic table are not original but formed from this one element. This is the element from which the Sun, the Moon, the Earth etc. are made. This primary element is called '**Prakruti**'. Prakruti literally means 'original' and the substances formed from this Prakruti are called 'Vikruti' (literally imbalance or distortion) meaning its manifestations.

Even though the element is one, if it had a single Guṇ or Guna (quality/attribute), it couldn't lead to multiple attributes according to Satkāryavāda (Theory of Causality). If we look at all the objects in the universe, they possess various, innumerable properties. Hence, observing different substances, Sānkhya have classified these attributes into three classes – Sattva, Raja and Tama. Every substance has its purest or complete form and the opposite or inferior form. We observe that it always tends to move from its inferior form to its purest form. The three states among this constant transformation are listed as follows – The purest state is called Sāttvic, Inferior state is called Tāmas and transformational state is called Rājas. Sānkhya say that Sattva, Raja and Tama are the three attributes which are present in Prakruti since the beginning; rather these three attributes are Prakruti. Initially, all three are in equal proportion and Prakruti is in equilibrium. This equilibrium was at the beginning of the universe and would be at its end, too. There's no movement in equilibrium. Everything is still. However, as these three attributes become imbalanced, transformational Raja causes original Prakruti to get transformed into different objects and the universe comes into existence. There's a catch here – If Sattva, Raja, Tama were in equilibrium, what made the imbalance? To this Sānkhya simply call it the inherent quality of Prakruti. Even though Prakruti is inanimate, it orchestrates all these activities. Of the three Gunas, knowledge or consciousness is the virtue of Sattva, ignorance or lethargy is the virtue of Tama and Raja Guna is transformational, promoting activity – either good or bad. These three Gunas can never occur in isolation. Every substance in this universe is a combination of these three. As the combination of each component is different in different objects; each substance is different – Gold, Iron, Water, Sky, Human body etc. In every substance, there's a competition of the three Gunas and whichever Guna dominates decides its character. When we say a substance is Sāttvic, it doesn't mean Sattva Guna is present in isolation but simply in dominance. Similar is the case with Rājas and Tāmas. If Sattva dominates Raja and Tama in our body, we start getting knowledge and we start seeing everything in its true form and mind becomes peaceful. It doesn't mean Raja and Tama have vanished, but they are dominated by Sattva and are thus not expressed. If Raja dominates, person develops greed and becomes active to do many things. If Tama dominates instead, a person develops sleepiness, laziness and dementia. In summary, all the variety in the universe is because of different combinations of Sattva, Raja and Tama and study of how this variety exists despite there being this one original element (Prakruti) is called Vidnyān (Science). Physics, Chemistry, Astronomy etc. are different branches of science.

In equilibrium, Prakruti is **Avyakta** (unmanifest), meaning it's not perceivable to senses. Due to the fight of Sattva, Raja and Tama within it, many substances which are formed are perceivable by our senses and are called **Vyakta** (manifest). They may be visible, audible etc. depending on the sense which can perceive it. Of these, substances like rock, gold, water are Sthool (Gross) while other substances like mind, intellect, ether etc. are Sookshma (subtle). Subtle doesn't mean minute, however, as ether may be subtle yet it's virtually everywhere. Sookshma and Sthool depict the constitution of a substance while Vyakta and Avyakta depict the perceptibility. Hence, two different Sookshma objects may be such that one is Vyakta and other is Avyakta. E.g. Air is Sookshma (subtle) but Vyakta (perceptible) while Prakruti is Sookshma (subtle) but it's so subtle it can't be perceived by senses and hence is Avyakta (imperceptible). One may argue here about the existence of Prakruti if it's imperceptible. However, Sānkhya counter this argument by saying that as per Satkāryavāda (Theory of Causality), every effect must have a cause and thus we conclude that every substance can be traced back to a single building block which may not be perceptible but its existence can't be denied. That is Prakruti. Vedānti use the same logic for proving the existence of Brahman. Once we consider Prakruti to be extremely subtle and imperceptible, the Naiyāyiks' Parmānu vāda (atomic theory) automatically gets defeated. Parmānu may be imperceptible and infinite. However, as every Parmānu is a separate entity, the question of the contents of Parmānu remains. Hence, Sānkhya say – Prakruti doesn't have distinction as in Parmānu and it is continuous, homogenous, imperceptible and omnipresent.

Although Parabrahma (Supreme Absolute) of Vedānta may seem to have the same description as Prakruti of Sānkhya, they're poles apart. While Prakruti is inanimate/unconscious and Trigunātmak (made of three Gunas – Sattva, Raja and Tama) or Saguna (with attributes); Parabrahma is Chaitanyaroopi (conscious) and Nirguna (attribute-less). We shall, however, discuss this later. Let's focus on Sānkhya principles for now. We defined Sookshma, Sthool, Vyakta and Avyakta. At the beginning of the universe, every object was Sookshma but Avyakta like Prakruti and it becomes Vyakta (either Sookshma or Sthool but perceptible); while at the end of the universe this perceptibility is lost and it goes back to being Avyakta as Prakruti. Gitā seconds this opinion (Gitā 2.28 and 8.18). In another terminology of Sānkhya, Avyakta Prakruti is called Akshar (permanent) and all the substances formed from it are called Kshar (impermanent). This Prakruti is called Māyā (appearance) in Vedānta.

Once we classify all substances into Avyakta and Vyakta or Kshar and Akshar, the entities Ātmā (soul), Man (mind), Buddhi (intellect), Ahankār (ego) and Indriye (organs) which were explained in Kshetrakshetradnyavichār should be classified as Vyakta, as they are part of body (physical). However, how to classify mind, intellect, ego and especially soul as Vyakta, if they can't be perceived? Famous modern naturalist Haeckel says that mind, intellect and soul are all bodily constituents. If a person's brain gets damaged, he loses memory. If one part of brain gets damaged, that particular function is lost. In short, all psychological aspects are properties of physical and can't be separated from it. Hence, soul along with other such entities must be classified as Vyakta or perceptible. Once we classify them so, only Avyakta and

Inanimate Prakruti remains as it's the original element from which everything has been formed. There's no creator of the universe other than Prakruti herself. Once the power of Prakruti crossed a certain level, it became soul or consciousness. The rules of the original Prakruti, and thus that of the whole universe, are governed by the theory of causality and we're all its prisoners. Soul is neither independent nor permanent. What's the relevance of Moksha (liberation) then? The concept of free will is a myth and one must follow the instructions of Prakruti. This is what Haeckel proposes and as everything is attributed exclusively to Prakruti, he calls it Advaita (Monism). As it's rooted entirely in physical, we call it Jadadvaita (Physical Monism).

Sānkhya philosophy disagrees with this completely. They agree with and explain the development of Man, Buddhi and Ahankār as physical entities which are developed from Prakruti. However, consciousness can't be born from Prakruti. Moreover, just as one can't sit on their own shoulders, knower of Prakruti can't say "I know this" or "I see this" without being different from Prakruti. Hence, 'knower' and 'to be known' or witness and the scene have to be different. The same entity we called 'Kshetradnya' or 'Ātmā' in the previous chapter is called 'Purush' (spirit) or 'Dnya' (knower). As this Purush is different from Prakruti, it's naturally free from the Sattva-Raja-Tama Gunas and hence is Nirguna (attribute-less), inert and is only a witness to what's happening. Sānkhya philosophy thus proposes that Prakruti and Purush are these two primordial, independent and self-manifested entities where Prakruti is inanimate while Purush is conscious, Prakruti is a doer while Purush is apathetic and inert, Prakruti is governed by three attributes while Purush is attribute-less and Prakruti is blind while Purush is witness to everything. Gitā seconds this by saying Prakruti and Purush are primordial (Gitā 13.19). We must note here, however, that Gitā doesn't agree with the notion that Prakruti and Purush are independent or self-manifested.

Sānkhya believe that all substances in the universe are classified into three groups viz. Prakruti, its manifestations and Purush. However, the manifestations are transient and impermanent. Thus, we're left with only two entities – Prakruti and Purush. As Sānkhya believe that both these entities are primordial and self-manifested, they're called Dvaiti (dualists or believers of duality). They don't believe in any entity beyond Prakruti and Purush like Almighty, Time, Nature etc. As almighty with form, time or nature are all manifest and thus a part of other manifest substances arising from Prakruti, according to Sānkhya; and if we believe almighty to be attribute-less, how can it give rise to Trigunātmak (with attributes) Prakruti defeating the Satkāryavāda? Thus, depicting Prakruti and Purush as two primordial entities, they've discarded the concept of any third entity and also propounded the origin of universe through these two. They say that although Purush alone can't do anything; once Prakruti and Purush meet, Prakruti starts spreading out the manifestations of its Gunas (Sthool and Sookshma) in front of it. Although Purush is knower and conscious, being attribute-less it can't perform any actions; while despite being capable of actions, Prakruti is inanimate and unconscious thus not being able to act. Just as a handicapped man can sit on the shoulders of a blind man to jointly walk the path, actions begin in nature once Prakruti and Purush meet. Just as in a play an actress dances for audience's entertainment, Prakruti dances with all different combinations of its Gunas in front of Purush. Once Purush, due to its vanity or through desire, needlessly attaches the consequences of Prakruti's actions to itself, it gets entangled and shall never get Moksha (liberation) (Gitā 3.27). Once, however, it realizes that Prakruti is separate and so am I, it's already liberated (Gitā 13.29,30; 14.20). If you see clearly, Purush is neither the doer nor bound. It's naturally independent and inert. Whatever happens is an act of Prakruti. Rather, even mind and intellect are manifestations of Prakruti. Thus, whatever intellect realizes is a consequence of Prakruti's actions. This realization or knowledge is of three types – Sāttvic, Rājas and Tāmas. Once intellect realizes Sāttvic knowledge, Purush understands clearly that it's independent from Prakruti. Once Purush realizes this, Prakruti blushes and stops dancing in front of Purush. Once this stage is attained, Purush is free from all bindings and attains Kaivalya (its naturally liberated state). Kaivalya means solitude, knowledge of being detached from Prakruti; and this natural state of Purush is called Moksha or liberation. There's a delicate question of whether Purush leaves Prakruti or Prakruti leaves

Purush. Some may shrug off this question as immaterial. However, it's not invalid. As Purush is inactive, attribute-less and apathetic; there's no question of Purush 'leaving' Prakruti. Hence, it must be considered that Prakruti leaves Purush as action is a virtue of Prakruti and gets liberated from Purush. This is the final conclusion drawn by Sānkhya. In summary, Moksha isn't something one receives from outside. It's the natural state of being which Purush forgets by being tangled in Prakruti's actions and by falling in the trap of desire. However, once they realize this reality, they are liberated instantly. Enlightened, Aware, Realized etc. are other names for this very state of being.

Although Vedānti agree with Sānkhya principle that Purush (Ātmā) is Nirguna, Inert and Apathetic, they don't believe that there are infinite Purush witnessing the same Prakruti. They say that this separateness is apparent whereas in reality it's the same Brahman. However, Sānkhya say that as birth, life and death of different beings is different and their happiness and sorrow are different, every Ātmā or Purush is different and they're infinite. Sānkhya claim that although whole universe is consisting of only two entities – Prakruti and Purush, Purush here means a collection of infinite Purush. The whole universe is operational through the union of infinite Purush with the Trigunātmak Prakruti. The Purush whose surrounding Prakruti becomes Sāttvic gets liberated and it reaches Kaivalya. Even though the particular Purush has reached Kaivalya, other Purush continue with Samsāra (the cycle of birth and death). Even after one reaches Kaivalya, one may assume they're free from the manifestations of Prakruti. However, Sānkhya say that just as a potter's wheel keeps rotating for some time after the pot is made, Purush having attained Kaivalya still continues with the body and its organs for some more time. However, it doesn't continue to be affected by sorrow or problems from the mundane life. Whoever has not understood that it's separate from Prakruti is destined to live in Samsāra (the cycle of birth and death); and it gets born in Deva Yoni (incarnation as celestials) due to development of Sattva Gunas, Manushya Yoni (incarnation as human) due to development of Raja Gunas or Pashu Yoni (incarnation as animals) due to development of Tama Gunas. Fruits of these cycles of birth and death are acquired by

Purush due to the development or reduction of Sattva, Raja and Tama in its surrounding Prakruti (its Buddhi). Development of Sattva Gunas leads you upward to heaven and respectively that of Tama Gunas leads you downward to netherworlds. However, if one wants to attain Kaivalya or liberation, one must go beyond the boundary of these Gunas and assume ascetic life, according to Sānkhya. Kapilāchārya was born with Vairāgya (dispassion) and Knowledge. However, not all are born so and must attain it through acquiring of knowledge and understanding of the difference between Purush and Prakruti. According to Sānkhya, Dharma is categorized as Sāttvic but would only lead you to Swarga (heaven). Only knowledge and Vairagya (ascetic dispassionate life in Sānkhya philosophy) would lead you to Moksha or Kaivalya (liberation) and all sorrow would end. This is the final conclusion stated by Kapilāchārya.

Sānkhya depict attaining Kaivalya through super development of Sāttvic Gunas and so does Gitā. However, Gitā doesn't believe in separate origins of Prakruti and Purush and hence whenever these words are used in Bhagavad Gitā, they're used as Kshetra and Kshetradnya respectively. We've elaborated on this difference in approach in a later chapter (Adhyātma). However, we found it worth clarifying here as one may infer from the terminology that Gitā follows Sānkhya philosophy due to usage of the terms Prakruti and Purush. Gitā considers Parabrahma as the ultimate. According to Bhagavad Gitā, knowledge of its existence beyond Prakruti and Purush leads to Moksha.

CHAPTER 8

Vishwāchi Ubhārni Va Sanhārni (Birth and Death of the Universe)

After learning that Prakruti and Purush are the two independent primordial entities and understanding their properties in the previous chapter, let's now understand the sequence in which Prakruti manifests itself as the entire universe. This manifestation is called birth and death of the universe. Gitā covers this in the 7th and 8th Adhyāyas and is part of Ksharāksharvichār. Dnyān (Knowledge) is what makes you understand that all manifest substances have one single unmanifest element as their basis and Vidnyān (Science) is what explains how this single element gets transformed into a plethora of different substances.

Gitā proposes that Parmeshwar (Almighty) activates Prakruti into its manifestations while Sānkhya regard Prakruti as independent and its union with Purush is enough for starting the cycle of the universe. It then begins to blossom into new substances like a tree does during spring season. On the other hand, Vedas, Upanishads and Smruti consider Parabrahma as the original element from which Hiranyagarbha (literally golden womb) was formed and through this truth was born the entire universe. There are some variations of this occurring in different scriptures. However, Vedānta Sutras finally iterate that Ātmaroopi Parabrahma (Parabrahma in the guise of Ātmā or soul) led to formation of the five elements and other manifestations. The steps after Prakruti in the formation of the universe are thus common between Vedānta and Sānkhya schools. This is why all knowledge of history, Purānas and economics etc. is said to have come from Sānkhya as mentioned in Mahābhārat. It doesn't mean Vedānta was inspired from Sānkhya. However, Kapilāchārya has described the evolution of universe particularly in detail and Gitā agrees with this evolutionary path and hence we shall discuss the same in this chapter. Modern scientists agree with the Sānkhya principle that all manifest universe has originated from an imperceptible, homogenous, infinitesimally small and omnipresent element. Moreover, they also agree that this development of universe has happened gradually from this element and not suddenly to today's state. This is the theory of evolution. When this was proposed in 19th century Europe, traditional religious Christians attacked it vehemently as it opposed their theory that God has created the five elements and each species separately. However, as scientific truth holds more water, evolutionary theory has unanimously been accepted now. Our solar system was initially a homogenous system from which the planets were separated and cooled down to where they are now. Subsequently, air, water and the solid earth was formed on our planet. Darwin said that from this, unicellular organism was formed and slowly evolved to today's living world. However, there's a lot of debate on whether a separate principle called 'soul' exists or not. Some like Haeckel consider that inanimate gradually became animated or conscious while others like Kant propose that all our knowledge is collated by the soul and we must regard soul as a separate entity. Including soul to be a part of the same environment that it exists in, is like saying one can sit on their own shoulders which is logically wrong. This is why Sānkhya consider Purush and Prakruti as two originals. Despite substantial advent of science, it's still being debated whether process of origin of universe is to be treated separately from how we treat events in the universe today. If we consider the evolution of universe post its birth, however, we see that there's little difference between modern science and Sānkhya principles. Advanced science speaks of universal principles such as momentum, heat and gravity instead of Sattva, Raja and Tama of Sānkhya. Although these principles have undoubtedly become much more measurable through technological advancement, in principle they're the same. The concept of evolution is equally accepted in both and Gitā accepts this notion, unlike Christianity where it's vehemently opposed.

Let's now see what Sānkhya say about the evolution of the universe. This process is termed Gunotkarsha or Guna Parināmavāda (Transformation Theory). Intent to perform any action first needs to be born in a human being through their intellect. Upanishads also say that solitary Parabrahma first 'thought' of becoming multitudinous. The same way, Prakruti 'thinks' of leaving its state of equilibrium to become the universe. This thought or resolution is called Vyavasāy (profession). Being professional is the property of Buddhi (intellect). Hence, Sānkhya have postulated that Buddhi gets originated in Prakruti as the first Guna (attribute). As human beings have a union of Purush and Prakruti within them, they're conscious and possess the knowledge of their own Buddhi. On the other hand, Prakruti being inanimate or unconscious, doesn't have this knowledge. This is the major difference. This happens because of the union with Purush and is not an attribute of Prakruti. Modern science assumes that even inanimate objects have this power similar to living things, albeit involuntary, for explanation of principles like Gravity and Magnetism. This in a way explains the significance of Buddhi as the first attribute as per Sānkhya theory. Thus, this intellect of Prakruti and human intellect are principally the same. This Buddhi (intellect) also has other names such as 'Mahat', 'Dnyān', 'Mati', 'Āsuri', 'Pradnyā', 'Khyāti' etc. As this Buddhi is a consequence of a combination of Sattva-Raja-Tama, it can assume an infinite number of combinations of these three Gunas in different proportions. Hence, there can be infinite types of Buddhi as well. Like Prakruti, this Buddhi is subtle. However, unlike Prakruti which is Avyakta (unmanifest) Buddhi is Vyakta (manifest) and hence can be perceived by humans. Similarly, all subsequent forms of Prakruti are Vyakta according to Sānkhya, making Prakruti the only Avyakta principle.

Even after formation of professional Buddhi, Prakruti is still homogenous. Leaving this homogeneity to become heterogeneous is called Pruthaktva (distinction). It's impossible for variety to occur before this heterogeneity. This separate attribute formed subsequently after Buddhi is called Ahankār (ego). Differentiation between You and I creates the first distinction and hence ego, which distinguishes everything else as different from I, is the first attribute from this distinction. This attribute is involuntary on its own. Hence, humans or animals who have consciousness realize and express this distinction while inanimate objects such as rocks, water etc. don't voice out their distinction. Yet, like Buddhi, Ahankār in living as well as non-living things is the same principle. This Ahankār is also called 'Taijas', 'Abhimān', 'Bhootādi', 'Dhātu' etc. Ahankār is an attribute subsequent to Buddhi and hence can't appear before Buddhi. Like Buddhi, Ahankār can also be of infinite types based on its constitution of Sattva-Raja-Tama. Similarly, all subsequent attributes are infinite and thus everything in this universe has Sāttvic, Rājas and Tāmas nature according to which Gitā propounds Gunatrayavibhāg (Three types of Guna) and Shraddhātrayavibhāg (Three types of reverence) (Gitā Adhyāyas 14 and 17).

Although Prakruti has become manifest and heterogeneous, its subtlety is still there. Till Ahankār, Prakruti was homogenous and singular. Hence, rather than calling it generation of Buddhi or Ahankār 'from' Prakruti, we must say they're formed 'within' Prakruti. From here onwards, one can say, that the minute atoms of Naiyāyik come into the picture. Once Prakruti becomes heterogeneous, the transformation branches out into two – One branch leading to generation of the living entities with organs and second branch generating non-living entities without organs. Here, by organs we mean the power or energy that animates the physical organs as the physical body is inanimate without it. The soul which controls these powers is classified under a separate category 'Purush'. 'With organs' and 'without organs' are the only two possible types of substances in this universe and hence there can't be more than two branches possibly originating from Ahankār. Out of this, everything with organs is called Sāttvic (as the power behind the organs is considered superior) while everything without organs is called Tāmas. In short, once Ahankār branches out, development of Sattva Gunas creates five sensory organs, five action organs and Man (mind), totaling 11 basic organs of the universe; while development of Tama Gunas creates Five Tanmātre (subtle matter) without organs. However, Prakruti has still maintained its subtlety and thus all these 16 manifestations of Prakruti are still Sookshma (subtle).

Five Tanmātre belonging to the sensory perceptions - smell, sound, touch, vision and taste, independent without overlap, are the ultra-subtle, basic building blocks of the non-living universe without organs. Similarly, eleven basic organs are the seeds of the living universe with organs. The Sānkhya logic behind these specific numbers (5 and 11) of basic elements is interesting and worth mentioning. While naturalists have divided substances into three states viz. solid, liquid and gaseous; Sānkhya approach to classification is different. They say – All five sensory organs of our body are beautifully unique and exclusive. Ears can't taste, Tongue can't smell, Nose can't see, eyes can't touch while skin can't hear. If the five sensory organs and the subtle perceptions (smell, voice, touch, vision and taste) are fixed, attributes of matter cannot exceed five. Even if we assume that they do, there's no way for us to perceive them anyway. There may be different types of these five perceptions depending on variation and degree (voice could be soft, harsh, rough etc. taste could be bitter, sweet, sour etc. vision could be red, yellow, blue etc. and so on) pertaining to each sense. However, original attributes of matter would always be five as our five senses can sense only one attribute each. Even though we may not encounter substances with only voice, only smell, only touch, only vision and only taste independently; the governing subtle matter yielding a particular type of these perceptions to a substance is only of five kinds according to Sānkhya. We'll discuss the take of Vedānti on the Panchtanmātre or the Panchmahābhoote (five elements) arising from them later.

After we establish that there are five basic principles of the non-living universe, we observe that no living being has more than 11 basic organs. Even though action organs like hands, legs etc. appear Sthool (gross), they must have a subtle element at its root without which it wouldn't have been differentiated into what they are. Modern evolutionists have pondered a lot over this. According to them, microscopic unicellular organisms had just the skin with touch as the only sensory organ. From this skin, various sensory organs evolved. E.g. when light fell on the skin, eyes got developed over time. This principle is also accepted in Sānkhya. However, Sānkhya say that if Prakruti didn't have the seed of different sensory organs, how would eyes or nose develop (and at a specific place) on the body. Darwin only talks about survival of the fittest. However, western modern science doesn't tackle the question of why different organs evolve in the first place. Although skin might've appeared as the first sensory organ, Sānkhya say that the principles of the five senses didn't evolve from one another but are inherently prevalent in Prakruti and the 11 attributes (five action organs, five sensory organs and Man) originated simultaneously from Ahankār when heterogeneity originated and further gave rise to the living universe with organs. Of these, Man (mind) does both tasks – that of being Sankalp-Vikalpātmak (the presenter of inputs) to the intellect as well as that of being the executive, prompting action organs to act. We studied this in Chapter 6. Upanishads call organs collectively as Prāna. This Prāna don't trace their origins to the five elements but are separately evolved from the Parmātmā (Ultimate soul), according to both Sānkhya and Upanishad authors. There are some variations about the number of these Prāna. However, finally the number arrived at is 11, even in Vedānta Sutras and Gitā (Gitā 13.5).

After the manifestation of 11 attributes of living universe with organs and 5 attributes of non-living universe without organs from Sāttvic and Tāmas Ahankār respectively, the five Tanmātre (subtle matter) subsequently give rise to the five gross Panchmahābhoote (also called Vishesh) or the five elements we famously know which form the entire non-living universe. Union of these substances with the 11 subtle organs then develops living universe with organs as we see them on living beings.

After aggregating the entire sequence of events from Prakruti till now as propounded by Sānkhya, we see following chart of evolution:

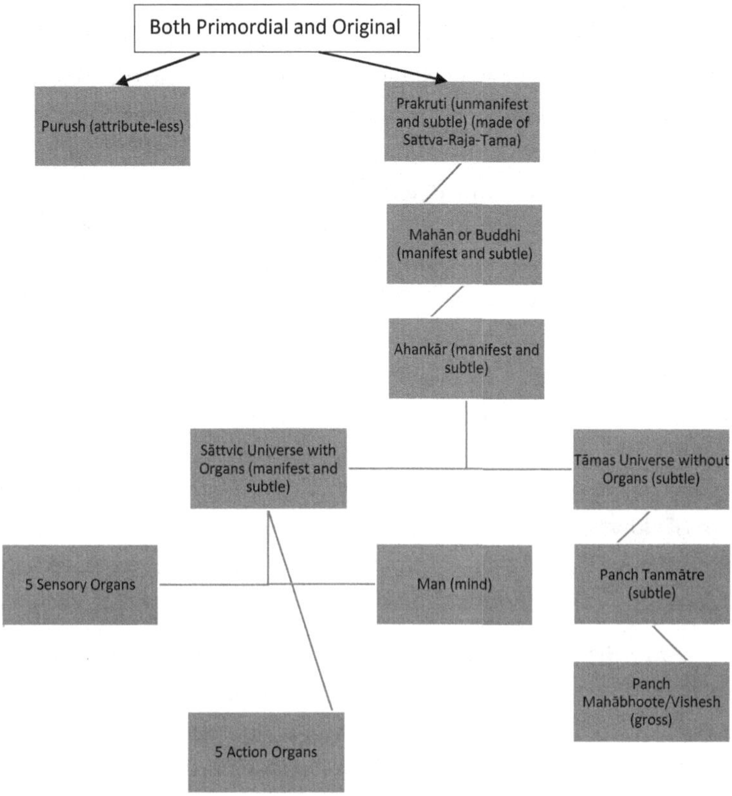

Including five Sthool (gross) elements and Purush, there are totally 25 attributes or principles. Of these, the 23 attributes from Buddhi onwards are manifestations of Prakruti. Out of these, five subtle Tanmātre and five gross Mahābhoote are manifestations in the form of Matter while Buddhi, Ahankār and organs (11) are manifestations in the form of Energy. These 23 are manifest while original Prakruti is unmanifest. Sānkhya include Time and Space within the Ether attribute (one of the five gross Mahābhoote or elements). Prāna, according to Sānkhya is nothing but the operations of 11 organs. Vedānti, however, regard Prāna as a separate principle/attribute. While Sānkhya regard Prakruti and Purush as independent and original; Vedānti consider them two incarnations of the same Parmeshwar. Apart from these differences, the rest of the sequence of evolution of universe is common between Sānkhya and Vedānta schools.

Anugeetā in Mahābhārat describes this evolutionary path as an allegory to a massive tree of which the 25 attributes are various parts – Prakruti as the seed, Buddhi as the tree-trunk etc. The same tree is also called the spread of Māyā. Upanishads call it the Sanātan Ashwatthavruksha (Eternal Ashwattha Tree). However, there it's described as inverted with roots up and branches downward. Combining these two descriptions, Gitā has its own description of Ashwatthavruksha in 15th Adhyāya (Gitā 15.2).

Sānkhya also divide these 25 attributes into 4 categories as:

1. Prakruti is primordial and original and hence is classified as 'Avikruti' (Original)
2. Buddhi, Ahankār and Panchtanmātre are classified as Prakruti-Vikruti (manifestations which also manifest further into others, acting as Prakruti for the subsequent attribute)
3. 11 basic organs of the universe and Panchmahābhoote don't lead to any further attributes and are called simply 'Vikruti' or 'Vikar' (manifestations)
4. Purush is independent and apathetic and hence called 'Na Prakruti Na Vikruti' (Neither Prakruti nor manifestation)

They're also classified as Avyakta (unmanifest), Vyakta (manifest) and Dnya (knower). Purush is Dnya, Prakruti is Avyakta and everything else is Vyakta.

Vedānti have a slightly different classification as they propound that Purush and Prakruti originate from Parmeshwar. The 16 Vikruti (11 basic organs and Panchmahābhoote) are manifestations and hence are not treated as Prakruti or elements. Of the remaining 9 (1. Purush 2. Prakruti and 3-9. Buddhi, Ahankār and 5 Tanmātre), they classify Prakruti and subsequent 7 together as Ashtadhā Prakruti (Eight types of Prakruti) and Purush as Jeev. This is the terminology used in Gitā as well. Purush is called Parā Prakruti (Superior form of Parmeshwar) whereas Prakruti is called Aparā Prakruti (Inferior form of Parmeshwar) (Gitā 7.4,5). Now while describing the subsequent manifestations of

Aparā Prakruti, we can't include Prakruti itself, so Ashtadhā Prakruti in Gitā includes Man instead (Ashtadhā Prakruti – Buddhi, Ahankār, Panchtanmātre and Man) (Gitā 7.5). Here, Man also includes Ten organs (Action and Sensory) while Panchtanmātre includes Panchmahābhoote in Gitā. However, enumeration aside, principally the total attributes are identical in Sānkhya and Vedānti approach. They add up to twenty-five in all.

Following table elucidates different classifications of Sānkhya, Vedānti and Gitā in simple form:

<table>
<tr><th>Sānkhya Classification</th><th>Attributes</th><th>Vedānti Classification</th><th>Gitā Classification</th></tr>
<tr><td>Na Prakruti – Na Vikruti</td><td>1 Purush</td><td>Superior form of Parabrahma</td><td>Parā Prakruti</td></tr>
<tr><td>Avikruti (Original Prakruti) or Mool Prakruti</td><td>1 Prakruti</td><td rowspan="4">Inferior form of Parabrahma (eight types)</td><td>Aparā Prakruti</td></tr>
<tr><td rowspan="3">7 Prakruti – Vikruti</td><td>1 Buddhi</td><td rowspan="4">Eight types of Aparā Prakruti</td></tr>
<tr><td>1 Ahankār</td></tr>
<tr><td>5 Tanmātre</td></tr>
<tr><td rowspan="4">16 Vikruti/Vikar (manifestations)</td><td>1 Man</td><td rowspan="4">These 16 are not counted as basic elements according to Vedānti as they're pure manifestations</td></tr>
<tr><td>5 Sensory Organs</td><td rowspan="3">These 15 are not counted as basic elements according to Gitā as they're pure manifestations.</td></tr>
<tr><td>5 Action Organs</td></tr>
<tr><td>5 Mahābhoote</td></tr>
<tr><td>TOTAL</td><td>25</td><td>9</td><td>10</td></tr>
</table>

This concludes the evolution of various manifestations from the primordial element (Prakruti).

Sānkhya only mention that Panchmahābhoote are produced from Panchtanmātre by Guna Parināmavāda (Transformation Theory). Let's understand in detail how this process happens and subsequently how all the substances come into existence. Only Vedānta texts explain this and not Sānkhya. Upanishads tell how the Panchmahābhoote (Five elements viz. Earth, Water, Fire, Air and Ether) were made in sequence as – Parmātmā or Ultimate soul (not Prakruti like Sānkhya say) first leads to Ākāsh (Ether), Ākāsh leads to Vāyu (Air), Vāyu leads to Agni (Fire), Agni leads to Aap (Water) and Aap leads to Pruthvi (Earth). Uttar Vedānti explain this sequence with a reference to one attribute getting added in each member of this sequence. Ākāsh (Ether) only has Shabda (Sound) so this was made first. Then was made Vāyu as Air has both Shabda (Sound) and Sparsha (Touch). After Vāyu comes Agni as Fire has Shabda (Sound), Sparsha (Touch) and Roop (Vision). Then comes Aap as Water has Shabda (Sound), Sparsha (Touch), Roop (Vision) and Ruchi/Ras (Taste). The last element to be made was Pruthvi as Earth has the fifth attribute of Gandh (Smell) in addition to the previous four attributes. Upanishads further say that, from these five elements first Plants were made, from this food and finally humans. The whole nature is born out of these five elements by their innumerable combinations in different proportions. However, we must not forget that five elements can only lead to non-living things by themselves and need union with subtle organs first and then with soul for a conscious living being to be born. One must also note that this explanation given by Uttar Vedānti is not from Upanishads. Most Upanishads only mention three (Fire, Water and Earth) elements from which they explain development of all visible universe including bodies of living beings. However, some like Taittiriya, Prashna, Bruhadāranyak etc., Vedānta Sutras and Gitā mention five elements making up human body. This concludes evolution of conscious and unconscious entities of the universe.

Let us now discuss more about the living beings and their path. We know that Sānkhya say Kaivalya is attained when one realizes that Purush is separate from Prakruti. However, we have not discussed how someone dying without this knowledge has to go through the cycle of rebirth. This is obvious, as otherwise there'd be no importance of knowledge or good/bad actions. We can't say Purush takes these births as it's been long established that Purush is inert and apathetic while all actions are taken by Prakruti. Moreover, if we say soul takes new births itself, there'd possibly be no end to this cycle. Hence, a person's rebirth after death without knowledge must somehow be linked to Prakruti. However, as with death the gross body gets destroyed, it can't be with the Panchmahābhoote. Once we remove these five gross elements, we're left with 18 attributes. Thus, someone dying without knowledge retains the link to these 18 attributes. They are – Buddhi, Ahankār, Man, 5 Action organs, 5 Sensory organs and 5 Tanmātre. They're all subtle and the continued union of Purush with these 18 is together called Sookshma or Linga Shareer (Subtle body). If an animal dies without knowledge, this subtle body leaves the Sthool Shareer (Gross body) and compels the Purush to take rebirth again and again. Many argue that while Buddhi, Ahankār, Man and 10 organs are visibly seen to leave the body, there's no reason to include Panchtanmātre (subtle matter) in Linga Shareer. Sānkhya counter this by stating that just as a shadow needs a substrate to fall on, these 13 attributes need a material support to hold on to. Purush being inert and apathetic can't act as a support. A living person has the support of the Panchmahābhoote (five elements). However, upon death there's no other support except these five subtle elements and thus they must be included as a part of Linga Shareer. Upon a little deliberation we notice that there's little or no difference between this Sānkhya definition of Linga Shareer and that of Vedānta. Once we add Prāna and Dharmādharma (Karma) to the Sānkhya Linga Shareer, we get the Linga Shareer of Vedānta. However, as Sānkhya include Prāna in the tendencies of 11 basic organs and Karma in the operations of Buddhi; overall constitution of Linga Shareer is identical between Sānkhya and Vedānta.

We discussed the existence of Linga Shareer and its constituents. It is beyond doubt that this subtle body would accumulate gross elements from the parents' body and later from nourishment to develop the gross body. However, we still don't know why and how this subtle body takes different life forms such as animals, birds or humans. Sānkhya call the consciousness in the living world as Purush and although this

Purush may be innumerable, it can't make the decision of getting into different bodies like animals, birds or humans as it's naturally inert and apathetic. Vedānta explains this as a consequence of Karma or actions; however, we shall cover that later. Sānkhya don't accept a third principle other than Purush and Prakruti. Now as Purush is inert, cause of manifestation of Karma has to be bequeathed to Prakruti. Among the 18 attributes of Linga Shareer, Buddhi is the principal attribute as it leads to the other 17 attributes. Thus, what Vedānta calls Karma is the manifestation of Buddhi differing depending on the constitution of Sattva-Raja-Tama in it and is called 'Bhāva' (attitude). Just as a scent is inherent to a flower, a Bhāva is inherent to the subtle body. Depending on this Bhāva (Sānkhya) or Karma (Vedānta), the subtle body takes up a new birth and while taking birth also accumulates more Bhāva or Karma from the parents' body. Depending on the aggregation of Bhāva or Karma, birth or incarnation is decided. When all Bhāva develop Sāttvic Gunas to achieve knowledge and Vairagya (detachment) and the person realizes the difference between Prakruti and Purush, they attain Kaivalya where Linga Shareer is released and Dukkha (sorrow) is permanently destroyed. If there's just the development of Sāttvic Gunas without the realization of difference between Prakruti and Purush, the subtle body takes rebirth in Devayoni (heaven). Development of Raja Gunas leads to birth in Manushyayoni (on earth as humans) while development of Tama Gunas leads to birth in Tiryagyoni (as a beast or animals). Once being born as a human, Sānkhya describe subsequent development from a zygote to the full body through theory of transformation. Although this terminology of Bhāva is not mentioned in Vedānta texts, Gitā mentions it a couple of times with a similar meaning; most probably referring to the Sānkhya terminology.

Just as we saw the evolution of the entire universe from original unmanifest Prakruti (Sānkhya) or from original true Parabrahma (Vedānta), the manifestations follow the reverse route to go back to Prakruti or Parabrahma. Although the time (duration) of the complete cycle of birth and death of the universe is not mentioned by Sānkhya, it appears that they accept the chronology mentioned in Gitā (8.17), Mahābhārat or Manusamhitā. Our Uttarāyan (Period between winter solstice and summer solstice of northern hemisphere) is considered the day of the Devas (celestials) while our Dakshinayan (Period between summer solstice and winter solstice of northern hemisphere) is considered the night of the Devas. This is because, Devas are believed to reside on Mount Meru (North Pole of the earth) according to Smruti as well as astrological texts. Thus, our year (total period between solstices) is one full day and night of the Devas, while our 360 years mean 360 days or 1 year of the Devas. We have four Yugas (ages) viz. Krut/Sat, Tretā, Dwāpar and Kali. Krutyug lasts for 4000 years, Tretāyug for 3000 years, Dwāparyug for 2000 years and Kaliyug for 1000. However, at the beginning and end of each of these ages there are small transitory periods (400 years each side of Krutyug, 300 for Tretāyug, 200 for Dwāparyug and 100 for Kaliyug). Thus, including the Yugas (4000+3000+2000+1000=10,000 years) and the transitory periods (800+600+400+200=2000 years) it is a total of 12,000 years. There's a question of whether to consider these as human years or those of the Devas? However, had it been human years and Kaliyug having started 5,000 years ago, it would mean today we're in Tretāyug of the next cycle as it would mean even Krutyug of the next cycle is over. This simply doesn't match. Hence, it must be 12,000 Deva years (360 x 12,000 = 43,20,000 human years). This period is called human Mahāyug (Great age) or Deva Yug (age). Now, there are 71 such Deva Yugas in 1 Manvantar and there are 14 such Manvantars. At the start and end of each Manvantar, there are transitory periods (total 15) each of which is equal to Krut Yug (including its transitory period) which equals 4,800 Deva years or 1.728 million human years. This total period (14 Manvantar and 15 transitory periods) equals 1,000 Deva Yugas and it makes 1 day of Brahma, which is also called Kalpa and equals 4.32 billion human years. Just as much as the day, there's 1 Brahma night. This day and night together form one cycle of birth and death of universe.

At the start of the day of Brahma, Avyakta (unmanifest) starts turning into Vyakta (manifest) and the universe starts evolving, whereas at the start of the night of Brahma, reverse process begins (Gitā 1.18, 9.7).

If you add 360 such days and nights of Brahma, you get 1 year of Brahma. If you consider Brahma's life to be 100 years, it amounts to 311.04 trillion human years! Accordingly, today's period is calculated as 51st year and 1st day of Brahma, of which we're in 7th Manvantar (out of 14) and 28th Mahāyug (out of 71). Of this Mahāyug, we're in Kaliyug which started in 3101 BC, making today (2022 A.D.) the 5,123rd year out of the 4,32,000 years of Kaliyug!

The description of birth and death of the universe as explained till now is the one followed by Vedānta, Sānkhya (except the existence of Parabrahma) and Bhagavad Gitā. Other descriptions could be explained as different nomenclature for the same concept. E.g. what some call Hiranyagarbha or Brahmadev is basically Prakruti. Let's now delve into the investigation of whether there's anything beyond Purush and Prakruti, and at the origin of all Vyaktāvyakta (Manifest and unmanifest) and Ksharākshar (Impermanent and Permanent). This study is called Adhyātma or Vedānta and this is what we shall study in the next chapter.

CHAPTER 9

Adhyātma (Spirituality)

Last two chapters discussed how Purush and Prakruti are the primordial elements, how their union results in evolution of the universe and how Purush attains Kaivalya or Moksha (liberation) by knowing that it's different from Prakruti. About the evolution, modern scientists differ partly from Sānkhya philosophy and as modern science advances more and more, these differences may become more pronounced to explain the process in a more accurate way. However, the central idea, of an unmanifest having transformed into manifest to create different substances sequentially, is unlikely to be proven wrong. However, Vedānta considers this as a subject of other disciplines and moves on to decipher the single basic principle behind everything in this universe; and to find out how someone can become one with it.

Sānkhya say that resultant product of Kshetrakshetradnyavichār (Purush or soul) and resultant product of Ksharāksharvichār (unmanifest Prakruti) are both independent and original and thus assume an approach of duality. Vedānta says – Rather than assuming that Prakruti has the knowledge and knowhow of handling the innumerable, formless Purush; why not extend the same logic which we used to narrow down origin of innumerable substances of the universe to a single Prakruti and aggregate innumerable Purush and Prakruti to a single ultimate indivisible principle? It seems both logical and plausible. Distinction is a virtue of Ahankār. If Purush is attribute-less, how can it assume the status of being innumerable or distinct? Rather, they're not actually innumerable but only appear so because of the virtue of Ahankār developed within Prakruti. Another question that arises, is whether to consider the union of the independent Purush with the independent Prakruti as truth or illusion. If we consider it as the truth, then it's inseparable thus rendering the possibility of liberation impossible; whereas if we consider it as an illusion, the assumption of Prakruti spreading out manifestations of its Gunas in front of Purush becomes baseless. There's also the question of debating the metaphor of the actress dancing in front of Purush. If Purush and Prakruti are independent and original, one being inanimate and other being conscious, why would the tendency of one be for benefit of the other? If we consider it as Prakruti's inherent nature, why not accept Haeckel's Jadadvaita (Physical Monism)? Haeckel proposes that Prakruti develops a desire to look at itself and to become conscious. However, Sānkhya deny it and argue separate existence of witness and the scene in front of it. Why not extend the same logic further? Is there any way to further investigate the nature of the Purush or the Prakruti? Sānkhya declare that there's no answer to this question and propose that Purush and Prakruti are originally different. Looking at this strictly from a corporeal or physical view, it's not unreasonable. If the witness, the knower or the soul is imperceptible, how can one perceive it through their senses? In summary, all physical tests or ideas to evaluate the existence of soul become meaningless. How then could one do it? It looks like an unsolvable question, but it really isn't. How did Sānkhya arrive at the nature of Purush as independent and attribute-less? By introspecting, isn't it? Why not implement the same method for tracing the origin of the true nature of Purush and Prakruti? This is the fundamental difference between Adhibhautik Shāstra (Physics) and Adhyātma Shāstra (Spirituality). Physics deals with things that can be perceived through senses. The subjects of spirituality are beyond perception of the senses and purely personal or subjective. Someone may argue, that if soul is personal, let each person experience it and know it as they may. Why is there a need for spirituality? However, this is acceptable only if everyone is of equally pure mind. As not everyone is of equally pure, virtuous and broad mind; we must accept the experiences of those who have it. There's no point in simply arguing about random opinions. Adhyātma doesn't ask us to give up logic. It just says that as the topics of spirituality are personal and undecipherable by physical tests, we can't accept the theories that are against the personal experiences of great scholars with broad and stable mind. It declares that the original principle behind the universe is thus imperceptible and hence must not be attempted through senses. Pātanjal Yog became a separate discipline dedicated to stabilize mind. Those born with such a stable mind or those who stabilize it through study and exercise have experienced this knowledge and described it in Upanishads. Thus, to make any decisions in spirituality, we need to resort to these principles stated in these great texts. Depending on the intellect of a person, there can be different ideologies about this experience. However, it would not alter its significance. Let's now study the theories proposed by Gitā and Upanishads about this unthinkable principle beyond Prakruti.

Gitā doesn't accept the duality of Prakruti-Purush postulated by Sānkhya and proposes that there's a third, all-encompassing, unmanifest and immortal principle at the base of everything in this universe. This is the first principle of Adhyātma Shāstra and Vedānta. Although Prakruti is unmanifest, it's with attributes (Trigunātmak or governed by Sattva-Raja-Tama Gunas) and thus impermanent. Gitā thus describes this third entity which is 'beyond' manifest and unmanifest, permanent and impermanent; describing it as 'Purushottam' (Supreme Being). Bhrugu tells Bhardwaj – "Soul when bound inside a body is called Kshetradnya or Jeevātmā (Personal soul) while when it's liberated from this physical body it's called Parmātmā (Ultimate soul). One may feel that these two definitions of the soul are different. However, as there's a single Parmātmā behind both Prakruti as well as Purush, it can be described as the one beyond Prakruti or as the one beyond Purush. Bhagwān Shri Krishna says in 15th Adhyāya describing himself as – "Prakruti is an incarnation of mine and Jeev or Ātmā (soul) is my incarnation, too". Bhagavad Gitā as well as all texts of Vedānta unanimously say, that the ultimate principle is beyond all (Prakruti or Purush, Knower or knowledge) and is one, permanent, unmanifest and immortal. While Sānkhya describe Prakruti as Avyakta (unmanifest) and Akshar (permanent), Gitā or Vedānta describe only Parabrahma (Ultimate Absolute) as Avyakta and Akshar. However, for matters other than these, Gitā accepts the principles of Sānkhya about evolution of manifest universe from unmanifest Prakruti and mentions it as well. It employs terminology such as 'Akshar beyond (Sānkhya) Akshar' and 'Unmanifest beyond (Sānkhya) unmanifest' to denote Parabrahma. One must always remember that the words Avyakta and Akshar are used sometimes as Prakruti (Sānkhya) and sometimes as Parabrahma (Vedānta) and one must know which meaning is intended by looking at its context.

Once we say that Prakruti and Purush are not the ultimate original elements and that Parmeshwar or Purushottam is at the base of the universe, the next natural quest is to find the nature of this principle and its relation with the two. The trinity of Prakruti, Purush and Parmeshwar are called Jagat, Jeev and Parabrahma respectively in Adhyātma. Vedānta and Upanishad deal with the interrelationship among the three at its core. Depending on differing opinions of Vedānti, there are different communities within Vedānta as Advaiti, Dvaiti, Vishishtādvaiti etc. Communalist critiques tend to ignore the heart of Gitā and keep on arguing which community of Vedānta it belongs to. Anyway, let's see what Bhagwān Shri Krishna has said about Jagat, Jeev and Parabrahma himself. This agrees with Upanishads as well and this proves that Gitā traces its origins to Upanishads.

While describing Purushottam, Parmātmā, Parmeshwar or Parabrahma; Gitā has first described its two forms viz. Vyakta and Avyakta (here meant as perceptible and imperceptible). It's obvious that the perceptible form is Saguna (with attributes). The other form may be imperceptible to senses. However, that doesn't make it Nirguna (without attributes) as it might as well have all Gunas in Sookshma (subtle) form. Hence, Avyakta has been further divided into three categories – Saguna, Saguna-Nirguna and Nirguna. Here, by Guna they mean all attributes perceptible by senses or mind. As the incarnation of Parmeshwar (Shri Krishna) himself told Gitā to Arjun, he's used phrases such as – "Prakruti is my form" (Gitā 9.8), "Jeev has my essence" (Gitā 15.7), "Focus your mind on me and become my devotee" (Gitā 9.34) etc. about his own form in 1st person. He also asks Arjun after showing him Vishwaroop (his cosmic form) to worship him, as it's easier to devote to Vyakta rather than Avyakta (Gitā 12.8). This and other such examples may show that Gitā predominantly describes the Vyakta form of Bhagwān. However, this doesn't prove that Vyakta Parmeshwar is considered ultimate in Gitā. While describing himself as above, he also says that his form is just his Māyā (appearance) and that his Avyakta (imperceptible) form is the principal one. E.g. He says – "Although I'm imperceptible, ignorant consider me perceptible and don't recognize my superior, imperceptible version (Gitā 7.24). He also mentions on several occasions about 'Māyā' as – "As I'm engulfed in my Māyā, people don't recognize me" (Gitā 7.25) before finally declaring "Ishwar is present in every living being and operates everyone like a machine through his Māyā" (Gitā 18.61). Thus, although Shri Krishna appreciates the perceptible form for devotion, Gitā firmly says that Parmeshwar in its superior form is imperceptible and becoming perceptible is just its Māyā (appearance). It further tells that one doesn't attain Moksha (liberation) till they overcome this Māyā and gain knowledge of the pure and imperceptible version of Parmeshwar. Later, we shall discuss this word 'Māyā' in detail. For now, just note that 'Māyā' and its description wasn't coined by Ādi Shankarāchārya but was originally there in Gitā, Upanishad and Mahābhārat.

Although it's clear that the superior form of Parmeshwar is Avyakta and not Vyakta, whether it's Nirguna (without attributes) or Saguna (with attributes) still needs to be decided as there's an example of Prakruti which although imperceptible is Saguna (made up of Sattva-Raja-Tama). Many thus believe, that as Avyakta Parmeshwar creates Vyakta nature, operates everyone by being inside them, is the receiver of all Yadnya & prayers; it must be Saguna (with attributes) even though it's Avyakta because all Bhāva originate from it. However, Bhagwān Shri Krishna also says – "I am never impacted by any Karma or Gunas yet foolish people who delusively attach themselves to Prakruti, consider themselves to be the doers" (Gitā 3.27; 14.19) thus indicating that it is in fact Nirguna (without any attributes of its own). In addition to these two versions (Saguna and Nirguna), Parmeshwar is also described as a mix of both Saguna as well as Nirguna in some instances. "I'm the support of the five elements but not in them" (Gitā 9.5), "Parabrahma is neither Sat (true) nor Asat (false)" (Gitā 13.12), "I'm both far and near" (Gitā 13.15) etc. are some of the examples of seemingly paradoxical descriptions of Parabrahma or Parmeshwar. Similarly, in Upanishads the description of Avyakta Parmeshwar is sometimes Saguna, sometimes Nirguna and sometimes both Saguna-Nirguna. One may not need an idol for worship. Still, even if the object of worship is imperceptible to the five senses, it must be perceptible to one's mind. Otherwise, there's no worship possible. Worship means remembrance of something. And if the object is without any perceptible attributes, what can one worship? Thus, wherever Upanishads have asked us to worship something, Saguna Parmeshwar is imagined. The Gunas assumed by Parmeshwar are shown more or less pervasive or Sāttvic; depending on the capability or maturity of the worshipper. "Worshippers of deities go on to meet deities and worshippers of ancestors go on to meet ancestors" (Gitā 9.25) mentions this very principle. Taittiriya Upanishad mentions ascending levels of worship – Anna (physical), Prāna (energy), Man (mind), Vidnyān (ether) and Anand (bliss) levels. Other Upanishads also mention various levels of worship depending less and less on an idol or an icon. Final verdict of all Upanishads is however, that true Parabrahma is beyond this. In the story of Nachiketā, Death asks him to leave all Dharma and Adharma, manifest and unmanifest, past and future; and to go beyond all of this to recognize the true Brahman. Bruhadāranyak Upanishad first mentions Earth, Fire and Water as the visible forms while Air and ether as the invisible forms of Brahman but later mentions that Parabrahma is actually neither of these and can only be denoted as 'beyond this' or 'indescribable'. Rather, whatever can be named can't be Parabrahma; so 'Neti Neti' ('Na Iti, Na Iti' meaning not this, not this) is the only small possible description or Sutra which is often used to denote it. Kathopanishad describes it as 'Devoid of any of the five elements, primordial, eternal, perpetual'.

While it's established that Avyakta form of Parmeshwar is the superior one, we now have the question of collating these three contradicting versions of Avyakta Parmeshwar (Saguna, Saguna-Nirguna and Nirguna). Upon a little bit of thinking, we can decipher that Saguna-Nirguna is a transitory phase between Saguna and Nirguna. After gaining knowledge of Parmeshwar with attributes, one must slowly get rid of the attributes one by one to reach Nirguna version.

Similar gradual form of worship is recommended in Upanishads. Varun recommended Bhrugu to first worship Anna (food which is physical) and then slowly to rise through Prāna, Man, Vidnyān and Anand to make him decipher Parabrahma. Moreover, as it's impossible to describe the indescribable, contradicting adjectives are the only way of denoting it. By saying "Parabrahma is neither Sat (true) nor Asat (false)" (Gitā 13.12) or "I'm both far and near" (Gitā 13.15), they're trying to depict this indescribability and universality of Parabrahma. As it's omnipresent, we can't describe it as far or true because then we indirectly accept that there's something else which is near and/or false which is not Parabrahma. This is not the case and that's why the description as mentioned above.

While we can agree to describe Parabrahma by calling it as both extremes simultaneously this way, we still need an explanation as to how we get these descriptions of both Saguna (with attributes) and Nirguna (without attributes) to the same Parmeshwar. Even if we accept that Avyakta Parmeshwar assumes a Vyakta form which is its Māyā (appearance); we still need an explanation as to which form is better (Saguna or Nirguna) and how did the entire universe evolve or arise from this Avyakta Parmeshwar. Calling the almighty Parmeshwar Saguna and rejecting the Nirguna description given in Upanishads and Gitā as false and exaggerated is like axing the root of spirituality itself. Great sages arrived at something through immense concentration and deep meditative thinking. They mentioned it as 'Difficult to decipher even through mind and indescribable through words' and declared it as the final form of Parabrahma. Calling their personal experience exaggerated and calling Parabrahma Saguna just because your mind can't grasp the Nirguna, eternal Brahman is like calling your little bulb as being brighter than the sun! It would've still been acceptable if both Gitā and Upanishads had not given an explanation of the Nirguna description. However, that's not the case. Gitā on several occasions states that the true and superior form of Parmeshwar is Avyakta while the forms we see are nothing but its Māyā (appearance) (Gitā 4.6). There are also instances where Gitā clearly tells the superiority of Nirguna Parmeshwar – "Although Avyakta soul is Nirguna" (Gitā

13.31), "Assigning Karma to it through attachment or ignorance, people make it Saguna" (Gitā 7.24). This reinstates that there are 3 clear conclusions about the principles put forth by Gitā:

1. Although there's a lot of description about the Saguna form of Parmeshwar, original and superior form is actually Nirguna and Avyakta while people make it Saguna through attachment and ignorance
2. Sānkhya Prakruti or its manifestations (all universe) is Māyā (appearance) of Parmeshwar
3. Sānkhya Purush or Jeevātmā is actually Nirguna and inert like Parmeshwar; yet people consider it as a 'doer' due to ignorance

Uttar Vedānta mentions Māyā and Avidyā as two different concepts depicting the difference between them. However, Gitā doesn't do so and mentions only the word 'Māyā' on various occasions considering Māyā, Avidyā and Adnyān (ignorance) synonymous. Let us now study what's the general philosophical form of this Māyā and how it scientifically explains the principles of Gitā and Upanishads.

While Nirguna and Saguna might appear as small words, we see literally the entire universe once we start to see what it covers. How does the primordial Parabrahma while being one, inert and apathetic generates characteristics perceptible to senses? How does the homogenous singularity get converted into different objects? These and many such questions are raised while discussing these two words. In short, we shall now discuss how one becomes many, single becomes dual, Advaita becomes Dvaita or detached becomes attached. Sānkhya, by declaring two originals (Prakruti and Purush), have escaped this question. However, the natural curiosity of human mind to find out the ultimate origin of universe isn't satisfied through this dualistic explanation. Moreover, this duality defies reason. Hence, Upanishads have declared that Nirguna Brahman, which sits above Prakruti-Purush and also above Sacchidānand or Sat-Chit-Anand (Existence-Consciousness-Bliss) Brahman, is at the root of the universe. However, now we must explain how Nirguna (without attributes) led to Saguna (with attributes). Like Sānkhya, Vedānta too agrees with the principle that 'something' cannot be created out of 'nothing'. Thus, Nirguna couldn't lead to Saguna. Then where did Saguna come from? If we deny Saguna, it is visible. If we consider Saguna to be real, its form which is perceptible to our senses changes constantly and is thus impermanent. This would render the all-pervasive Parmeshwar, at least for this Saguna part, perishable. How can one call something as Parmeshwar; when it is divisible, dependent and is governed by the rules of Prakruti? In short, whether one considers all Saguna substances to be sourced from Panchmahābhoote (five elements) or considers them to be formed from Avyakta but Saguna Prakruti (like Sānkhya or Modern Science); they can't call either of them the eternal, independent and immortal principle because both (Panchmahābhoote and Prakruti) are perishable. They should either stop calling Parmeshwar immortal, independent and eternal or go beyond the five elements and/or Prakruti to find what lies there. If we deem immortality false, we see humans seeking immortality since the beginning of time, from Vedas to modern European philosophers. Where did this concept of everlasting blessing beyond mortal life originate? If we call it natural, we must accept there's something beyond the body that's eternal. If we deny it, on the other hand, we can't explain this state of mind observed universally. Modern Adhibhautiks call this question unanswerable and ask us to move on. It appears easy, only it isn't. How could we deny this innate urge for the original and immortal principle observed from last thousands of years? How else then would our knowledge increase, if we kill this drive? Humans have been seeking the origin of this universe since they were born on the earth for the first time. However advanced the modern science becomes, this natural and innate, insatiable hunger for immortal principle shall never recede and this philosophical drive shall always be a step ahead of science. The moment we lose this drive would be the day we shall be like any other animal.

The explanation that we find in the Upanishads which explains the origin of Saguna universe from the principle which is unlimited by time and space, immortal, primordial, independent, homogenous, unitary, ceaseless, omnipresent and Nirguna (without attributes); is more apt than any other explanation ever. Modern German scientist

Kant has explained the reason behind our understanding of this varied world as one through modern science. While Hegel has gone one step ahead of Kant, his theories have not gone as far as Vedānta. Schopenhauer in his own book credits Upanishads for his thoughts and calls Upanishads 'Best among global literature'.

To move beyond the duality of Purush-Prakruti given by Sānkhya, we've to move beyond 'the witness' and 'the scene' to the true essence of the knowledge that witness gets of the scene. Although other animals also see the same universe, humans have a special ability to aggregate multiple phenomena and decipher properties of the matter. We've discussed in Kshetrakshetradnyavichār that the ability of aggregation is beyond Buddhi (intellect) and Man (mind) and it belongs to Ātmā (soul). Many such phenomena which we call laws of nature, are not directly perceptible by our senses but we make sense of them through the power of mind. E.g. If we see an object passing by, through its appearance and speed we decide that it was a soldier and remember it. If there's another object that passes by, our mind starts processing this input and our Buddhi decides that it was another soldier. Similarly, by processing subsequent incidents and using memory we decide that an army is passing by. After looking at the object passing by after the army has and after interpreting its appearance, we decide that it's the king leading his army. Thus, knowledge of the universe isn't the 'scene' that we see but it's the fruit of the aggregation of impressions done by 'the witness'. To describe this, Gitā defines knowledge as 'Avibhaktam Vibhakteshu' (That through which we understand the unity among the diversity). Now if we minutely observe the impressions made by the different senses on our mind, we never understand the intrinsic structure of the objects we see, hear etc. While we may say that a pot was made out of wet clay, we never understand the true intrinsic nature of this 'wet clay'. After observing the different properties of clay like stickiness, colour and wetness through our senses to our mind, our soul who's 'the witness' aggregates it and calls it 'wet clay'. Later when this same object changes form (as the intrinsic principle in the clay doesn't change) into a round, hollow object; our soul observes its appearance and starts calling it a 'pot'. Another classic example of this is of Gold where the same metal is called by various names like earring, bangle etc. when it's molded into different shapes, sizes and designs. Sea and the waves are another such illustration. These names and different shapes or forms leading to these names are called 'Nāmroope' (name-forms) in Upanishads. All other properties are also covered under the same term as despite any changes in physical characteristics of these substances, the base element or principle is eternally unchanged. Like a ripple on water, these are superficial changes in the objects. As our senses can only sense these factors and not perceive the unchanged original principle, we call them by different names. However, through our Buddhi (intellect) we must infer the existence of a single, eternal, imperceptible, true element behind all these 'Nāmroope' or name-forms. Without these name-forms there wouldn't be a way to distinguish between them and know them separately. However, just like we say the bangle is made of gold; we shall extend the same logic and say that all the objects in this universe are nothing but name-forms and they differ in physical properties perceptible to our senses but are made of the same homogenous principle.

Vedānta calls these changing name-forms as 'Mithya' or illusion and the undying principle as 'Satya' or 'Amrut' (Truth or Immortal). Normally, people say that "What we see is the truth". For most practical purposes, this definition works perfectly fine. However, this definition is only good enough to the extent that what you see is more believable than any hearsay. When we're discussing the eternal principle at the core of any substance, these name-forms are not permanent and hence called Mithya (untrue or an illusion). If we see a penny made of copper and also see other objects made of copper; our soul aggregates all these inputs and decides that it is all copper. If we say only what we see is the truth, this decision-making process which is made not by eyes but by the processing mind would be deemed untrue. We know that's not the case. Knowing this and many other possibilities where what we don't see is truer than what we see, Upanishads have decided that 'That principle or element which is never destroyed even after everything is destroyed is the Satya (truth)'. Just as we call someone who changes their statement as a liar, the things we see are termed 'Mithya' or untrue as they keep changing forms; while that which is covered with these Mithya Nāmroope (name-forms) is called the truth even though we don't see it – because that underlying principle is eternal and doesn't change form or get destroyed. In Vedānta, the word Mithya is used for physical appearance of the object and it doesn't mean they're calling the object completely useless, false and non-existent. It recognizes that the underlying principle is true and is only interested in the study of this principle. This is the true subject of philosophy. Even in practical life, we see this in many examples. E.g. when you try to sell an ornament to a goldsmith for money, they'd only pay you for the weight of gold in it and won't consider the making charges you might've paid while molding it. While selling your house, a buyer would only be paying you according to the area and the structure rather than considering how aesthetically you've built it or what decoration you've done. Just as the goldsmith looks at the underlying metal (Gold) in the ornament, Vedānti go further and look at the eternal and permanent underlying principle behind everything. As this principle has no Gunas, it would never be perceptible through our senses. However, we can decide its presence through our intellect and also infer that this unchanging, undying principle is the only 'Truth' in this universe.

However, not understanding this rationale and terminology in detail, some blame Vedānti for calling the world an illusion and ridiculing their theory. However, just as comments of a blind person don't alter the existence of a pillar in front of them; Vedānta philosophy stands tall despite ignorant comments by such people. Gitā calls this appearance or these ever-changing name-forms as 'Māyā', 'Moha' or 'Adnyān'. The original principle which was without name-forms, Nirguna and Avyakta; later manifests itself into various name-forms and becomes Vyakta and Saguna. Thus, all these Nāmroope (name-forms) or Vikar (manifestations) are termed 'Māyā' and this entire universe is called a 'Leela' or play of Parmeshwar. Once we see this way, Sānkhya Prakruti, being Saguna or with Nāmroope, also comes under the umbrella term Māyā, even though it is Avyakta (unmanifest). The entire process of 'Birth and Death of Universe' that we discussed in 8th chapter comes under this. Any Guna which is perceptible through our senses has to be with name-forms. Thus, all modern sciences such as Physics, Chemistry, History, Geography etc. which deal with how substances change from one form to another and what their structure is; come under the purview of Māyā according to Vedānta. Whoever wants to study Parabrahma or Truth which lies beyond this must broaden their horizon beyond these disciplines which deal with Nāmroope or physical aspects. The conclusion of this deliberation we did is that while our senses can't perceive it, there's an Avyakta (imperceptible), eternal principle through which we gather the knowledge in totality through aggregation. As Ātmā (soul) gains this knowledge, it becomes the Dnyāta (knower); whatever knowledge it gains is of these Nāmroope (name-forms), so the perceptible universe becomes the Dnyān (knowledge) and that imperceptible underlying principle at the base of this universe becomes Dnyeya (to be known). Further, Gitā divides knowledge into three parts viz. Sāttvic, Rājas and Tāmas as follows – The narrow knowledge of considering the object of desire as everything is 'Tāmas' knowledge, the knowledge of different objects in the universe as separate is 'Rājas' knowledge while the knowledge of all the things in this universe as one underlying, eternal principle is 'Sāttvic' (Gitā 18.20,21,22).

Many criticize this by calling this tripartite classification as invalid, because there's no evidence to prove existence of anything other than the knowledge we gain. Although we know about various things in the universe and this knowledge is true, there's no way of saying 'of what' this knowledge is; other than the knowledge itself. We can't say that there are things beyond their knowledge or that there's an underlying principle behind these things. If there's no Dnyāta (knower), there's no question of the universe. There's nothing separate called Dnyeya (to be known). If we extrapolate this further, even Dnyāta (knower) is one kind of knowledge and thus there's nothing that remains in this universe except Dnyān (knowledge). This philosophy is called Vidnyānvāda (doctrine of consciousness). This was founded by the Buddhists from Yogāchāra sect. They consider that knowledge is all that there is, in this universe. However, Vedānti disagree with this and it has been proven wrong by Bādarāyanāchārya in Vedānta Sutras and also by Shrimad

Shankarāchārya. It's true that humans understand various impressions made on their mind and that's what we call 'knowledge'. However, if there's nothing apart from knowledge, how does our intellect identify knowledge of different objects as distinct (Cow, Horse, Rock etc.) from 'I' (or self)? If the action of gaining knowledge is a universal psychological phenomenon and there's nothing apart from knowledge, how come there are different kinds as Cow, Horse, and Rock? If we say our mind dreams up these different kinds of knowledge, there's no explanation of distinction between randomness of knowledge in dream state and coherence of knowledge in the awakened state. Moreover, if there's nothing other than knowledge and we consider that the 'knower' dreams up different objects, one must see everything (Cow, Horse or Rock) as themselves (in the first person). However, as we see Cow, Horse or Rock to be distinct from ourselves, there must be some entities in the universe that the knowledge in based on; according to Shankarāchārya. Hearing this argument, one would surely say – "On the one hand Shankarāchārya calls the universe 'Mithya' whereas on the other hand denies the Buddhist view and proclaims existence of various objects along with the existence of a 'knower'. How do you explain this paradox?" We've already answered this question. When he calls the universe 'Mithya', he means that the different name-forms that we see are impermanent or perishable; and doesn't deny the existence of an underlying, imperceptible principle at the base of this universe. Thus, just as we said in Kshetrakshetradnyavichār that there's an eternal principle beyond the perishable body of a living being; we must also say that there's an underlying eternal principle at the base of this universe. Thus, Vedānta proposes existence of a principle at the base of both Body and the universe. There are different schools within Vedānta depending on whether they consider both these principles as same or different. Before discussing this, let's first debunk the allegation debating the antiquity of this opinion of Vedānta.

Many argue that although Buddhist Vidnyānvāda is denied by Vedānta, the Māyāvāda (Calling Nāmroope as 'Mithya' and the underlying eternal principle as 'Satya') was proposed by Shankarāchārya and was not proposed in Upanishads. Upon careful studying of

Upanishads, one can easily prove that this allegation is baseless. In common parlance, whatever we see with our eyes is called 'Satya' (Truth). Using this terminology, some Upanishads have called ordinary visible substances 'Satya' while the underlying principle as 'Amrut' (immortal). E.g. Bruhadāranyak says – "Tadetadamrutam Satyen Chhanam" (That Amrut is covered with Satya) where Amrut refers to the Parabrahma while Satya refers to the Nāmroope (name-forms). What latter Upanishads called 'Mithya' and 'Satya' were formerly called 'Satya' and 'Amrut'. At many places, Amrut is called 'Satyasya Satyam' (Truth behind the visible truth). When philosophers started, they considered the visible world as 'Satya' (Truth) and later they started looking for the underlying truth. Slowly, they started understanding that what we see is perishable and impermanent whereas the underlying principle is permanent and immortal. As they began differentiating between these two, 'Satya' and 'Amrut' changed to 'Avidyā' (ignorance) and 'Vidyā' (knowledge), finally leading to 'Māyā' and 'Satya' or 'Mithya' and 'Satya'. Although terminologies were different, the concept of outer appearance being perishable or ever-changing and the underlying element being true was ancient. Even Rig-Veda which is the most ancient of them all has verses such as – "Ekam Sat Viprā Bahudhā Vadanti" (Learned give different names to that which is actually one and permanent). It also has the word 'Māyā' in the same sense as it has been used later. It was not invented later during the times of Shankarāchārya.

Whatever knowledge our soul gains of the name-forms of the universe must be based on and correspond to 'something' which is the basic and eternal principle; otherwise, the knowledge is impossible. However, the job of Adhyātma doesn't end here. Vedānti call this principle 'Brahma' and now we must find the nature of this Brahma. It's obvious that it wouldn't be Sthool (gross) as it's unmanifest. However, there are still other unmanifest contenders like Man (mind), Smruti (memory), Vāsanā (desire), Prāna (life energy), Dnyān (knowledge) etc. which are not gross; and it's not completely improbable to imagine Parabrahma as one of these. Many equate Prāna as Parabrahma. Schopenhauer associates Parabrahma with desire indirectly linking it to the mind. Some Upanishads define Brahma as 'Sat-Chit-Anand'

(Truth-Knowledge-Bliss). Another version of Brahma is Omkar. It's explained that all Vedas originated from Omkar and from these words of Vedas the universe was made. Thus, there was nothing but Omkar at the beginning of the universe and thus Omkar is the true form of Brahma. However, from pure Adhyātmik (spiritual) point of view, all these versions of Parabrahma are somewhat 'with Nāmroope (name-forms)' as all these are perceptible by human mind and all that's perceptible comes under the purview of Nāmroope. How then shall we fathom the true nature of this primordial, omnipresent, homogenous, eternal and permanent principle? As it would always remain imperceptible, some spiritualists like Kant have quit the effort. Some Upanishads describe it as 'Neti Neti' meaning that which can't be described or is beyond. However, Adhyātma has decreed that even in this inexplicable form, there's a way of fathoming the Parabrahma through our intellect. When we evaluate the Avyakta (unmanifest) entities listed above (Prāna, Man, Dnyān etc.) to find out which is the broadest of them all, it shall lead us to the greatest one which shall be considered the true form of Parabrahma. Desire, memory, hope etc. are all properties of the mind so mind is superior to them; Knowledge is superior to mind; knowledge is the property of intellect so intellect is superior to knowledge and intellect is the slave of the soul so soul is superior to them all (Gitā 3.42). It thus becomes obvious that Ātmā (soul) which is the greatest among the unmanifest is the true form of Parabrahma. English author Green assumes a similar standpoint with a slight difference. Whatever impressions the Nāmroope create on our mind through senses are aggregated by our soul to attain knowledge. This knowledge needs a common base which shall be permanent despite different impressions of different objects; otherwise, the soul's knowledge would prove to be imaginary and baseless just like Vidnyānvāda. We call this base 'Parabrahma' while he, along with Kant, calls it 'Consciousness'. Whichever terminology you use, we're left with only two – Parabrahma/consciousness and Ātmā (soul). Of these, soul is beyond mind and intellect and is imperceptible. Based on our understanding, we decide that soul is not gross but takes the form of consciousness. Once we decide this, we're left with the task of deciding the nature of the Parabrahma (absolute). This Parabrahma or consciousness could either be the same as Ātmā or something different, as there's no third possibility.

In any science, we decide the distinction between two objects by proving that their purpose, actions or consequences are different. If we see carefully, we find that the aggregation done by soul to make sense and attain knowledge; is the same as the aggregation or homogeneity at the base of diverse objects in the universe. If it was not the case, all knowledge would be baseless. Being so alike and evenly matched in all respects, Ātmā (soul) and Parabrahma (absolute) cannot be different and thus, they are proven to be having the same nature. In short, whichever way you approach this, we not only conclude that the principle underlying all name-forms is subtle (not gross), but also understand that all different forms proposed (Prāna as Brahma, Dnyān as Brahma, Omkar as Brahma etc.) are lower forms of Brahma. True Parabrahma is even superior and pure, like soul. This is also the principle propounded in Gitā. However, this is not the only basis of arriving at the true nature of Parabrahma employed by our ancient Rishis (sages). We can't establish any theory based purely on reasoning. It must be corroborated with experience, as we said at the start of this chapter. Just as in modern science where findings of an experiment precede the theory devised to explain it; our ancient sages said through experience – "Neh nānāsti kinchan" (The diversity appearing in this universe is not true) and there's one common, immortal, eternal and permanent principle underlying everything. Then they also saw through introspection that the principle at the core of a living being (Ātmā) and the principle at the core of the entire universe (Parabrahma) is the same. The famous notion "Je pindi te brahmāndi" means literally this. Various Upanishads have different characters telling this very concept to others. "Aham Brahmāsmi" (I am Parabrahma) is one such quote which hints that whoever knows this – 'whatever is within me is everywhere else' knows everything. "Tattvamasi" (You are that) is another variation of the same quote where Shwetaketu's father tells him that he's the underlying principle at the core of everything as it's the same principle at the core of his body.

We established that Parabrahma and Ātmā are nothing but different forms of the same principle. However, looking at some anecdotes of Ātmā being comparable to knowledge may force one to believe if Parabrahma is also comparable to knowledge. Let's discuss this to clarify the doubt. Chit or knowledge is the property created in the gross Buddhi (intellect). However, just as we can't associate this property of Buddhi to Ātmā, the form of Ātmā must be considered as Nirguna (attribute-less) and Adnyeya (unfathomable). Hence, calling either Ātmā or Parabrahma as Chit (knowledge) is incorrect. Similar is the case with Sat (truth), as the moment you call something Sat (true), you automatically accept the existence of Asat (untrue). However, if Parabrahma is the one absolute or ultimate, how could dualistic characteristics be attached to it? Nāsadiya Sookta from Rig Veda says "At the start of the universe, there wasn't Sat (truth); whatever it was, it was one" as Sat and Asat or Hot and Cold etc. are dualities formed afterwards. Whoever gets liberated from these dualities is truly free and attains the one true Brahma beyond them (Gitā 7.28, 2.45). We can understand from the above discussion how deep and subtle the Adhyātmik thoughts are.

Although Parabrahma is imperceptible and unfathomable, every human has an understanding of its own soul and hence can access the true nature of Parabrahma through that; and thus, the theory of Brahma and Ātmā being identical doesn't become baseless or meaningless. This way, there's nothing more left to be said about Parabrahma other than that it's the same as Ātmā; everything else is left to experience and is beyond the purview of description or explanation. However, during intellectual or scientific discussions, we must clarify as much as possible with words. Hence, while Parabrahma is unfathomable, omnipresent and indescribable; to distinguish it from the gross manifest universe we describe it by the closest possible property of Chaitanya (consciousness) given by it to the beings in this universe. Hence, in Adhyātma we say Ātmā and Parabrahma are Chaitanyaroopi (in the form of consciousness); otherwise, there would be nothing else to say or describe both of them. We'd have to keep saying 'Neti, Neti' (not this, not this) to any and every description with words as it would render them to have attributes, which they don't. Hence, Chit (Knowledge or Consciousness), Sat (Truth or Existence) and Anand (Bliss) are commonly considered as the properties or descriptors of Ātmā or Parabrahma. One must remember here, however, that while these are the best possible ways to describe the principle; the only true way of understanding it is through one's own experience. Let us now delve into ways in which one can experience this.

As soon as we accept and experience the identity of Ātmā and Parabrahma, the difference between Dnyāta (knower) and Dnyeya (to be known) doesn't remain. However, as long as a person is alive and perceives everything through their senses, how would the diversity disappear? And how shall one experience the identity of Ātmā with Parabrahma? This is a valid and difficult question, but has an answer in Adhyātma. If we think carefully, sensory organs can't perceive anything merely by themselves but need support of Man (mind) as discussed earlier. If mind is at shoonya (zero) state, one won't see things right in front of their eyes. Even in day-to-day activities, we experience this – if we're not involved in the present but lost in our own thoughts, we miss sights right in front of our eyes or miss hearing even the loudest of noises. Thus, if mind is fully focused on Ātmaroopi Parabrahma (Parabrahma present within us as Ātmā) we'd realize Brahmātmaikya (identity of Brahma and Ātmā). One who achieves this state through Samādhi (Transcendence), Dhyāna (Meditation), Ekānt Upāsanā (solitary devotion) or Atyant Brahmavichār (Extreme concentration on Brahma) gets free from the duality of the universe even if it is right in front and automatically has the epiphany of Advaiti Brahma (singular absolute). The tripartite existence of Dnyāta (knower), Dnyān (knowledge) and Dnyeya (to be known) gets dissolved and the duality of devotee and deity doesn't remain either. Hence, this state is indescribable to anyone else, as the moment one says 'someone else', the state is disturbed and you come out from Advaita to Dvaita. It's beautifully described by Yādnyavalkya in Bruhadāranyak Upanishad – "Till the time there was the duality of witness and the scene, one was seeing, smelling, feeling or listening to the other; but when everything became one, who'd see, smell, feel or listen to whom? Who'd know that who's the knower himself?" In this state, there's no concept of happiness, sorrow, fear or grief. For one to fear someone; that someone has to be separate from oneself and that's not the case here. The essence of the sentence "Although the Parabrahma is imperceptible and unfathomable even by mind, it can be perceived through self-experience" is this. While we can't understand it as long as there's duality between 'I' and the 'Universe'; it can be understood by becoming one with it. A river can't fathom the ocean but it can enter it to become one with it and then there's no river anymore but just the ocean. There's a very witty description of this in Ken Upanishad – "Those who say they've understood Parabrahma actually don't; while those who don't know that they know it actually know it". This paradoxical sentence beautifully explains the invalidity of the understanding the moment one mentions that they experienced it; because saying 'I understood' means they're distinguishing themselves from others which defeats the whole concept. Conversely, when an enlightened being is unable to describe it in dualistic language, they most likely have experienced it. While difficult to imagine being in or attaining, this state of 'Nirvāna' (literally departure) is achievable by detachment and practice, according to Adhyātmik philosophers. A devotee rises from worshipping the manifest to worshipping the unmanifest at a later stage, ultimately reaching the stage of "Aham Brahmāsmi" (I am Brahma) becoming one with the Parabrahma. As the devotee is fully conscious, the state of being can't be called Sushupti (Sleep) or Swapna (dream). It is different from the regular state of consciousness that all of us are in which is Jāgruti (consciousness). This is thus believed to be a fourth state of being called Turiya (super consciousness). This state of being detached from everything is attainable through Pātanjalyog. As the person has attained the state of knowing 'Avibhaktam Vibhakteshu' (That through which we understand the unity among the diversity) to the maximum, no more knowledge is possible. As they've experienced the immortality beyond Nāmroope (name-forms), they're beyond birth and death as even those are manifestations with such name-forms. This is Moksha or the state of liberation. Pātanjalyog describes attainment of mystical abilities in this state. However, Gitā doesn't mention anything about these powers as they're neither the goal nor the part of attaining this state. They may even be attained; however, they're never highlighted as at that purest state of being, it's pointless to still engage in puny tricks of Māyā.

As this state of liberation is indescribable, no language can depict the accurate nature of Parabrahma. Thus, all the descriptions of achievement of this state given in Upanishads become secondary or figurative. Many descriptions of creation of universe by Parmeshwar thus become trivial. If Parmeshwar or Parabrahma is everywhere and in everything, it's principally invalid saying Parmeshwar 'created' something. However, to explain structure of the universe to common people, this practical or dualistic language is the only way. This is the reason behind various such descriptions we find in Upanishads. Still, we can find many anecdotes pointing to the true Advaiti (monistic) nature of Parabrahma reiterating the essence these Upanishads wish to convey. Even Gitā uses many such terminologies like "I create the universe" (Gitā 4.6) where Shri Krishna says this. However, there are also other instances where he says "My true form is imperceptible and unfathomable" (Gitā 7.25) where he's pointing to the true concept. However, some intellectuals hold on to the statements like the former and claim dualistic nature of Parabrahma being advocated in Gitā and Upanishads. They claim that true Advaita can't explain how the unmanifest Parabrahma led to the manifest as it's logically impossible to expect Nirguna (attribute-less) to transform into Saguna (with attributes) Māyā. Rather, they consider it more apt to accept existence of a Saguna original with attributes (Prakruti) and fit another original (Parabrahma) operating within it; like steam operating a steam engine. They compare the two to become one like different seeds of a pomegranate make the whole fruit. However, we don't agree with such inference of the Upanishads. We accept that we need to aggregate and explain the seemingly paradoxical descriptions in Upanishads which are sometimes Dvaiti (dualistic) and sometimes Advaiti (monistic). The best explanation is provided by considering Advaita vāda (monist approach) as primary and assuming that this singular 'appears' as plural when the unmanifest becomes manifest. Assuming Dvaiti approach doesn't explain all the things as aptly as our approach does. E.g. While

Tattvamasi clearly means "You are that" in Sanskrit and is purely Advaiti, Dvaiti try to force-fit the meaning according to their school of thought by incorrectly translating it as "You are theirs". Unless you throw away some of the important verses from Upanishads, there's nothing other than Advaiti point of view proposed in them. We shall thus not indulge in proving it any more, as truth is clear enough for those who want to see it. While there are many Upanishads, there's only one Shrimad Bhagavad Gitā and thus there shouldn't be any conflict while inferring from it. "That one which doesn't get destroyed even after everything else is" (Gitā 8.20) and "Only that's the truth and that is present in both body and the universe" (Gitā 13.11) are proof enough for substantiating Gitā's Advaiti point of view. Rather, the doctrine of becoming one with the universe proposed in Gitā can't be explained by anything other than Advaita Vedānta.

We must now answer the pressing question of how this one Nirguna (attribute-less), Avyakta (unmanifest) evolves into Saguna (with attributes) universe. We already discussed how Sānkhya have dealt with this by accepting two originals (Saguna Prakruti and Nirguna Purush). If we accept Saguna Prakruti as a second original, it contradicts with the Advaiti (monistic) point of view; whereas if we deny the existence of Saguna Prakruti as original, we can't explain how one Nirguna element manifests into Saguna universe. Moreover, theory of causality – Nirguna (attribute-less) can't lead to Saguna (with attributes) is agreed by Advaiti. This seems like a deadlock. Rather, many consider this as an obstacle to accept Advaita vāda (monism) and accept other dualistic schools of philosophy. However, Advaiti geniuses have found a perfect and logical way out of this predicament. They say that Satkāryavāda (Theory of causality) or Guna Parināmavāda (Transformation Theory) apply when cause and effect belong to the same class of objects. Thus, even Advaiti agree that Satya (True) and Nirguna Brahma can't lead to Satya and Saguna Māyā. However, this question would arise if both are considered Satya. Where one is Satya (true) while the other is just its appearance, theory of causality isn't applicable. Sānkhya considers both Purush and Prakruti as Satya and hence can't explain origin of Saguna Prakruti from Nirguna Purush. However, in Advaita, although Māyā is primordial, it's not Satya or independent but is 'Moha', 'Ignorance' or 'Appearance' as described in Gitā. Hence, the objection of the theory of causality doesn't apply to Advaita theory. If Sun gets transformed into something else we shall apply the theory of causality to it. However, if we see a mere reflection of the Sun in water, we can't expect the reflection to follow the rules of cause and effect with Sun. Once we observe a planet through binoculars properly, the form of planet perceived by the naked eye is described as a mere appearance due to limited ability of our eyes looking at an object too far. Similarly, Adhyātma says that the Nirguna Parabrahma seen through the binoculars of knowledge is 'True' while the Nāmroope seen by the eyes is a mere illusion or an appearance. As the appearance we see is because of the inability or limited ability of our senses to perceive clearly; what we see, hear etc. isn't described as the 'Truth'. Take examples of the power of hearing and vision. It's established that sound is nothing but vibrations of air or waves. Similarly, different colours like Red, Orange, Yellow etc. are manifestations of the same sunlight and are nothing but waves. Just as our ears and eyes perceive these waves as sound and colours, everything we perceive is nothing but an appearance created by our senses. Thus, we can positively conclude that Nirguna Parabrahma need not have any of the attributes or name-forms that we see in its appearance perceived by us. As we'd never be free of our perception through senses, it's ok to live with it. However, one shouldn't insist on calling it the original and eternal principle. Tomorrow if humans develop a new sense or lose a sense, the universe as we perceive it would appear different. Thus, if one asks what true, permanent underlying principle of the universe is; we should answer that it's Nirguna but appears Saguna to our senses. These kinds of questions don't arise in Adhibhautik discipline as it only deals with objects perceivable through senses. However, in Adhyātma which deals with finding the original principle at the base of the universe, we've to move beyond the subjective view of the senses and think only using knowledge or through intellect. Who and how to describe this Nirguna Parabrahma? Hence, it's also called indescribable and Advaita proposes that we perceive Saguna appearance in this Nirguna form through abilities of our senses. A question arises as to what gives this power to the senses. Advaita answers this by saying that waves of human knowledge stop at the appearance and hence it's the ignorance of the senses that they perceive Saguna appearance in the Nirguna Parabrahma; or that senses are a part of the universe and hence the Saguna universe is nothing but 'Daivi Māyā' (Divine appearance) of Parabrahma and leave it at that. We'd now understand the essence of following description in Gitā – "Uninitiated people only relying on their senses may perceive Parmeshwar (almighty) as Saguna (with attributes) and Vyakta (manifest) but the real and superior form of Parmeshwar is Nirguna (without attributes) and recognizing it using knowledge is supreme" (Gitā 7.14,24,25).

Let's now clarify what we mean by 'Nirguna' (without attributes) in Adhyātma. When we perceive sound waves as words or a dewdrop as honey, we may accept that we perceive attributes in these objects which may not be real. However, who's to say that these objects are completely attribute-less (Nirguna)? Upon careful observation we can infer that even if Parabrahma did have any attributes, if they're beyond our perception we'd anyway never understand them; and hence we call it Nirguna (attribute-less). Advaita doesn't claim there'd be no attributes at all but only says there are no attributes in Parabrahma that humans can perceive. Rather, the appearance we see (Māyā) is attributed to the power of Parabrahma as stated earlier.

Naiyāyiks consider that the universe is made up of innumerable, small, indivisible atoms and they say that once these atoms start aggregating, the universe is formed. This is called Parmānu vāda (atomic theory) or 'Ārambha vāda' (Theory of creation or beginning). Sānkhya on the other hand reject this possibility of innumerable atoms and accept development of a 'Homogenous, True and Trigunātmak (made up of 3 Gunas)' Prakruti as the cause behind the gross universe. They propose that development of these Gunas results in evolution of universe. This is called 'Guna Parinām vāda' (Theory of Transformation). However, Advaita Vedānti deny both these theories. As Parmānu are numerous and different, they can't be considered original according to Advaita while the dualistic originals Prakruti and Purush differ from the monistic Advaiti view. They must, however, provide an alternative and better explanation or theory than these two for evolution of universe.

Advaita says that it's not true that the Nirguna Parabrahma transforms into Saguna universe. It's just an illusion created by our sensory perceptions that we see the different Nāmroope (name-forms) in the same homogenous Parabrahma. This is called 'Vivarta vāda' (Theory of illusory manifestation). Advaita Vedānta has proposed Vivarta vāda to explain Nirguna Parabrahma (which appears to) transform into Saguna universe. It's a popular misconception that Advaiti reject validity of Guna Parinām vāda altogether. Advaita School only rejects it for explanation of the 'apparent' transformation from Nirguna Parabrahma into Saguna Prakruti. Once it's clear that it's merely an appearance that we see Nirguna Parabrahma as Saguna Prakruti, entire subsequent Guna Parinām (transformation) of Prakruti into various substances is well-accepted by Vedānta. In fact, after Bhagwān Shri Krishna says "Prakruti is my own Māyā (appearance)" (Gitā 7.14; 4.6), it's also said in Gitā that "Gunas (in one thing) transform into (another) Gunas resulting in us seeing different manifestations" (Gitā 3.28). This proves that Gitā and Vedānta accept that Saguna universe is governed by the Guna Parinām vāda (Theory of transformation). They consider both – Prakruti and the Guna Parinām vāda that it follows – as illusory, and regard Parmeshwar as the ruler of all these illusions who's beyond them. It's Parmeshwar and not Prakruti that has governed these laws.

We understood the nature of and interrelation between Māyā, Ātmā and Parabrahma. Adhyātma divides everything into two types – 'Nāmroope' and the 'Eternal principle' underlying them. If we apply this to a human body, Adhyātma regards the flesh, organs etc. as impermanent Nāmroope and the underlying Ātmā (soul) as eternal Parabrahma. Readers must've realized by now the intrinsic difference between the Buddhist school and Advaita school. While Buddhists consider everything as an illusion only regarding knowledge as true; Vedānti consider the external appearance as untrue while regarding the underlying Parabrahma (in the form of Ātmā or soul) as true. While Sānkhya have agreed with aggregation of entire universe into a single Prakruti they regard Ātmā (souls) in human bodies as innumerable Purush. Vedānta however, by removing the clause of theory of causality or transformation, has aggregated these innumerable Purush along with Prakruti into a single, homogenous Parmātmā (Ultimate soul).

There's a lot of trivial confusion and debate around calling Brahma as Sat (True) and visible universe as Asat (Untrue). We shall resolve it quickly. This is basically because of the two different interpretations of the word Sat or Satya – 1. Sat is what we see clearly in front of us (whether it later changes its form or not) and 2. Sat is what's permanent and eternal (whether it's perceptible to us or not). Those following the first definition call the visible universe as 'Sat' and the underlying Parabrahma as 'Asat'. However, even in instances where it's called so, the all-pervasive nature of Parabrahma is retained. Those following the second definition call the visible universe as 'Asat' and the underlying Parabrahma as 'Sat'. This second definition is adopted in Gitā. However, the other terminology is useful in explaining only one verse from Gitā where the doctrine of "Om Tat Sat" (Gitā 17.23) calls Parabrahma as Tat (that) meaning 'that which is beyond' while calling visible universe as Sat (truth) meaning 'what you see'. The meaning of the verse is "Parabrahma is that beyond what you see as truth".

After understanding the interrelationship between Jagat, Jeev and Parmeshwar (same as Māyā, Ātmā and Parabrahma respectively), we should move to understanding the meaning behind statements in Gitā such as "Jeev is my 'essence'" (Gitā 15.7) and "I've occupied the whole universe with my 'essence'" (Gitā 10.42). While Parmeshwar or Parmātmā is universal, it is also homogenous and indivisible. How then do we make sense of Parmeshwar being divided among all? The answer to this is that it shouldn't be considered as 'parts' or 'components' of Parmeshwar. When you imagine a pot in front of you, the air inside and outside the pot is the same despite being in different places. Similarly, Ātmā is the same Parmātmā merely existing within the confines of a body. As time, space, numbers and measures are also nothing but types of Nāmroope (name-forms), everything measured by them is limited and impermanent. Parabrahma is beyond these concepts of time, space etc. Many descriptions in Gitā and other Upanishads describe this single concept in different beautiful words. All Adhibhautik advancement happens within the purview of perceptions and limited by sensory capabilities. Even if modern science advances multifold and we fathom nature of the far-reaching galaxies and minutest of particles, it would never be able to grasp the eternal principle as it's beyond everything measurable or perceptible. To understand it, one must resort to Adhyātma (spirituality).

All that we learned till now about the universal, eternal and homogenously omnipresent Parabrahma is good enough to explain the meaning of Gitā verses and make sense of other literature. However, this can be understood by anyone who's literate enough and has a decent level of intellect. To completely understand the true and omnipresent nature of Parmeshwar, to inculcate this reality in our being and to behave in a truly egalitarian manner even in difficult times, requires generations of impressions, restraint of senses, persistent practice, meditation and devotion. Hence, only the person who's attained the stage of living by the code – "one soul in everyone" all the time irrespective of situations; and whose behavior naturally exhibits this reality is the one said to have attained 'Moksha' (liberation) or to have been enlightened (Gitā 5.18-20;6.21,22). This is the core essence of all theories and the final doctrine of Adhyātma Shāstra (spiritual discipline). Whoever lacks any of the said characteristics has still not attained the highest stage of Moksha. This is why Gitā describes true knowledgeable person not as someone whose intellect has grasped the essence of what the underlying principle at the base of the universe is; but someone who "Through peace, resolution, equanimity and humility has purified their mind and exhibits the same in every aspect of life" (Gitā 13.7-11). Once someone attains this stage, their Vyavasāyātmak (professional) intellect stabilizes to become subjective and they know the principle of "one soul in everyone". Then their Vāsanātmak (desirous) intellect also undoubtedly gets purified. One should remember that colloquially the word Dnyān (knowledge) or Samabuddhi (stoic calm) includes pure professional intellect, pure desirous intellect and pure behavior.

Moksha or Mukti isn't something that's 'achieved' or 'received'. We naturally use these terms loosely; however, one must remember that one can receive something only as long as there's duality of 'I' and 'Everything else'. Moksha is therefore an instantaneous phenomenon that happens without the person having to go anywhere. Neither is it received 'from' anyone or anywhere. Whenever and wherever one becomes conscious of Ātmadnyān (spiritual knowledge), Moksha is in that moment itself. This Moksha (liberation) can be attained by Bhakti Mārg (way of devotion), Pātanjalyog Mārg (way of Pātanjalyog), Sānkhya Mārg (way of analysis of Gunas given by Sānkhya) or Adhyātma Mārg (way of Spirituality). Gitā says that while Adhyātma Mārg is the most direct way, it is also the most tedious to understand through one's intellect and hence declares Bhakti Mārg as the easiest way for a common person. We shall discuss this one in detail in Chapter 13.

We see that Adhyātma has been prevalent since the times of Upanishads. However, even before Upanishads, in the ancient times of the Vedas there was development of this pragmatic school of thought. We'd take a brief look at one of the Sooktas (hymns) from Rig Veda. No other religion has tackled such pragmatic, independent, original and fundamental thoughts in its sacred texts and it's worthy of mentioning in our book. It's the 129th Sookta (hymn) in 10th Mandala of Rig Veda and is called 'Nāsadiya Sookta'. Following is its brief translation:

1. At that time (birth of the universe), there was neither Sat (True) nor Asat (Untrue). There was neither air nor the space beyond. What should we call being engulfed by what then, in such situation? For whose happiness? Was there even deep water?
2. Then there was neither Mrutyu (literally death, meaning impermanent or perishable universe) nor Amrut (literally immortality, meaning permanent or eternal) [This means there was no difference between permanent and impermanent]. There was no way to distinguish between day and night. Whatever was there was alone breathing by itself without air. There was nothing beyond it.
3. There was darkness. At the beginning it was all occupied by darkness and homogenous water or all-pervasive Brahma was covered by illusory Māyā. Whatever is said to be there, was that one, manifested as the other.
4. The seeds of its mind that arose first became Kāma (desire to create the universe). This was the first link between the Parabrahma and

the impermanent universe. This was decided by scholars using Buddhi (intellect) through deep introspection.
5. This ray spread across, above and below. Of these, some took the form of seed and grew bigger. Their inherent energy occupied this side while its effects occupied the other side.
6. Who else could explain better than this, how the universe evolved? Who knows for sure, as even deities; who were created after creation of this universe, wouldn't know where it came from.
7. Origin of this manifestation of universe that happened, or didn't happen, is known only to the Parmeshwar or Hiranyagarbha (golden womb) positioned in the space... or may not be known (to him either) ... who's to say?

Moving beyond the normally perceptible, impermanent name-forms and knowing that there's a single, immortal principle at the core of the universe is the essence of Vedānta philosophy and the sage who wrote this Sookta (hymn) seems to have captured it spot on right in the first attempt! We can notice how sharp and clear their introspection was. Moving beyond all perceptible dualities in this universe, he tackles the question of dualistic existence and declares that all these subjective jargons have appeared after the birth of the universe. Before that, there was no question of anything but the homogenous principle uniformly pervading everything without anything else being there. Gitā reiterates part of this Sookta as "Parabrahma is neither Sat (true) nor Asat (untrue) (Gitā 13.12). The beauty of this Sookta is that by saying that homogenous, Nirguna Parabrahma 'desired of' becoming heterogeneous and Saguna; the sage also admits later by saying we don't know exactly how. He doesn't, however, reject the Advaita logic attained through pure intellect and own experience. He doesn't resort to existence of two originals (Prakruti and Purush) like Sānkhya do. He stands by the Advaiti (monistic) approach. Occurrence of this Sookta in Rig Veda is incredible and it tells us how human mind freely roams around in unfamiliar terrain using sharp intellect, talent and pure credence. Even though subsequent Brāhmanas, Upanishads and other Vedānta texts have elaborated on the same idea first given in this Sookta using different anecdotes, explanations and simplifications, they haven't gone beyond that idea and are not likely to go either.

This concludes the chapter of Adhyātma (spirituality). Let's review what we've seen so far lest we waver from the main objective. After covering the prologue and delving into Karmajidnyāsa (Passion for knowing Karma or Action), we showed how Karmayogshāstra is the principal subject of Gitā in the third chapter. In the 4th, 5th and 6th chapters we proved how Adhibhautik and Adhidaivik disciplines fall short in explaining Karmayogshāstra and we also discussed Sukhadukkhavivek (Comparative scrutiny of Happiness and sorrow). Covering Kshetrakshetradnyavichār (Discussion of Body and Soul) in the 6th chapter to take a peek into what soul is, we discussed Ksharāksharvichār according to Sānkhya duality in the 7th and 8th chapters. Finally in this chapter we understood the true form of soul and how the same immortal and attribute-less principle is present in both body and the universe. We also learned how achieving and maintaining stoic calm and the equanimous view of "one soul in everyone" is the ultimate achievement of spirituality. This naturally explains how we must conduct ourselves while living in this world, as all behavior must follow in a way that would help attain this state. This is the Adhyātmik principle taught by Shri Krishna to Arjun in Gitā. However, explanation of Karmayog isn't over yet. Many argue that day to day behavior in the illusory world of name-forms would be against spiritual knowledge and must be avoided by an aspirant. If that's true, then all behavior would have to be sacrificed and Karmayogshāstra would be deemed meaningless. To decide on this, we must discuss under the purview of Karmayogshāstra what the laws and effects of Karma are. We must also understand why it is important to perform Karma even after purifying our intellect. Even Gitā discusses these. Sanyāsi (ascetics) are disinterested in this discussion and hence wrap up the analysis of Bhagavad Gitā after completing understanding of Vedānta and Bhakti (devotion). However, doing that is ignoring the main purpose of Gitā. Hence, let us see what answers Gitā gives of the questions mentioned above.

CHAPTER 10

Karmavipāk and Ātmaswātantrya (Fruition of Karma and Freedom of Soul)

We studied Adhyātma (spirituality) in the last chapter. Using the principles of Adhyātma, we shall denote two broad categories 'Brahma' and 'Māyā' into which we shall categorize everything through knowledge. By this classification, although human soul belongs to 'Brahma'; it's also covered with body and organs which are Nāmroope (name-forms) like other things in this universe. There's always a calling in human beings to liberate themselves from these and attain immortality. To fulfill this and to understand how one must behave in the practical world, we must now delve into this dualistic 'Māyā' world governed by laws of Karma. If it's the same Ātmā within the body and outside, natural questions that arise are – What is the impediment for the Ātmā within to recognize the Ātmā without? How to overcome that? To solve these, we must analyze the Nāmroope (name-forms); as there are only 2 categories – Ātmā and the Nāmroope. This envelope of Nāmroope is sometimes thin and sometimes thick. According to Vedānta, there are different types of living beings – animals, birds, humans etc. depending on thickness of this envelope. Ātmaroopi Brahma (Parabrahma in the guise of Ātmā) is everywhere, even in non-living things like rocks. Imagine it like being a source of light. When you keep a bulb inside a clear glass, light passes clearly through it. On the other hand, if you keep it in a metal container it's invisible from outside. Similarly, depending on the kosh (envelope) of Nāmroope on soul, there are two kinds – living and non-living. This is also the reason why not all animals can grasp what humans can. Ātmā can't do anything without the support of Buddhi (intellect) and Nāmroope; as despite being equally present within everything, Ātmā is intrinsically inert and Nirguna (attribute-less). This is why human birth is considered most superior. Once born as a human, there are two types of kosh (envelope) – Sthool (Gross) and Sookshma (Subtle). Of this, Sthool kosh is the combination of shukra-shonit (sperm and blood) of which sperm gives rise to the muscles, bone and nerves while blood gives rise to skin, flesh and hair. Vedānti call these collectively as Annamaykosh (physical envelope). Once we go deeper, we subsequently get Prānamaykosh (life energy envelope), Manomaykosh (Mind envelop), Dnyānamaykosh (Intellect or Knowledge envelop) and finally Anandamaykosh (Bliss envelope). Ātmā is further beyond. According to Vedānta, all kosh except the Annamaykosh are subtle and collectively with subtle organs and 5 Tanmātre (subtle elements) form Sookshma or Linga Shareer (Subtle body). However, the explanation for different births that Ātmā takes is attributed to Karmavipāk (fruition of Karma) in Vedānta; unlike Sānkhya who attribute it to the Bhāva (attitude) of Buddhi (intellect). This Karma remains attached to the subtle body and leaves with Ātmā when it leaves the physical body, making it take different births. While discussing requirements of soul to become one with Parabrahma, one must discuss both subtle body and Karma. We've discussed subtle body from Sānkhya as well as Vedānta point of view already. Let's now discuss the form of Karma that prevents human beings from attaining spiritual knowledge and ties them up in the cycles of birth.

At the birth of the universe, Nirguna, unmanifest Parabrahma began to appear as Saguna and manifest Māyā, which includes Karma as well. In fact, Māyā and Karma could be considered synonymous, as without Karma (action) unmanifest can't become manifest. Gitā describes a property of Karma as "The process of evolution from eternal Parabrahma to the universe consisting of elements" (Gitā 8.3). Karma is action or process; be it human, natural or even that of creation of the universe. However, any Karma simply changes name-forms, as the underlying principle is eternal. Māyā is often defined as Nām and Roop (name and form). However, while discussing Karma we understand that the form of Karma and Māyā is same. Māyā, Karma and Nāmroope are thus interchangeable words. As a matter of fact, Māyā is a general term. While its appearance is called Nāmroope, its processes are called Karma. However, in common parlance, this distinction isn't done and the three words are used synonymously. This Māyā is what Sānkhya call Trigunātmak (made of three Gunas) Prakruti where along with Purush it's considered primordial, independent and original. However, as Māyā/Nāmroope/Karma is ever-changing, it's inappropriate to call it original or independent as only Parabrahma is permanent, original and primordial. While there's still a question of why and when the Parabrahma was illusorily transformed as Māyā; this question is not answerable anyhow. This is the reason why we consider Māyā or Karma to be as ancient as Parabrahma according to Vedānta Sutras. Gitā mentions it as well – "Prakruti (Māyā) and Purush are both primordial" (Gitā 13.19). We can thus see that while Vedānta accepts the primordial nature of Māyā, they still don't accept its original or independent nature. The same is said about Karma – "Karma, Karma-like Yadnya and Universe were created simultaneously". In summary, Karma is the process by which Nirguna Parabrahma became visible universe. As its exact time is unfathomable, it's regarded as primordial, although not original.

While we discussed the evolution of universe from this Māyā or Prakruti in 8th chapter, we didn't discuss the common principles of what consequences humans have to bear with during this evolution. We're going to study this now, under the title 'Karmavipāk' (fruition of Karma). First rule of Karmavipāk is that once the process of Karma starts, it continues perpetually. Even if the whole universe gets destroyed, Karma remains in the form of a seed and the same process is initiated again and again from this seed. No one escapes the purview of Karma, neither celestials nor humans. As we don't know when this Karma came into being, the time or way in which human life got entangled in Karma is inexplicable. Even after death, you're not rid of your Karma which continues in the next birth; as the consequences of actions continue to exist in different name-forms. Adhyātma calls this as the cycle of birth and death or Samsāra and the power associated with these name-forms as Jeevātmā (soul). As Ātmā is immortal, it's neither born nor does it die. However, because of its entanglement in Karma, it's unable to escape this cycle. Consequences of what you do today, you experience tomorrow. Similarly, what you do in this birth, you put up with in the next. Some fruits of Karma even carry over to the grandchildren and great grandchildren. A live example of this is the existence of a hereditary disease which carries over for 3 to 4 generations. The explanation of where we're born also needs to be given by Karma vāda (doctrine of actions). Once this cycle of actions and consequences starts, even Parmeshwar (almighty) doesn't interfere in it as the whole universe is functioning as per will of Parmeshwar. This is why Bhagwān says – "Humans get the fruit I have decreed for them" (Gitā 7.22). While it's the prerogative of Parmeshwar to decree the fruits of Karma, these fruits are decided depending on the goodness or evilness of one's Karma and technically Parmeshwar is inert according to Vedānta.

This Karma is governed by the laws of this universe which are the rules of processes that the name-forms undergo. If we see this way, all Adhibhautik (physical) sciences come under the purview of Māyā. Pure Adhibhautiks like Haeckel propose that free will is an illusion while also denying existence of a soul. Whatever you do today is a result of what your ancestors did. E.g. Kleptomaniacs involuntarily get an urge of stealing whenever they find something attractive, owing to the hereditary impressions in their genetics. All that happens with a person is thus declared as 'fate' by this school of thought, as fruits of previous actions. This invalidates any need to correct or improve one's actions. Some evolutionists advise changing our behavior with changing laws of the universe. While delving into whether we can or should change our behavior, we must first know whether or not we have a choice between giving in to our tendencies and restraining our behavior. Going by Adhibhautik logic, everything is predefined and there is no 'free will' and we're bound by the relentless wheel of Karma. However, if we introspect, we realize that although we can't make the sun rise from the west; we have the right to decide between just and unjust, good or bad, righteous or unrighteous action. We shall now see if this belief is true or false. If we try to call it false, there's no logic behind punishment in our society for theft, murder etc.; whereas if we believe it to be true, the theories like Karma vāda and the laws of universe fall flat. While this question doesn't arise in Adhibhautik schools of thought, Karmayogshāstra discusses ethics and duties of a knowledgeable person, and must discuss and answer this question. If we realize there's no free will, all talks about ethics and morality would be rendered meaningless and we'd be deemed slaves of nature, bound to suffer fate. There has been a lot of pondering over this topic through time. However, we shall discuss the answer given in Bhagavad Gitā and Vedānta.

Adhyātma claims that there's still a way out of this, as Ātmā being an essence of Parabrahma is a part of a parallel, eternal universe of its own; uniformly underlying the visible universe of name-forms. Before getting into it, let's conclude the discussion of Karmavipāk (fruition of Karma). The doctrine of "As you sow, so shall you reap" is not just applicable individually to a person but also to a family, society, country or rather the entire universe. As every human being is part of some such units, they're liable to experience the fruits of familial, social Karmas etc. along with their individual Karma. Still, as we're discussing individual Karma, the Karma is mainly divided with the perspective of individuals. E.g. Manu divides Karma as Kāyik, Vāchik and Mānasik (Physical, Verbal and Mental) and tells us their fruits. Still, these are not the only ones. There are also the types Sāttvic, Rājas and Tāmas which are similar to the ones in Gitā. Now Karmavipāk classifies Karma by yet another method and mentions three types viz. 'Sanchit', 'Prārabdha' and 'Kriyamān'. Any Karma performed by a human being, may it be from this birth or previous, is their 'Sanchit' or accumulated Karma. It's also called invisible or unique as only its effects are visible once it's over. It's impossible to experience the fruits of these as they get accumulated. Some of the fruits may be favorable while others may be unfavorable. E.g. some fruits may be worthy of sending you to heaven while others may be worth banishing you to hell. They must be experienced subsequently and not simultaneously. Hence, out of the accumulated fruits, those which one has started experiencing, are called 'Prārabdha' meaning 'accumulation that has started'. In Marathi, Prārabdha is often used interchangeably with Sanchit. However, it's incorrect because Prārabdha is actually a subset of Sanchit. This is why it's also called 'Ārabdhakārya' or 'that which we've begun experiencing'. Other than these two, there's a third type called 'Kriyamān' which means 'ongoing' or 'the karma we're currently doing'. As our ongoing Karma is a function of the fruits of Sanchit Karma which we've started experiencing (which essentially means Prārabdha); we don't feel there's a need to have this third type. While Prārabdha is the cause and Kriyamān is its effect, this difference isn't relevant in the process of Karmavipāk. There's still a need to denote the Karma left after deducting Prārabdha from Sanchit. Vedānta divides Prārabdha as 'Prārabdhakārya' (experiencing currently) and 'Anārabdhakārya' (not yet being experienced). This would replace Prārabdha and Kriyamān with Prārabdhakārya and Anārabdhakārya respectively. While we agree with this sub-classification, it's not followed as 'Kriyamān' is considered as the ongoing Karma. However, if we do so, there's no term left for Anārabdhakārya. To solve this predicament, we've kept aside the tripartite classification of Sanchit, Prārabdha and Kriyamān; accepting a dichotomous classification of 'Arabdhakarya' and 'Anārabdhakārya' which is also scientifically accurate. While there are three types of experience based on the tense viz. 'experienced', 'experiencing' and 'to be experienced'; they're not relevant in Karmavipāk as fruits of the Prārabdha Karma (part of Sanchit being experienced) get added in Sanchit again. Hence, there's no need to classify any further than **'Prārabdha' (begun to experience)** and **'Anārabdha' (yet to begin experiencing)**. After zeroing in on this classification, Karmavipāk says that Sanchit is the total accumulation which is to be experienced. Out of these, once we start this birth with Prārabdha (the subset of Sanchit Karma to be experienced), there's no escape till we experience them all. However, it's not the case with Anārabdha Karma. With knowledge, one can completely extinguish this Karma. Hence, someone who's attained knowledge must live out their Prārabdha Karma patiently. If they don't do so, they'd have to take another birth to experience the remaining Prārabdha Karma even if they've extinguished all the Anārabdha Karma through knowledge. In fact, if one tries to end life before that, there's

Karma of suicide added to the tally. For experiencing the fruit of that, another birth becomes inevitable.

After discussing the types of Karma, let's now discuss the ways of escaping the cycle of Karma. One way is that of Karma vāda. Anārabdha Karma is that which is yet to begin, be it in this birth or another, as mentioned above. Ignoring this, Mimāmsaks have devised their own simple way of escaping the cycle of Karma. As discussed in 3rd chapter, Mimāmsaks classify Karma as Nitya (periodic), Naimittik (causal), Kāmya (desirous) and Nishiddha (prohibited). Of these, performing Nitya and Naimittik is mandated by Mimāmsaks. Nishiddha are sinful and prohibited so one should avoid them. If we do Kāmya Karma, we've to take rebirth on earth for experiencing their fruits so we must avoid them. By doing this, one lives out the Prārabdha Karma by living this life; avoids Narak (hell) by performing Nitya and Naimittik Karma while avoiding Nishiddha Karma; and also avoid Swarga (heaven) as we didn't perform Kamya Karma. By thus escaping these three places (Earth, Hell and Heaven) one is left with nothing but attaining Moksha. This doctrine is called 'Karmamukti' or 'Naishkarmya Siddhi' (freedom from fruits of Karma). The phenomenon of not having to experience the fruits even after performing Karma is called 'Naishkarmya'. However, Vedānta declares that this is not achieved in the aforementioned way employed by Mimāmsaks. Even Gitā says – "Quitting Karma achieves neither Naishkarmya nor Siddhi" (Gitā 3.4). Avoiding all prohibited Karma is virtually impossible. Even if one manages to do so, the Mimāmsak logic of exhausting all Sanchit Karma by living out Prārabdha Karma and following the code as mentioned above is flawed. If Sanchit includes relatively opposing experiences (one heavenly and other hellish), it's impossible to live both out in the same time and space. So, it's impossible that by living out Prārabdha Karma one can exhaust all Sanchit Karma. Vedānta thus declares this simple way of achieving Moksha devised by Mimāmsaks as false and illusory. No Upanishads mention this way of escaping the binds of Karma. Rejecting this way of Mimāmsaks and choosing to quit all Karma doesn't help either; as not only does it leave out Anārabdha Karma but stubbornness to quit Karma and sitting idle are both Tāmas

Karmas which add to the Anārabdha Karma and lead to another birth (Gitā 18.7,8). Moreover, Karmas like breathing, sleeping, eating etc. are unavoidable as long as we're alive and hence stubbornness to quit Karma is foolish.

We now face the question of finding a way to escape this cycle of Karma filled with Nāmroope and become one with the eternal and immortal principle. Even if we perform so called 'Good Karma' of Yadnya-Yaag (ritualistic fire) for the divine well-being, the fruits of those Karmas would lead you to heaven and land you back to earth once you exhaust experiencing them. Thus, they'll not yield Moksha. 'Knowledge' is the only way according to Adhyātma Shāstra. By knowledge, we don't mean practical knowledge or universal knowledge here. It's Brahmātmaikya Dnyān (knowledge of identity of Brahma and Ātmā) or Vidyā. There are only two types of objects viz. Māyā and Parabrahma as mentioned earlier in this chapter. Thus, the only way of escaping the cycle of Karma is to attain the form of Brahma. However, it's important to know it fully before attempting to attain it. "As I'm not attached to the Karma, I'm not burdened with the fruits of it" (Gitā 4.14, 13.23) essentially describes this. Here, the knowledge doesn't only mean mental knowledge but to assimilate that knowledge in oneself and achieve victory over your senses to ingrain this in every aspect of one's life. We also explained this in the last chapter as a doctrine of Adhyātma. Adhyātma Shāstra can only show you the way. Once on this way, one must take immense efforts to attain this goal. However, one may get confused due to availability of many options such as Pātanjalyog, Adhyātmavichar, Bhaktiyog, Karmayog etc. about which path to choose. Hence after explaining the principal way of Karmayog, Gitā talks about the path of eight steps of Pātanjalyog (Yama-Niyama-Āsana-Prānayāma-Pratyāhāra-Dhārana-Dhyāna-Samādhi) in the 6th Adhyāya to help on the path of Karmayog. From 7th Adhyāya it explains how on the path of Karmayog one attains this knowledge of Parmeshwar through Adhyātmavichar, or easier still through Bhaktiyog (Gitā 18.56).

Even though we've seen that the way of attaining Moksha is through Karmayog with knowledge, we're yet to see if this is humanly possible. Many scriptures including Gitā describe how compulsive urges pull humans towards following their inherent tendencies and Karmavipāk advocates the same. If we consider that all inspirations are born of past Karma, we've to conclude that one must get from one Karma into another. Rather, Karma and the inspiration to get rid of Karma are mutually opposite. If that's true, no one would appear to be capable of freeing themselves though knowledge. Adhyātma Shāstra answers this by stating that as Ātmā (which is the fundamental principle of a person) is same as Parabrahma (which is the fundamental principle of this universe), we've to think about a person's karma through both perspectives – Body and Soul. Although enveloped with name-forms or Karma, soul is inherently independent and thus can't be bound by Karma. Moreover, Karma/Māyā are but an illusory transformation of Parabrahma and hence can't control the soul. Thus, Parabrahma or Jeevātmā (Personal soul) are beyond the purview of Karma. Soul is pure, independent, Nirguna and Inert. However, as it is bounded within the confinements of body and organs, we can perceive through experience the inspiration it generates in our mind. Just as expanding steam trapped in a metal pot pushes the lid outward while trying to escape, human soul develops a tendency in its body and organs to perform Karma that's conducive for Moksha. Practically, this is called the 'Free will of the soul'. Reason we say 'practically' is that 'technically' soul is inert while all inspiration is of Prakruti. However, Vedānta doesn't attribute Prakruti to voluntarily perform Karma conducive to Moksha like Sānkhya do. If we assume that, it would mean that Prakruti would blindly liberate ignorant as well. We can't even call the inert Ātmā to naturally induce inspiration without a cause. Hence Vedānta needs to explain this phenomenon of Ātmaswātantrya (freedom of soul) calling it apparent, temporary inspiration given by the soul because of its entrapment. This inspiration is independent of the laws of Karma as soul is outside the purview of Karma as stated earlier. We've to remember two things here. One, independent doesn't mean that it doesn't cause anything. Second, while Soul creates this inspiration in the trapped state, it is always inert in its pure state. However, without always telling this whole story we simply call this 'Ātmaswātantrya' (freedom of the soul). Inspiration of the senses is to perform Karmas that let you indulge in sensory pleasures while inspiration of the soul is to perform Karmas that help attain liberation. These two inspirations are from different planes and opposite to each other. Due to these opposing inspirations, humans live in a state of constant conflict throughout their lives. Once a person stops following their indulgent inspirations and follows inspirations of its pure soul, they're said to attain Ātmadnyān (spiritual knowledge). Their behavior then automatically becomes conducive for Moksha and ultimately Moksha is attained through knowledge as said earlier. Once a person realizes the notion of "one soul in everyone", their behavior according to that is the one we call righteous or liberating behavior and because this is the independent tendency of the trapped soul, conscience of even an evil person takes the side of righteousness. This is the reason behind guilt and this is what Adhidaivik people call the deity of 'Conscience'. However, technically speaking Buddhi is an organ of Prakruti and thus it wouldn't voluntarily escape the laws of Karma. Hence, it's clear that this inspiration has to come from the soul, outside the purview of these laws. Similarly, the term 'free will' used by western intellectuals is incorrect as will or desire is virtue of Man (mind); and like Buddhi, Man is part of Karma/Prakruti and can't escape voluntarily. Hence, Adhyātma has finally declared that this freedom is of the soul. The feeling of being capable of free will, despite seeing the apparent binds of Karma is explained only by this explanation of separate universes of Karma and Brahma given in Vedānta. Whoever doesn't agree with Adhyātma should either reject the concept of freedom of choice or give up on knowing the explanation of it. Depending on whether one follows Advaita School or Dvaita School, this capacity of Jeevātmā is owed to oneself or to Parmeshwar respectively. Nevertheless, relentless efforts are advocated everywhere, even in Buddhism where the concept of soul is rejected. Kant who rejects all spiritual concepts indirectly agrees with the concept of deliberate efforts to improve one's behavior.

Although freedom of the soul is possible, this freedom doesn't come automatically or instantly. Just as an experienced craftsman needs intense practice and appropriate tools to achieve a certain level of skill, soul needs to achieve its freedom by inspiring the intellect and senses.

Since one may not be born with pure and Sāttvic Buddhi, they may need a lot of time and practice of Vairagya (detachment). Even then, bodily Karma like hunger, thirst etc. is not avoidable. Hence, one must patiently and courageously train their body and senses lest they go out of control. 6th Adhyāya of Gitā mentions help of Dhruti (determination or courage) in addition to Buddhi for this. In 18th Adhyāya of Gitā, it's mentioned that Dhruti, like Buddhi (intellect), is of three types (Sāttvic, Rājas and Tāmas). Getting the Buddhi from being Tāmas or Rājas finally to Sāttvic requires restraint of the senses and hence 6th Adhyāya teaches about the place, seat and diet required for the study of controlling one's senses. It's mentioned that with time and efforts one stabilizes their mind, gains a control over their senses and then attains knowledge of Brahmātmaikya (identity of Brahma and Ātmā) to become free from the binds of Karma. While occasional solitude is advised to stabilize one's mind and gain control over one's body and senses, it's never stated in Gitā that one must quit all social life. Rather, restraint of senses is advocated for conducting day to day operations without attaching desire to them.

It's mentioned in Mahābhārat that if a person is intelligent and determined, they can attain the stoic calm through Pātanjalyog within 6 months. However, if someone is unstable and lacks determination, they may not attain this even in 6 years. Rather, there appears to be a risk of failure to attain it in this life and having to start over from scratch in the next. There's also a fear that even in the next birth if we have to start from zero, what if we never achieve it and also whether we must learn Pātanjalyog and reach Samādhi stage. Arjun asks this question in 6th Adhyāya of Gitā to which Bhagwān Shri Krishna answers saying – "As Ātmā is immortal, whatever progress is made in this birth is carried forward through Linga shareer (subtle body) to the next and you start from there. In such a way, one attains Moksha after multiple births" (Gitā 6.45). Thus, one must not lose hope but keep at it. One must also not insist on achieving everything in one birth by engaging in extreme measures of Pātanjalyog and by wasting life merely straining the organs. Whatever potential you have, must be realized and progress has to be made so that slowly intellect would become Sāttvic and you'd attain

Moksha in this birth or the next. Even the smallest of curiosity in the direction of Karmayog doesn't go waste.

Let's see what Karmakshay means and how it's achieved. The meaning of Karmakshay is complete riddance from the bindings of Karma. One may wonder that if survival demands basic Karma from even a knowledgeable person, how one would achieve Karmakshay and Moksha. Vedānta answers this by saying that while Karma of name-forms is unavoidable even for a knowledgeable person, whether or not to attach this Karma to itself is the prerogative of Ātmā. Thus, if one wins over senses and gives up the desire towards actions they're performing, the Karma is inconsequential; because by nature it's blind, unconscious or dead. By itself, it neither binds anyone nor frees. It's neither good nor bad. Individuals attach themselves to the Karma and deem it as good or bad. Once this attachment is gone, the binding is gone; whether Karma remains or not. "Real Naishkarmya is in this, not in quitting Karma" (Gitā 3.4) or "Your right is only in performing the Karma, getting the fruits or not is not your prerogative" (Gitā 2.47) etc. are teachings of Gitā reiterating this notion. The question of whether or not a knowledgeable person should continue Karma is a different question which we shall discuss in the next chapter. We wanted to know the meaning of the sentence 'Knowledge extinguishes all Karma' and we saw what Gitā conveys on this subject. Even in matters of law, unintentional crime is treated differently from deliberate one. Emphasis is given more on the intent than on the action. This is a small example of this principle from our day-to-day life. Just renouncing social life or assuming inaction doesn't extinguish Karma. On the other hand, once someone detaches themselves from the Karma they do, they are free from its binding automatically; even if they continue performing all Karma. Just as water spilled on a Lotus leaf falls off without wetting it, one must remain detached from the fruits while still continuing to do all Karma. Thus, the 'extinguishing' of Karma is figurative. Literally, Karma is Nāmroope (name-forms) and thus would only change form. What one can do is extinguishing the implication given to the Karma due to one's attachment. Just as fire burns everything instantly, the extinguishing during Moksha is instantaneous, as soon as the knowledge is attained. However, the time of death is considered particularly crucial in this matter. Death is the last time of this birth. Even if one attains Brahmadnyān (Knowledge of Brahman) and extinguishes Sanchit Karma, it must be continued till death; lest fruits of the Karma done till then would cause another birth. While we agree that one who's truly attained Moksha need not worry, technically we should consider the possibility of this knowledge not persisting till death. This is why time of death is considered critical and Adhyātma insists on someone being in this state at the time of death for ensuring Moksha. Hence Shri Krishna says in Gitā – "One gets liberated by unconditionally remembering my name at the time of death" (Gitā 8.5). By this theory, one may claim that someone may spend their lifetime committing evil Karma and still get Moksha by attaining Brahmadnyān at the time of death. On the face of it, the claim is valid and upon a little thinking we can accept it. However, someone who's followed the path of evil all their life is unlikely to suddenly get the knowledge of Parabrahma at the time of death. Just as in case of any other discipline, one attains this state after a considerable level of practice and inculcation of these thoughts in their mind. Thus, it's highly unlikely, if not impossible, for someone who's never learned or practiced it to suddenly attain it at the time of death. Thus, one must keep at it throughout their life so that they can maintain that state at the time of death. Still, let's consider the possibility of someone attaining it suddenly at the time of their death. In such case, the enlightenment extinguishes all Anārabdhakārya Karma and fruits of all Ārabdhakārya Karma have been experienced in this life. Thus, the person is left with no fruits of any Karma and gets liberated. The beauty of this knowledge of Parmeshwar is such that as and when it's attained; all Anārabdhakārya Karma gets extinguished instantly. This is why it's said – "Even if wrongdoers unconditionally worship Parmeshwar, they're liberated" (Gitā 9.30). However, one must understand that we're talking about a person who's become one with the principle completely and not someone simply chanting the name of some deities. Time of death is considered critical because arising of desire before death may result in rebirth and hence maintaining this state till death is crucial.

Let's now see what Vedic Dharma says about the fate of someone who's unbound and someone who's still bound to Karma. Bhagavad Gitā has depicted two paths of Vedic Dharma – Karmakānd (Ritual centric) and Dnyānkānd (knowledge centric). Karmakānd advises worshipping of deities like Soorya (Sun), Agni (Fire), Indra, Varun, Rudra etc. earning material wealth and achieving liberation with death. As this practice (called Shrauta Dharma) is not prevalent in the modern times, people have replaced this with charity and devotion in temples. In ancient times, people used to perform Yadnya-Yaag (ritualistic fire) for both selfish and selfless motives, as evidenced in Rig Veda. As this way was unanimously accepted by the three Vedas, it was called 'Trayi (Triple) Dharma' and Vedic Samhitās along with Brāhmanas describe different rituals and guidelines for them. Afterwards, there were found to be many variations and inconsistencies between different practices given and hence Rishi (sage) Jaimini compiled and consolidated them all in his scripture called 'Poorvamimāmsa' which is also called as 'Mimāmsā Sutras'. This is why this path came to be called Mimāmsak path. Gitā doesn't use this name but calls it Trayi Dharma. The subsequent texts Aranyaks and Upanishads consider this ritualistic path inferior. They insist on focusing on knowledge instead and hence are called 'Dnyānkānd' (knowledge centric). Bādarāyanāchārya compiled these and formed 'Vedānta Sutras' which are also called Brahma Sutras, Shāreerak Sutras or Uttarmimāmsa. Practitioners of Karmakānd path are called 'Mimāmsak' while practitioners of Dnyānkānd are called 'Vedānti'. Mimāmsaks claim that rituals are vital and only the one who practices these attains Moksha, others do not. They claim that rituals like Yadnya-Yaag were born along with the universe and everyone must follow this timeless practice. We don't consider this path significant as it's no longer prevalent. Gitā, however, mentions this as an alternative path as it was prevalent back then. Still, we can see that ritualistic path had begun to be trivialized with the advent of knowledge centric path of Upanishads. This was accentuated further with the rise of Buddhism and Jainism. Today, there are hardly any Mimāmsaks left who practice these rituals religiously. Some rituals still persist today and are practiced by a few. Other than Shrauta Dharma, Smārta Dharma (advocated in

Smrutis) enlists many other rituals for every class of society depending on their profession.

Now the question arises whether one attains Moksha and escapes the bindings of Karma by following this ritualistic path. If so, what then is the importance of knowledge? Dnyānkānd says that there's no escape till one becomes detached from the Karma while Karmakānd is all about doing different types of Karma. Even Brahmadev (the Creator deity) has advised Karma for maintaining the cycle of universe. How then should one proceed? Gitā answers this by saying that it doesn't advise anyone to quit doing Karma at all. Rather, it agrees with the notion that the world would come to a halt if everyone gives up Karma and hence it advocates continuing Karma. Gitā says that if someone performs Yadnya-Yaag with the desire of entering heaven, they'd undoubtedly get into heaven. However, the fruits of Karma getting you to heaven are limited and once they're exhausted, you're bound to be born on the earth again. Thus, you do not escape the binding of Karma. For true Moksha, Gitā advises doing all these Karmas with knowledge of Brahmātmaikya (identity of Brahman and Ātman) and without desire or attachment. This way, you're liberated while maintaining the cycle of universe. This is the final message given in Gitā.

"Rather than sacrificing grains, food or animals in Yadnya, it's better to sacrifice tendencies like desire, anger etc. in the Yadnya of achieving stoic calm" (Gitā 4.33). Getting rid of one's possessive mind is the biggest sacrifice in the act of Yadnya, rest is symbolic or supplementary. Once we accept this broader and essential definition of Yadnya, all selfless acts and acts done without desire become a great Yadnya and the actions performed are non-binding. As these acts are done without expectation of their fruits, there's no question of going to heaven and back; it would simply lead to Moksha. Thus, there are two types of people doing Karma – One type that perform all Karmas with an eye on their fruit who are destined for heaven and another type that perform all Karmas with knowledge and without desire who are destined for Moksha. Gitā never asks us to quit actual Karma. In fact, by sacrifice, it's always meant the sacrifice of desire/expectations as mentioned in 18th Adhyāya.

The path of above-mentioned categories of people after death is also mentioned in the 8th Adhyāya. "Once a knowledgeable person dies, its Shareer (body) passes through (cremation) fire, day, Shuklapaksha (fortnight of waxing moon) and Uttarāyan (Northward movement of Sun) to Brahmapad (abode of Brahmā) and attains Moksha and there's no rebirth. Once a ritualistic (without knowledge) person dies, its Shareer (body) passes through (cremation) smoke, night, Krishnapaksha (fortnight of waning moon) and Dakshināyan (Southward movement of Sun) to Chandralok (abode of the celestials) and returns to take birth on earth once the fruits of their Karmas are exhausted" (Gitā 8.23-27). This was composed considering the position of people in the northern hemisphere and North Pole as the abode of the deities. Looking at the different steps given in the description of these paths makes one wonder if the process is associated with passage of time. However, they're not meant as periods but are symbolic of deities who take one through the journey of Moksha/Heaven according to Vedānta Sutras. Gitā's stand on this is still debatable as Gitā and Mahābhārat seem to suggest that the time of death also plays a role in deciding the path during afterlife. However, later this doubtful clause about significance of time is done away with and it's stated that a knowledgeable person, irrespective of time of death, is destined for Moksha. Now both these paths are destined for those who perform good deeds either with or without knowledge. For people who spend their lives with no regard to their actions and commit evil deeds, a third path of rebirth either as animals or in hell is described.

While we saw the different destinies of humans according to their Karma, Adhyātma says that someone whose Buddhi has become fully realized with clear understanding of Brahmātmaikya (identity of Brahma and Ātmā) and behave accordingly; there's no need to go anywhere or wait for death. As worship of Saguna (with attributes) Parmeshwar may result in some form of attachment (at least with the Saguna form), the knowledge may remain incomplete. However, someone who's completely one with the Parabrahma with no dualistic discrimination left in their being; is destined for immediate Moksha. This is what we saw in previous chapter as the state of "Aham Brahmāsmi"

(I am Parabrahma) and there's no reference of time and space for this stage as it's a complete union (Yog) with Parabrahma. Even Buddhists considered this stage as the ultimate goal even though they rejected existence of Ātmā (soul). While the mental state of a person at this stage may appear ascetic, Gitā doesn't insist on asceticism in practice for attainment of this stage.

CHAPTER 11

Sanyās and Karmayog (Asceticism and Action-Oriented Yog)

After learning the ways of attaining Moksha and how it translates to performing various actions, we should now come to an important question – Once we achieve complete knowledge of Brahman and continue to perform all actions without desire or expectations, we achieve Moksha. After achieving this, should we continue performing Karma till death, or should we quit all Karma by considering it meaningless and against knowledge? Karmasanyās (*Quietism* or quitting all action) and Karmayog (*Energism* or Action Oriented Yog) are the two logical paths ahead. It's prudent to choose that path right from the start which proves to be the better of the two. Thus, this discussion of Karmayogshāstra is not complete without finding the answer to this important question. Even in Gitā, it was not enough to tell Arjun that one doesn't accumulate any more fruits of Karma once they've achieved the attitude of equality towards all. The message to be conveyed to Arjun was to "Get ready for war" (Gitā 2.18). There was a different explanation needed rather than just making him feel indifferent about whether he wages war or not. Rather, it was trying to explain to him why the seemingly destructive act of starting the Great War was the necessary thing for him to do. Although Karma binds you and Dnyān (knowledge) liberates you, Gitā told Arjun why it is still important to perform Karma. While it has been clarified that it's impossible to quit all Karma, it still doesn't prove why one should not avoid as much Karma as possible. This is why Arjun asks Krishna at the beginning of

3rd Adhyāya – "If according to you, Nishkām Karma (Action without desire) and attitude of equality towards all is better than Karma; I shall maintain the purity of my intellect like a 'Sthitapradnya' (someone with stoic calm). Why are you pushing me to start this ghastly war" (Gitā 3.1)? Shri Krishna then explains to him the significance of Karma by explaining how Karma is inevitable. Still, it doesn't clarify why one should not freely choose between Sanyās (asceticism) and Karmayog (Action Oriented Yog) as the way of life. Hence, Arjun again bluntly asks Shri Krishna at the start of 5th Adhyāya – "Don't mix both the paths (Sanyās and Karmayog), please tell me definitively which one is better" (Gitā 5.1). This question isn't unique to Gitā. Lord Rām (from another great epic Rāmāyan), asks Guru Vasishtha in the scripture 'Yogavāsishtha', a similar question. Similar question also appears in the literature of great Greek philosopher Aristotle. Across world history, there have been these two paths and similarly they've been prevalent in India since ancient Vedic times. One of these is called Sanyās Mārg (ascetic way), Sānkhyanishthā (allegiance to Sānkhya) or simply 'Sānkhya' or Dnyānnishthā (allegiance to knowledge). Lokmānya Tilak prefers calling this first path 'Quietism' as this path advocates quietly spending life, immersing oneself in the pursuit of knowledge. The second path is called Karmayog (Action oriented Yog), simply Yog (literally union) or Karmanishthā (allegiance to Karma). We've already illustrated in the 3rd chapter that the words 'Sānkhya' and 'Yog' don't denote 'Kāpilsānkhya' and 'Pātanjalyog' here. Additionally, let's clarify on the word 'Sanyās' a little bit as there are many interpretations drawn. It doesn't imply 'staying a bachelor' or if married then 'leaving your family to take up clothes of a monk'. The patriarch Bheeshma from Mahābhārat was a celibate but was overseeing the political happenings. Samarth Rāmdās from Maharashtra had taken celibacy but performed great deeds of spreading knowledge. The question is whether or not one, after attainment of Moksha, continues to perform all actions dutifully for betterment of others or quits everything considering it Mithya (false). Those who take up the former route are Karmayogi while those taking the latter are Sanyāsi. Marriage, clothing etc. are immaterial. Gitā only focuses on behavioral aspect of Karmayog and not dwelling on trivial points like clothing. These true meanings of the two words shall be the ones we'd use in this chapter.

While these two paths are prevalent after attainment of Moksha, many communalists have proposed a suggestion that both these paths are equally prudent even in the quest for attaining Moksha. Rather, they suggest Karmayog as the first step before ultimately reaching Sanyās for attaining Moksha. While Gitā describes these two paths separately in 2nd and 3rd Adhyāyas, these people try to imply that Gitā advocates Sanyās as the principal point. However, then they can't give any explanation for the verse – "Sānkhya (Sanyās) and Yog (Karmayog) are two disciplines (to attain Moksha)" (Gitā 3.3). There can be 3 interpretations of the path of Karmayog – (1) Irrespective of knowledge, ritualistic Karma like Yadnya-Yaag and Shrauta-Smārta Karma leads to Moksha. Gitā doesn't agree with this Mimāmsak meaning. (2) Karmayog is necessary for purifying one's mind and must be followed as a first step before Sanyās. This is also not what Gitā implies. (3) A knowledgeable person who knows the glory of their soul must perform requisite Karmas lifelong without desire and attachment. This is the meaning implied in Gitā and this can never be taken as a precursor to Sanyās. There's no end to performing Karma in this path. Knowledge and detached approach to Karma makes this path of Karmayog equally worthy of attaining Moksha as the path of Sanyās (Gitā 5.5) is a clear message given in Gitā. Even Mahābhārat mentions separate and unique existence of these two paths as independent ways to attain Moksha. The suggestion to call Karmayog as a precursor to Sanyās is a partisan attempt of trivializing it by communalist followers of Sanyās discipline. We want to highlight this glaring flaw in the communalist critiques of Gitā and show everyone that one can't grasp the true essence of Gitā unless they go past this communalistic view and objectively and impartially assess its true meaning.

Proving these two paths independent and equally capable doesn't serve the purpose intended in Gitā, as Arjun could then potentially choose any of the two paths and avoid going to war if the path of Sanyās was chosen. This is beautifully drafted as a question by Arjun (which we saw earlier) and its answer given by Shri Krishna – "While both paths are potentially capable in attaining Moksha, Karmayog is particularly special" (Gitā 5.2). Throughout the Bhagavad Gitā, there are many recurrences of such emphasis on pursuing Karmayog rather than following the path of Sanyās. It's not that followers of Sanyās discipline don't see the importance given in Gitā to Karmayog. However, if they accept it, it would make their sect deemed inferior to Karmayog by Gitā. This has resulted in far-fetched and illogical twisting of words to forcibly draw meaning of verses from Gitā in favor of Sanyās. Still, no one could draw any other meaning from the part "... Karmayog is particularly special" said multiple times by Shri Krishna in Gitā. This is why they've attempted to claim that this was a namesake praise of Karmayog done by Shri Krishna while the ultimate path is that of Sanyās according to them. Shankarāchārya has proposed that Gitā considers that only knowledge extinguishes all Karma and yields Moksha and that Karma is not required. He's then proposed that as this is said in Gitā, Karma is meaningless once the mind is purified and as Karma is naturally binding, it must be avoided. Even if it's proven that doing Karma is not necessary once Moksha is attained, insisting on not doing any Karma post Moksha is not satisfactory because – 1. While Karma with desire is binding, Nishkām Karma is not binding and hence need not be avoided and 2. While not for Moksha, there are many other strong reasons for which one should continue doing Nishkām Karma and one's not prevented from doing so even if we agree Karma is not necessary. What's ironic is that Gitā was narrated to Arjun to convince him for war because he was planning to renounce everything instead of going to war. Thus, it would be self-defeating if Gitā advocated path of Sanyās.

While Gitā strongly advocates Karmayog, it would be wrong to say that Gitā disrespects the path of Sanyās. It does regard it as an alternative path to attain Moksha. Even in Karmayog, one has to renounce desire or expectations. While both paths are equivalent in terms of attaining Moksha, looking at well-being of the universe, one must continue working for it and only renounce desires. This way, both Sanyās and Karma are maintained; says Bhagwān Shri Krishna. Many narrow-minded followers of Sanyās Mārg (Quietism) go on to say that although Shri Krishna advised Arjun to continue doing Karma, it was because Arjun was devoid of knowledge and it was in his interest to continue with Karma for purification of his mind. However, even Shri Krishna would advise Sanyās post enlightenment. If Arjun was told that he was devoid of knowledge, he would've insisted on attaining full knowledge and that would've meant him quitting the battlefield and taking up the path of Sanyās. There's no point in arguing against such theories as they're ridiculous to the point of showing Bhagwān Shri Krishna in bad light just to prove that their path is correct. We'd just say that Shri Krishna was more than capable of telling Arjun that he lacked knowledge and still telling him to initiate war to follow his duty. Anyway, Shri Krishna enlightened Arjun through Gitā and made him willingly go to war (Gitā 18.63). This clarifies Shri Krishna's opinion that a knowledgeable person must continue to do Karma without desires.

Let's now delve into the reasons given in Gitā to prove how Nishkām Karmayog is the better path even after attaining knowledge. Vedic Dharma has two paths Karmakānd and Dnyānkānd as we saw earlier. While Karmakānd advocates lifelong Karma, Dnyānkānd propounds asceticism the moment your Buddhi turns dispassionate. Even if we look at behavior of great beings, the history is divided with Shuka, Yādnyavalkya etc. having lived by path of Sanyās while Janak, Shri Krishna, Jaigishavya etc. having lived by Karmayog. One of the verses from Smruti mentions that a person with Brahmadnyān (Knowledge of Brahman) is indifferent and free despite performing Karma, like Janak and Shri Krishna. Sage Vyās had sent his own son Shuka to Janak for attaining Brahmadnyān. Janak tells Sulabha in their conversation – "I'm ruling this kingdom without any desire. Whether someone applies sandalwood to my hand or someone cuts off my hand, I'd feel the same". He then goes on to tell Sulabha – "Experts tell of three ways to attain Moksha. 1. Attaining knowledge and quitting Karma, which is also called Mokshanishthā. 2. Other learned scholars tell of Karmanishthā. However, aside from these two absolutes of only knowledge and only Karma, 3. He (Panchshikha) has taught me this third (Extinguishing desire with knowledge and continuing to perform

Karma) path. Nishthā usually means the ultimate goal or state. However, here and also in Gitā, it is used with the meaning – 'that way of life by which one finally attains Moksha'. Gitā also recommends this third Nishthā to Arjun with an addition of Bhakti (devotion). It doesn't call the Keval (absolute) path of Mimāmsak (2nd path in Janak's description with only Karma without knowledge) as Nishthā as it declares that it would lead one to heaven and not Moksha. If you see, even great sage Vyās sired two sons Dhrutarāshtra and Pandu to continue the lineage of Vichitraveerya and labored for 3 years writing the great epic Mahābhārat. Ardent proponent of Sanyās, Adi Shankarāchārya also worked so hard for propagation of his Dharma using his knowledge. Rather, Brahmadev (the creator himself) had to perform Karma to create this universe. This shows that both paths (Sanyās and Karmayog) have been in practice since time immemorial. Veda Vyās tells in his conversation with Shuka that Karma binds a person and knowledge liberates them. However, he also goes on to say – "Vedas tell us to both perform Karma and quit Karma. Hence, you must continue to perform Karma without keeping your ego in it. Continuing to perform Karma after achieving knowledge is an ancient practice/tendency of Brāhmans. There are two paths supported by Vedas. One is action oriented and the other is ascetic". Despite the clear indication of these two paths, communalist critics try to prove as if there's only one path, of Sanyās, advocated in Mahābhārat and consequentially in Gitā. This is completely wrong and driven by vested interests to find undivided acceptance of their sect.

As we've seen, these two paths have been given equal credit throughout history. However, Gitā emphasizes that Karmayog is better through sound logic – Our breathing is also a Karma and actions like eating, drinking, sleeping etc. are also unavoidable (Gitā 5.8-9). If followers of Sanyās are allowed to beg for food; what's wrong in performing all Karmas with Buddhi (intellect) free of attachment? In fact, giving up of Karma with the fear of losing the chance to attain Moksha is itself described as lack of resolve and Tāmas Karma according to Gitā (18.7; 3.6). Rather, a courageous person must continue with those Karmas which are entitled to them as their duty (Gitā 18.6).

Even if someone claims to avoid Karma for the fear of disturbing their purified mind by engaging in any Karma, it would be considered as a Rājas sacrifice (Gitā 18.8). If someone claims to quit Karma because it belongs to Māyā while Ātmā belongs to Parabrahma, we can counter argue by telling them that Parabrahma itself is enveloped by Māyā and Ātmā is enveloped by physical body which is a part of Māyā. How is it wrong for a person to continue with Karma while being in this universe? Rather, one should be aware of this unity between Ātmā and Parabrahma while continuing to perform all Karma with detachment so that it doesn't hinder Moksha. Moreover, it would mean that you have not avoided the cycle of universe. Bhagwān himself has lived by this path and worked for betterment of the good and execution of the evil in different Yugas (ages) (Gitā 4.8). This undoubtedly proves the significance of Karmayog. Prakruti would continue with its operations; you must quit the ego in all the actions you perform and you're free (Gitā 3.27; 13.29; 14.19; 18.16). Some argue that while it's enough to give up the desire and expectations in Karma to escape the binding, once the knowledge is acquired the wish to perform any Karma itself is lost. Thus, one gives up Karma due to apathy and not due to fear or ambition. To support this, they give reference of many verses in Gitā with different adjectives used to describe a knowledgeable person – "He doesn't need to do anything" (Gitā 3.17), "Quitter of all business" (Gitā 12.16) and "Homeless" (Gitā 12.19). These appear to hint that Gitā agrees with the notion that one quits Karma after gaining knowledge. However, this argument is hollow and without truth. Let us see how. We've shown in the chapter of Sukhadukkhavivek how Gitā doesn't agree with the notion that a knowledgeable person quits all wishes or desires. Having just a desire or wish to do something isn't considered a cause of sorrow. Attachment to Karma is the real cause of sorrow. Hence, it's advisable for a knowledgeable person to only quit attachment to all Karma rather than killing all desires. It's needless to actually stop doing Karma; rather it's impossible to quit all Karma. "Whoever it is, cannot survive without Karma" (Gitā 3.5) is a proof of this. Secondly, with the removal of attachment or desire, the Karma need not stop. There are many examples of Karma like breathing, sleeping etc. which have no involvement of either desire or attachment but are inevitable. Gitā says that as Karma is inevitable, you must do it without attachment. Thus, in the statement – "He doesn't need to work" (Gitā 3.17), emphasis is on 'He' and not on 'work'. What it means is, after knowledge he doesn't have anything as 'his' and that is why he must do all work selflessly from now on. Sure enough, in the following Shloka, Shri Krishna says – "Hence, you must continuously perform Karma that's your duty without being attached to it" (Gitā 3.19). This proves that a single Shloka chosen by communalist critics to stubbornly prove their point is an incorrect interpretation of Gitā's verses. Many subsequent verses have similar clear meaning but have been twisted by communalists to prove their point. Followers of Sanyās path say – 'There's nothing left that's yours, so don't do anything'; while Gitā says – 'There's nothing left that's yours, so do whatever you must, selflessly and without attachment'.

Upon attaining Ātmadnyān, there's no more feeling of 'I' and 'Mine'. This feeling is then replaced by 'Universe' and 'of the Universe'; or 'Parmeshwar' and 'of Parmeshwar' if we're speaking from the point of view of Bhakti (devotion). A common person does everything with the self-centered point of view. A Dnyāni (knowledgeable) person does everything from selfless point of view for betterment of the Universe. Similarly, proper understanding proves the true meaning of the snippets taken by Sanyāsi trying to portray Gitā advocating Sanyās. "Quitter of all business" or "Homeless" are thus said in the sense of this selfless view with which a knowledgeable person must continue their Karma. There are some other objections arguing that 'quitting desire' and 'quitting attachment' is the same and even in the Karmayog approach of quitting attachment, there's no drive to perform Karma and thus Sanyās or Quietism is the path ultimately taken by both disciplines. This is mainly due to ignorance or incomplete understanding of the word 'attachment'. Quitting attachment means keeping aside the thought that "**I'm** performing this Karma so that **I** get this fruit". It only means one must quit greed, adamancy or attachment to the Karma. It's nowhere implied that there needs to be any lack of motivation, enthusiasm or feeling of duty while performing Karma. Whoever is stuck with seeking personal interest as the motivation behind any Karma would surely see detachment being associated with lack of enthusiasm. However, it's not the same with someone who has attained knowledge of Parabrahma. The thought that 'whatever fruit I get is purely of my efforts' is itself wrong. There are so many other factors responsible for anything to happen, that are beyond our control. The fruit is thus an aggregate product of your efforts supported by these factors being favorable. One must also remember, however, that our efforts are absolutely essential as well. Whoever is knowledgeable and level-headed does their bit and leaves the occurrence of fruit of their Karma to destiny; or in case of Bhakti Mārg to Parmeshwar. When we keep this is mind, we never get sad if our Karma doesn't yield results. E.g. Medical science tells clearly that a medicine is effective only if the patient's body is strong and supports the action of the medicine. The composition of one's body is a result of generations of hereditary build up along with their lifestyle. Thus, it's impossible for a doctor to know the entire nature of patient's body. Still, a doctor treats thousands of patients by prescribing medicines as per their diagnosis. While working this way without getting involved, even if some patient doesn't get cured, the doctor doesn't get upset. They also calmly point out that the medicine only works in so many percent of patients. However, if ever this doctor's son falls ill, they might forget all about the statistics of medicinal action and the facts about a person's body composition and claim that their son must get cured. Often you see doctors inviting fellow doctors to treat their own children. This small example shall tell us what is meant by attachment to Karma and how one can function dutifully about anything if there's no attachment. This requires complete detachment of mind with knowledge. However, just as decolorizing a fabric doesn't mean destroying it, one must not quit Karma when we ask for detachment from it. Considering that Karma is inevitable, a knowledgeable person must perform all Karma (that ignorant people do while being attached to the fruits of Karma) while being indifferent about the results; yet with courage, enthusiasm and pure mind by being detached to their fruits or outcome. This is the central message of Gitā with Karmayog at the heart of it. Despite this if someone infers differently, they must be deemed unfortunate.

While we've proved that a Dnyāni must perform Karma throughout their life without being attached to the outcome, it's still not clear what's the cause and purpose of this Karma. Hence, "Considering 'Loksangraha' you must continue with Karma" (Gitā 3.20) is what Shri Krishna tells Arjun. However, Loksangraha (literally 'collection of people') doesn't mean just doing Karma to keep people together or pretending to be a part of the herd. 'Sangraha' means collecting, following, abiding etc. and we must understand the contextual usage of this word here which is 'Keeping them together while managing or motivating them so that they realize their maximum collaborative potential' and 'leading them on the path of achieving their goals'. One must also remember, by 'Lok'; Bhagwān Shri Krishna doesn't mean people or only humans. While human beings are superior to other living beings in this universe by virtue of their intelligence and mental capacity, entire universe is implied when he says 'Loksangraha'. The right of upbringing the entire universe, which belongs to the almighty, is bestowed upon the Dnyāni once they attain knowledge. People imitate the behavior of a knowledgeable person (Gitā 3.21). Thus, it is the duty of knowledgeable people to behave responsibly and set the right example for everyone to follow. They must impart this knowledge onto others. We can now understand what Bhagwān Shri Krishna means when he says – "If I don't do this work, entire universe would be destroyed" (Gitā 3.24). Without imparting knowledge, preaching would go waste as people would misinterpret it. A knowledgeable person must also lead by example, otherwise their inaction or Sanyās would become an example for common people to follow due to 'Buddhibhed' (misinterpretation). Thus, Loksangraha (welfare of the universe) is the strong reason given by Gitā for a person to continue with Karma post knowledge. While generally every human being works for themselves and is engaged in selfish motives due to ignorance; a knowledgeable person must think – "I am in all living beings and all living beings are in me" (Gitā 6.29) and once they do, they should care about others and definitely not quit all Karma. They have realized that there's no 'I' anymore and hence must work for the welfare of the entire universe. For them to look at only their own bliss by engaging in Samādhi (Meditative Transcendence) is selfish in a way. There's an argument that upbringing of the universe is the task of Parmeshwar, not mine. However, this thought is inherently flawed; because if you're enlightened, you and Parmeshwar are one and thus there can't be any distinction as 'I' and 'them'.

The Chāturvarnya (Four-tier) system recommended in Manu Smruti receives a lot of criticism as it allots specific Karma to specific 'classes' of people. It says that Brāhmans' Dharma is Dnyān (knowledge), Kshatriyas' Dharma is war, Vaishyas' Dharma is agriculture, husbandry and trade while Shudras' Dharma is service to others. This system is surely not ideal considering interests of an individual. However, it was created for the whole society to function properly. Some people must continue seeking more knowledge, some protect it by training in the art of war, some must conduct commerce and some must serve others; for the whole society to function in a smooth way. If any one class of this society fails, the whole society would crumble. However, this isn't and need not be the only system for allocation of work in a society. Different social systems would surely have less or more merit. However, that is not the topic of discussion here. Let's focus on how 'Loksangraha' is necessary. As Chāturvarnya system was prevalent during the time of Gitā, it is advocated as the system of achieving 'Loksangraha' (welfare of the universe). The only point tried to be made by Gitā is that one must continue the Karma entitled to them as per the prevalent social order for continuing the societal progress and act as a guide to the society after attaining knowledge. Arjun was a warrior and Krishna said this to convince him of his 'Dharma' and to go to war. 'Jeevanmukta' (liberated) state is a state of detached mind, stoic calm, pure intellect and is the epitome of spiritual progress; not a test of business acumen or monarchy. Thus, one must continue to perform the task that they're entitled to, from the point of view of progress of the society. There's another question raised as to whether this advice of continuing Karma post Moksha applies to everyone or only those occupying key positions. It shouldn't even be of any consequence. Still, just as a small part of a complicated machine is as important for its smooth functioning as a bigger part; even a seemingly minor person's work or Karma is as critical for smooth functioning of the society as a senior lawmaker.

Moreover, a knowledgeable person would add more value to the work than an ignorant one would.

Although we understand the unanimous message of continuing to perform Karma (before as well as after Moksha) as per one's profession and of spreading the knowledge, one may be curious about what is the significance of the 4th Ashram or stage that is recommended in Manu Smruti for a person. Manu Smruti recommends that a person must follow four Ashrams or stages in their life – Brahmacharyāshram (1st stage of learning), Gruhasthāshram (stage of family life), Vānaprasthāshram (stage of forest dwelling) and Sanyāsāshram (stage of renunciation). It appears that these four stages are four steps in ascending order of greatness and the final stage of Sanyās is considered the most superior. A person is supposed to get rid of the selfish tendencies and indulgent attachments to physical desires during the first three stages and reach the fourth stage of Sanyās to finally attain Moksha. While Manu Smruti advocates the above view, even Manu knew that there's a likelihood of people turning to jump to the fourth stage sooner and this would collapse the social order. Hence, even he has mentioned the importance of the first three ashrams before one could go to the fourth during old age (implying having completed all familial and social duties). To substantiate this, Manu has implied that everyone is born with three loans (duties) on one's head – Those of Rishis, Ascendants and Deities. Thus, one cannot take Sanyās (renunciation) before they have repaid the loan of Rishis by learning Vedas, Ascendants by siring children and Deities by performing Yadnya-Yaag. If one doesn't do so, they would be destined for rebirth in lower forms of life. If we see the motive behind Manu recommending such a system, we understand that it was so that one conducts their duties religiously through life and then slowly retires from the social life by renunciation and focuses on pursuit of Moksha. Still, somewhere during the history this set order of going through these four stages was broken by people who viewed Sanyās (renunciation) as the ultimate goal of life. They didn't find any point in going through these arduous stages set for the welfare of universe and decided to skip them and directly jump to the 4th stage. Even many Upanishads have verses claiming that Karma is mainly to eliminate the disease of attachment and desire from the mind and to attain knowledge on the way to Moksha. On the one hand Gitā tells us to continue with Karma all our lives whereas on the other are these teachings. How to make sense and arrive at final conclusion? Arjun faced this very question and asked in 18th (final) Adhyāya – "Tell me what Sanyās is and what sacrifice is, separately" (Gitā 18.1). Before delving into what answer Shri Krishna gave Arjun, we shall look at another path recommended by Vedas which is comparable to the path of 4 ashrams/stages.

To understand and organize the seemingly opposite instructions – 'Keep doing Karma' and 'Quit all Karma', Manu designed the system of Four Ashrams or stages, administering different duties during different stages of one's life. If one looks at renunciation of attachment to the fruits of Karma as the ultimate goal, this system is not inappropriate. This system ensures proper welfare of the universe by ensuring that people continue performing Karma through their life, discharging their duties. It also seamlessly combines the Karma from Vedas and Knowledge from Upanishads. In this system, the stage of Gruhasthāshram (family life or householder's stage) is considered most important by Manu and others alike. This is the most productive stage of a person's life where one contributes most to the family, society and universe in general. This is why Manu designated the stage of Sanyās well after a person is in their prime age. However, as we saw, people started breaking this norm and taking renunciation in their prime ages, causing damage to the society. In such a situation, Bhagwān Shri Krishna saw this and founded a new way of life called 'Bhāgwat Dharma'. This discipline doesn't limit itself to the spiritual thoughts but adds a dimension of comparatively easier tool of Bhakti (devotion). However, we shall discuss this tool in detail in the 13th chapter. For now, let's understand that even Bhāgwat Dharma advocates continuing with all Karma without attachment and expectations after attaining knowledge of Parmeshwar. As Nara and Nārāyan Rishis were the first proponents of this discipline, it is also called 'Nārāyaneeya Dharma'. This Bhāgwat Dharma favors action and acts as another parallel way of life which is based in action. This Dharma taught by Shri Krishna to Arjun in Bhagavad Gitā is called 'Yog' there. Many believe that 'Bhāgwat' and 'Smārta' (followers of Smrutis) are two sects based on the deity they revere. However, we believe that it's a misconception. Even though the revered deity is different in these two sects, the central spiritual knowledge is same. We don't think ancient greats would rival each other based on the deity revered; as the spiritual knowledge of both sects says that devotion of any deity makes the devotee become one with the same Parmeshwar. We don't deny that there would be two sects 'Shaiva' and 'Vaishnav' (devotees belonging to Smārta and Bhāgwat traditions who are worshippers of the deities 'Shiva' and 'Vishnu' respectively). We just feel that the reason behind formation of these two sects isn't the deity they revere, but it is the behavior they prescribe post attainment of knowledge. Subsequently, the action oriented Karmayog declined and got replaced by absolute devotion of Vishnu that almost resembled Sanyās. That is the time when both sects (Bhāgwat and Smārta) became proponents of Sanyās and the followers began rivaling each other based on the deities (Vishnu and Shiva respectively) they revere and 'Bhāgwat' and 'Smārta' became synonymous with 'Vaishnav' and 'Shaiva'. Later the Bhāgwat Dharma got modified from Advaita to Vishishtādvaita philosophy, started celebrating Ekādashis (particular dates of Hindu calendar) and started wearing a mark of sandal on their forehead in a particular way; which became different from the followers of Smārta tradition. However, all these petty differences are not original. This becomes clear by the word 'Smārta'. Smārta means 'inspired by Smrutis'. While it's understandable that followers of Bhāgwat sect revere Vishnu or his reincarnation if we trace the lineage of its proponents, the word Smārta doesn't indicate that the followers of this sect have to revere Shiva. No Smrutis mention worship of Shiva alone. Both Vishnu and Shiva are Vedic deities and thus it isn't decipherable why Smārta tradition would choose only Shiva. Thus, we should ignore the difference of deities in these two sects and stick to the original distinction between these two – Those that advocate conducting oneself through the three stages of life and then quitting everything to lead a path of renunciation are 'Smārta'; while those that along with knowledge and complete devotion advocate lifelong continuation of Karma without attachment are 'Bhāgwat'. Smārta can be considered synonymous with Sānkhya or Sanyāsi, while Bhāgwat can be considered synonymous with Yogi or Karmayogi. Later, Jainism and Buddhism accepted the opinion of Kāpilsānkhya and proposed that there's no Moksha (liberation) without Sanyās. Gautama Buddha famously took Sanyās from his palatial life at a young age. Although Adi Shankarāchārya debated and rejected the Jain and Buddhist views, he maintained similar choice of lifestyle as ideal in his Smārta tradition and maintained that this is the way proposed in Gitā. Even if Gitā describes path of Sānkhya or Sanyās at the start, it definitively advocates action oriented Bhāgwat Dharma right till the end. As a matter of personal choice, someone may find path of Sanyās more appealing. Yet, it doesn't mean Gitā has to be forcibly made into something that advocates that path. If you don't accept the final principle of Gitā, you should reject it; but you shouldn't twist the sentence "There are two independent paths of conducting life to attain Moksha" to "There's only one great and superior path which is the path of Sanyās". Rather if anything, Gitā states that "While both paths are potentially capable to attain Moksha, Karmayog is particularly special" (Gitā 5.2) Bhāgwat Dharma or Karmayog is also unequivocally recommended for people of all professions, classes and genders (Gitā 9.32).

While Gitā advocates Karma, one must remember that it doesn't encourage Karma without knowledge. There are two ways of performing Karma without knowledge – One, with ego and in a demonic way and the other with faith. The egoistic or demonic way is rejected by Gitā as well as by Mimāmsaks. Mimāmsaks claim that the other way of faith, by believing in doctrines and religiously performing the Karmas, is sure to yield Moksha to those who follow it. We saw in the last chapter that this path of Karmakānd is ancient. However, Veda Samhitā and Brāhmanas don't mention Sanyās as a way of attaining Moksha. Rather, Jaimini claims that one attains Moksha by continuing to be in Gruhasthāshram (family life) according to Vedas. Technically, he isn't wrong. While Upanishads belong to Vedas, they came after Samhitā and Brāhmanas. It wasn't that knowledge of Parmeshwar didn't exist. However, the opinion that 'one must renounce after gaining knowledge to attain Moksha' was first proposed during the times of Upanishads. This reduced the significance of Samhitā and Brāhmanas which advocate Karmakānd. Once this thought started prevailing, knowledgeable people started ignoring Karmas of Yadnya-Yaag as well as familial and social duties and the notion of performing Karma for 'Loksangraha' (welfare of universe) began to decline. While Smrutis advocate Karma in the Gruhasthāshram, even they regard Sanyās as the ultimate goal of life. Thus, they didn't help in Karma regaining popularity. At this point in time, Gitā was created to unify Karmakānd and Dnyānkānd with Bhakti (devotion) without trivializing either of them. Gitā agrees with the theories of Upanishads that there's no Moksha without knowledge and that the best fruit of Yadnya-Yaag Karma may be Swarga (heaven). However, according to Gitā it's necessary to continue Karma to ensure cycle of the universe and quitting Karma at any time is foolhardy. Hence, Gitā advocates that one must continue doing Shrauta Karmas like Yadnya-Yaag and Smārta Karmas like familial and professional duties with knowledge and detachment and as a responsibility so that they don't bind you and don't stop you from attaining Moksha. This idea of combining Karmakānd and Dnyānkānd (Sanyās and Karma) by Gitā is better than Smārta approach as it ensures the well-being of personal soul without compromising on the universal soul. It is different from Mimāmsaks (that advocate Karma with or without knowledge), most Upanishads (that depict Karma as inferior and suggest quitting them with renunciation) and Smrutis (that ask one to perform Karma during the first three stages but advise quitting them during old age). Thus, Gitā impressively combines the Karma with knowledge without letting fruits of Karma binding the doer and thus steering its followers clear of getting bound in the cycle of rebirth, in heaven or otherwise. It also avoids society losing knowledgeable people, without disturbing their journey of Moksha while also maintaining welfare of the universe.

Let's now see the difference between Karmayog from Gitā and Dnyānkānd from Smrutis. This difference is quite minute and honestly there need not be any debate pertaining to this. Till one achieves knowledge through the first two ashrams or stages, Gitā and Smārta paths agree. It's only regarding the phase after attaining knowledge that these two differ. Many might consider that these knowledgeable people are always going to be a small minority. How much difference would it really make? However, as common people follow the knowledgeable ones, behavior of knowledgeable people is very critical. Even in Smārta path of four ashrams, there have been exceptions like that of Janak who continued to perform Karma even after knowledge and this was not looked down upon. Bruhadāranyak mentions Yādnyavalkya advising Brahmadnyān (knowledge of Brahman) to Janak, yet never did he insist on renunciation. Rather, it's mentioned that post knowledge, those people quit social life who don't like it. Thus, renunciation is described as a choice, rather than a mandate. This and a few more examples prove that even Sanyās and Smārta paths allow, as exception, some people to continue with Karma post knowledge as duty. Expanding these exceptions as a general rule, Gitā is asking us to continue with Karma post knowledge with detachment and without expectations. This proves that Gitā Dharma is flawless even as per the point of view of Sanyās. Now, if one has to continue with Karma lifelong, we still need to explain what the fate of fourth ashram of Sanyās is. Arjun was expecting Shri Krishna to advise him to take Sanyās at some point in time during Gitā and that he would get to avoid going to war. However, when even till the end of 17th Adhyāya Shri Krishna didn't mention renunciation; Arjun asked at the start of 18th Adhyāya – "Tell me what Sanyās is and what sacrifice is, separately" (Gitā 18.1). Answering this, Bhagwān says – "If you think there's no Sanyās in the path of Karmayog I've been telling you, you're mistaken. A Karmayogi divides all Karma as 'Kāmya' (being attached) and 'Nishkām' (without attachment). Of these, he quits all Kāmya Karmas; meaning he renounces them. Remaining Karmas are Nishkām. While Karmayogi performs these, he has completely 'sacrificed' his expectations from them. Thus, even in these Karmas, there is Sanyās. Smārta followers give up Karma literally while Karmayogi give up the expectations from Karma" (Gitā 18.1-6). Rather, when one dedicates all Karma to Parmeshwar and does them without attachment, they are 'permanent Sanyāsi' (Gitā 5.3). This is the principle of Bhāgwat Dharma. Bhagwān Shri Krishna also says in Gitā – "One who sees that Sānkhya (Sanyās) and Yog (Karmayog) are the same from the point of view of Moksha, is truly wise" (Gitā 5.5). This is because the principles of renunciation and sacrifice are the same in both, just that the object of these principles differs.

From the above discussion, one may feel that Gitā is insisting so much on uniting Sanyās and Karmayog because the path of Sanyās is older while that of Karmayog may have come later. However, looking at history we see that most ancient path was of Karmakānd while Upanishads came later, bringing in the perspective of Sanyās through Dnyānkānd. At the same time, there were people like Janak who were practicing Karma with knowledge. From Dnyānkānd arose the third step of Smārta path which branches out into Sanyās and Karmayog. Thus, Sanyās and Karmayog were contemporaries. Another source of information is that of Dharma Sutras. While Manu and Yādnyavalkya mentioned Karmayog as an alternative path to Sanyās; Baudhāyan and Apastamb mention lifelong practice of Karmayog leading to Moksha while declaring that practitioners of celibacy and Sanyās lead to ruin. Looking at both these historical sources, Karmayog proves to be equally ancient as Sanyās, if not more. Most critics of Gitā have been from the paths of either Sanyās or Devotion with sacrifice of Karma. They've not emphasized on this chronology. People like Janak had been practicing this path of Karmayog. Shri Krishna modified it with the addition of Bhakti (devotion) and spread it further as Bhāgwat Dharma.

After studying all this, readers would now understand the essence of the line "Iti Shrimadbhagvadgeetāsu Upanishatsu Brahmavidyāyā Yogashastre..." at the end of every Adhyāya. The Upanishad which was sung by Bhagwān includes Brahmavidyā (knowledge of Brahman) for sure, but it also is an important scripture on 'Yog Shāstra' (doctrine of Yog or Karmayog). Gitā mentions the two paths of Sanyās and Karmayog as 'Sānkhya' and 'Yog' respectively. This explains the use of the word 'Yog' meant as 'Karmayog' in the word 'Yogashāstre'. Rather, one should say that Bhagavad Gitā is the principal scripture on Karmayog. While Karmayog is ancient and has been prevalent since Vedic times, Upanishads rarely mentioned it except on a few occasions. Bhagavad Gitā is a key scripture on Karmayog. It being included in Mahābhārat is also fitting, as Mahābhārat is an epic that describes the lives of many Karmayogi. We also see the relevance of Bhagavad Gitā in the Prasthānatrayi (Three texts to go through that include *Upanishads*, *Vedānta Sutras*/*Brahma Sutras* and *Gitā*). While

Upanishads are fundamental, they're scattered and co-authored by many Rishis (sages) and Vedānta Sutras that collate and summarize the Upanishads deserve an inclusion in it. If Gitā didn't add anything new to the table, there's no reason for it to be included in the trio. Upanishads, with a few exceptions, are mainly proponents of Sanyās with an inclination to pure knowledge. Bhagavad Gitā, along with knowledge, adds a dimension of Karmayog with devotion; thus, cementing its place in the Prasthānatrayi, making it comprehensive. If someone calls Gitā's place in Prasthānatrayi to be contradictory considering its advocacy of Karmayog; it would be wrong, as it acts as a key document representing Karmayog which has been considered an equally potent path of Moksha. To summarize and abridge the voluminous discussion we've had on these two paths of Sānkhya/Sanyās/Smārta and Yog/Karmayog/Bhāgwat Dharma, we have enlisted the similarities and differences between these two paths as follows:

Post Brahmavidyā or Ātmadnyān

KARMA SANYĀS (SĀNKHYA)	**KARMAYOG (YOG)**
1. Moksha is achieved by Ātmadnyān, not by Karma. Swargasukh (heavenly joy) achieved through Karma like Yadnya-Yaag, with faith but without knowledge, is impermanent.	1. Moksha is achieved by Ātmadnyān, not by Karma. Swargasukh (heavenly joy) achieved through Karma like Yadnya-Yaag, with faith but without knowledge, is impermanent.
2. For attaining Ātmadnyān, Buddhi must be stable, free of expectations, detached and equanimous.	2. For attaining Ātmadnyān, Buddhi must be stable, free of expectations, detached and equanimous.

3. Break the binds of desire of the senses.	3. Hence, without quitting the desire of the senses, control them with detachment (by leaving expectations). Nishkām (Without expectations) doesn't mean Nishkriya (Inactive).
4. Karmas arising out of desire are binding and the root of sorrow.	4. Inanimate Karma doesn't bind anyone; attachment and expectation of fruits of the Karma are binding and are the root of sorrow.
5. Hence, one must finally quit Karma, even if they're performed till mind is purified.	5. Hence, even after purification of mind continue to perform Karma with enthusiasm and without expectations. Universe is Karma, there's no escape.
6. Karmas performed for Yadnya are non-binding so it's acceptable to perform them in Gruhasthāshram.	6. Karmas performed without attachment or dedicated to Brahman are itself a Yadnya. Hence, one must always perform all Karmas entitled to oneself as duty without expectations.
7. As bodily needs are inevitable, it's acceptable to beg for alms.	7. Even begging for alms is Karma and a shameful one. Why not perform all Karmas then without expectations? If no one practices Gruhasthāshram, who'd give alms anyway?

8. There's no duty left after attaining knowledge and no need to worry about welfare of the universe.	8. Even if there's nothing attainable for oneself post attaining knowledge, Karma is inevitable. Hence, do whatever you're entitled to with a detached view and for welfare of the universe.
9. However, people at key positions may continue with their professional duties lifelong.	9. Everyone is entitled to duties, big or small. Everyone thus may continue with these duties lifelong without exceptions as this cycle is created by the creator for continuation of the universe.
10. Still, Sanyās by quitting all Karma is superior. Karma in three ashrams is preparatory and for purification of mind. Knowledge and Karma are antagonistic. Hence, one must purify their mind in the first three ashrams as soon as possible and renounce after attaining knowledge. If someone is born knowledgeable or attains it at a young age, there's no need to lead family life. Quitting all Karma is true Sanyās.	10. While it's true that mind gets purified by doing familial and professional Karma, it's not the only purpose of Karma. The cycle of universe propagates with Karma. While Karma with attachment is antagonistic with knowledge, Karma without attachment isn't. So, continuing with all Karma without attachment, for the welfare of the universe is true Sanyās. Quitting Karma altogether is neither possible nor correct.

11.	Even after renunciation, one must continue bodily Karma with peace and self-control.	11.	Once you quit attachment to Karma and continue to perform all duties with the feeling of oneness with the Parabrahma, you shall continue performing all Karma lifelong for welfare of the universe.
12.	This path is primordial and advocated in Shrutis and Smrutis.	12.	This path is primordial and advocated in Shrutis and Smrutis.
13.	Greats like Shuka, Yādnyavalkya lived by this path.	13.	Greats like Vyās, Vasishtha, Janak and Shri Krishna lived by this path.

Ultimately Moksha

Both these paths are rooted in Brahmavidyā (knowledge of Brahman), the state of detachment of mind is common through the two paths and both are destined for Moksha.

The paths we considered above are of a knowledgeable person. However, one can perform or quit Karma without knowledge as well. Let's now see the fate of those who follow this. The essence of different types of sacrifices and their description given in 18th Adhyāya is also this. The sacrifice of Karma without knowledge, out of fear or other reasons, is called 'Rājas sacrifice'. Similarly, some people perform Karma religiously but without knowledge. Gitā says that this path is destined for Swarga (heaven) but not Moksha (Gitā 9.20). As these people perform all their duties religiously, they're doing the correct things albeit without knowledge of Parabrahma. This makes them worthy of heaven. However, if one is aspiring Moksha; they must know, live and assimilate the concept of 'Sarvābhooti ek Ātmā' (one soul in everyone) in their being and continue to perform all Karmas without 'attachment to' and 'expectation of' fruits. This is regarded as the best way of life and called 'Karmayog'. Sometimes it's also called Karma Mārg or Pravrutti Mārg. However, the path of religious Karma without knowledge is also sometimes called Karma Mārg. Hence, to differentiate between these two types of Karma, Manu Smruti as well as Bhāgwat Dharma designated two different terms for them. The Karma without knowledge is called 'Pravrutta Karma' while that with knowledge is called 'Nivrutta Karma'. Nivrutta means retired, so they've added the word Karma next to it to specify that this doesn't mean quitting Karma. Still, we feel 'Karmayog' is the best name for the path which does justice to the path by adding the word 'Yog' which denotes 'idea which lets you do Karma without obstructing it'. If someone calls it by the other names such as 'Karma Mārg' or 'Pravrutti Mārg', it's perfectly fine as long as clarity is there on Karma with knowledge. Gitā's view on nature and fate of the types of doing or quitting Karma based on presence or absence of knowledge are as follows:

Way of leading life	Path	Grade	Fate
1. Considering fulfillment of desires as the only job of a person, performing Karma selfishly with ego, malice, vanity and greed.	Devilish/Evil	Lowest	Narak (Hell)
2. Despite knowledge of 'one soul in everyone', performing one's duties ethically and religiously by idolizing Vedic and Doctrine order. Called Mimāmsak path	Keval Karma, Trayi Dharma or Mimāmsak	Medium (High according to Mimāmsaks)	Swarga (Heaven) (Moksha according to Mimāmsaks)

3. After achieving knowledge of Parmeshwar by performing Karma without attachment, quitting all Karma by renunciation and being engrossed in knowledge.	Keval Dnyān, Sānkhya, Smārta	High	Moksha
4. First for purification of mind and post attaining knowledge continuing Karma without attachment for welfare of the universe, like Bhagwān.	Dnyānkar-masamucchay, Karmayog, Bhāgwat	Highest	Moksha

In conclusion, Gitā has declared lifelong continuation of Karma as the best path for a person, be it due to its inevitability or for welfare of the universe.

Now, let's talk a little bit about Upanishads. Most communalistic interpretations and critiques of Upanishads showcase all of them as pure advocates of Sanyās or renunciation. While we don't say they don't propose that path at all, it's clearly evident that most of them don't insist on Sanyās as the only proposed path. E.g. While it's mentioned in Bruhadāranyak Upanishad that after experiencing knowledge of Parabrahma, many quit the desire for having children, money or any worldly pleasures and blissfully live a life of renunciation begging for alms; it's never advocated that one must assume this path. Rather, Janak, whom the preaching is aimed at, is said to have achieved epitome of knowledge of Brahman yet he didn't live life of a recluse like Yādnyavalkya. Thus, it is clear that both paths – one of Sanyās followed by Yādnyavalkya and the other of Karmayog followed by Janak, are agreed with in Bruhadāranyak Upanishad. Similarly, Katha, Chhāndogya, Taittireeya and Shwetāshwatar are Upanishads which have verses praising Karmayog as a path for attaining Moksha. Ishāvāsya is an Upanishad with high credibility, which goes one step ahead to strongly recommend Karmayog. Even in Vedānta Sutras, the verse from Ishāvāsya Upanishad is given as a standard to explain the Dnyānkarmasamucchay (combination of knowledge and Karma) path. These examples show the connection of Upanishads with Gitā, especially about Karmayog. Adi Shankarāchārya was a great erudite with unparalleled knowledge. Yet, for establishing the communalist view held and propagated by him, he has twisted the meaning of many verses from such Upanishads and at times omitted explanation of a few verses whose clear meaning would advocate optional pursuit of either of the two paths. While Advaita Vedānta correctly mentions the exclusivity of Parabrahma as the only primordial element, it nowhere denies the possibility of multiple paths to attain unity with this Parabrahma. Gitā too mentions that there are two Nishthā (paths) of attaining knowledge. Once you see that there are two paths, it's understandable that some Upanishads would mention only one path, some would mention only the other while some would mention both paths as alternatives. However, once someone begins to prove that their path is the only correct one, it becomes natural for them to have a completely partial view and to start making forced interpretations of scriptures. When we see everything from an impartial and clear view, we take the pure meaning of these texts. Other scriptures like Manu Smruti, Nrusinha Purān, Hārit Smruti, Yogavāsishtha etc. also reiterate the importance of both Knowledge and Karma in attaining Moksha.

Looking at all the examples we've considered so far in this chapter, it shall be clear to the readers that accepting Advaita Vedānta doesn't necessitate acceptance of Sanyās path. Moreover, it shall also debunk the myth that the path of Dnyānkarmasamucchay (combination of knowledge and Karma) advocated in Samhitā, Brāhmanas, Upanishads, Dharma Sutras, Manu-Yādnyavalkya Smruti, Mahābhārat, Bhagavad

Gitā and Yogavāsistha etc. is not propagated in Shrutis and Smrutis and only Sanyās path is. We shall see in the next chapter how the persons following Karmayog conduct their life.

CHAPTER 12

Siddhāvasthā Va Vyavahār (Enlightened State and Way of Life)

The path of Sanyās considers familial or professional life as only an interim phase before purification of mind is achieved, post which one must renounce. Therefore, it doesn't emphasize much on how one must conduct themselves during this phase of life. We've discussed previously how communalistic critics have tried to prove that Gitā advocates Sanyās and all statements about performing Karma are supplementary or that it focuses on pure devotion (without action) or Pātanjalyog. We also showed how Gitā doesn't advocate the path of renunciation but proposes that a person must continue to perform all Karma (without attachment) after attaining knowledge, for welfare of the universe. We shall now see how a Dnyāni (knowledgeable) person conducts one's life post knowledge as this behavior of a Dnyāni person is, in a way, a guide for people to follow. Once we see how this path is set, we automatically access the key to decide what's righteous or not, what's ethical or not and what's moral or not. This is the distinctive feature of Karmayog as against path of Sanyās. A person whose professional Buddhi (intellect) has been stabilized through restraint of senses and who knows universality of Ātmā (soul), is ought to have a pure desire. As their desirous intellect is thus pure, equal, selfless and pious; they're unlikely to commit a sin or perform a karma that prohibits Moksha. As desire precedes Karma, a pure desire would always intend a Karma which is conducive for Moksha. We thus found the Guru we have been looking for, who'd solve the question of what's right and what's wrong through their own behavior. However, we saw in the 3rd chapter that we can't simply follow the behavior of great personalities. We must keenly study the behavior of these greats and understand the true essence of it. This essence is called Karmayogshāstra. The state and actions of these great personalities form the base of this discipline. The moment all people become knowledgeable and Karmayogi, the need for Karmayogshāstra would cease to exist and Krut Yug would dawn on earth. Everyone would behave with a thought about welfare of everyone else. This state was there long ago and shall return sometime later. This is what the ancient sages say. Modern scholars say such situation was never there but could occur in future. Either way, it is achievable through improvement of humanity as a whole. Ancient Indian and Western scholars alike, feel that behavior of truly knowledgeable people should be considered ideal as they've understood the true essence of philosophy or morals/ethics. Gitā's description of a Sthitapradnya (stoic) individual closely resembles that of an ideal person depicted in various Western philosophies – Whoever doesn't hurt people and is not tired of them (Gitā 12.15); Who's always blissful, free of dualities like happiness and sadness and is happy within oneself (Gitā 2.55); Whoever is not perturbed by the Trigunas (Three Gunas – Sattva, Raja, Tama), Who treats praise and blame alike and who recognizes the existence of common soul among all (Gitā 18.54). The same is also called enlightened or realized state in Gitā. While Kant says this state is more of an imaginary ideal described as attained by a human in Greek descriptions, such people have been recorded in history of India and it's mentioned that this state is attainable by mental resolve and sustained efforts. However, only one among thousands tries to achieve this feat and one among thousands who try actually achieves it (Gitā 7.3). However difficult achieving this state may be, it's clear from the characteristics mentioned above that someone who's attained it doesn't need any tutelage on ethics or morals anymore. The state is the epitome of all ethics. There's no place for desire and everything they do is as a duty. Characteristics such as solemn or sin, moral or immoral etc. don't apply to them as they've moved beyond these. Many great critics of ethics have praised such individuals with various similes. This description finds mention in many religious scriptures – Hindu,

Buddhist and Christian alike. Some who interpret anything blindly consider these descriptions as false and unrealistic. However, just as it's not the fault of a pole if a blind man doesn't see it; the theory about enlightenment or the enlightened people themselves are not at fault due to such misinterpretation of blind critics. It's understandable that the true test of knowledgeability is through evaluation of one's behavior and whoever falls short even slightly isn't considered an enlightened being even in Adhyātma. However, once a person is enlightened and has attained true knowledge, their acts are always through pure intellect and hence beyond critical evaluation. Just as the almighty creator is detached from any effects despite performing all Karma of the universe, an enlightened person is always pious and pure. Rather, the behavior of such people in different situations becomes an ideal or a model for everyone to refer to. They're said to set the rules, not be bound by them. We find these principles not only in Vedic Dharma but also in Buddhist and Christian religion; even Greek philosophers seem to agree with this. Kant has stated the same thing with detailed explanations in his treatise on ethics. Once we've thus established what the pure and unadulterated origin of ethics is, it is clear that seeker of the principles of ethics or Karmayogshāstra must carefully observe the life of such enlightened or realized people. The questions asked by Arjun about the characteristics of a stoic are precisely requesting Shri Krishna to provide guidance to him on these lines. Many argue that the answers given by Shri Krishna depict a knowledgeable Sanyāsi (ascetic), pointing to words such as Nirāshrayah (literally: without shelter) (Gitā 4.20), Sarvārambhaparityāgi (literally: one who's quit starting anything) (Gitā 12.16) and Aniket (homeless) (Gitā 12.19). However, once you ascertain the true meaning of the entire message given in Bhagavad Gitā, you realize that Nirāshrayah or Aniket actually depict one who doesn't give shelter to the fruits of any Karma; not the literal meaning of the words. We shall find this in the footnotes of our verse-by-verse translation. Moreover, the same verse that calls a stoic Nirāshrayah also mentions them as doer of all karma without being attached to their fruits. The 18th Adhyāya also mentions such enlightened person as an example of how someone achieves peace by doing everything without attachment. All these factors point to the conclusion that these depictions are of a Karmayogi and not a Sanyāsi. It's true that both of them are comparable in terms of their knowledge about universality of Ātman and Brahman, calm, detached intellect etc. However, while a Sanyāsi indulges in solitude with no concern for anything else, a Karmayogi uses calm and equanimity in practical life as much as possible. This is the major difference from point of view of Karma. Thus, while discussing practical ethics in daily life, a stoic Karmayogi needs to be set as an ideal; not a Sanyāsi. The essence of Gitā is that one need not and cannot quit Karma and hence must earn knowledge to keep their intellect balanced so as to remain calm, selfless and pure with no binding of any Karma.

Such a knowledgeable Karmayogi needs no more tutelage on Dharma and ethics as they are self-reliant and 'Buddha' which means aware or enlightened. As Arjun bore the potential to understand and implement this teaching, Shri Krishna simply asked him to stabilize his intellect, perform all karma entitled to him and forget about taking up asceticism. However, as everyone isn't as potent as Arjun to attain this in one birth, more discussion about the behavior of a Sthitapradnya (someone with stoic calm) is needed. We must also remember that this Sthitapradnya we're discussing is not one from Krut Yug where the entire society has attained fulfilment but from Kali Yug where one has to exist in a society where a majority of people are still engulfed in selfish motives. While a person may have attained complete knowledge, their behavior among an impure society riddled with lust and desire can't be entirely virtuous with non-violence, mercy, calm and forgiveness governing everything they do. Their behavior in a world full of similar people ought to be different from a world where selfishness dominates. This doesn't mean they've to quit the equanimity in their intellect. However, equanimity and equality are different. Treating everyone equal isn't the appropriate way. While Sanyāsis don't care about this, a Karmayogi must look at the environment they're a part of and then mold their behavior accordingly. This is the critical point of contention while discussing Karmayogshāstra. While being surrounded by selfish people, one must not change their stance but work for improvement of such people selflessly. As Rāmdās Swāmi, a saint from medieval

Maharashtra, has aptly said – a knowledgeable person must behave rowdily with a rowdy and nastily with a nasty when surrounded by such people. They've to modify their behavior to suit the need of the era and the surroundings they live in.

One may argue then, that this ideal behavior is simply a utopia, not a reality. However, this argument is hasty and baseless. Just as a sailor looks at the compass or the North Star and not wind and waves to decide the direction, one must look at epitome of ideals while deciding the course of action to be taken in any given situation; and that means resorting to the Adhyātmik view of knowing the universality of soul and not basing decisions on rules of ethics founded on Nāmroope (name-forms). Ātmā is the only eternal constant as we saw in 9th chapter and thus, we've to quit the yardstick of physical things and resort to timeless ideals of Dharma. It's true that we can't follow virtues such as non-violence and truthfulness in a world filled with cruel and greedy people. However, that doesn't take away the greatness of these virtues. Saying that the ethics applicable in an incomplete or imperfect society are the ultimate ones is like saying the shadow fallen on an uneven surface is also uneven and calling it the true form of the shadow. The imperfection is in the surface, not in the light or the shadow. While our scriptures recommend making some unavoidable exceptions in behaving among a world full of greedy people, they also suggest repentance for these acts. The Western Adhibhautik discipline glorifies these exceptions and forms ethical foundation based on these aberrations as we explained in previous chapters.

Let's now discuss the essence of the behavior of a Dnyāni or a knowledgeable person. As we've discussed earlier, we can approach this from two angles – one angle is to consider the intent of the doer and the other is to observe their actions. If we adopt the second angle, it would prove that behavior of a Sthitapradnya is towards betterment of everyone. We can see this being quoted at various instances across Gitā and other scriptures. If we go by this, it appears that betterment of society, which is the central characteristic of a Dnyāni is very similar to the principle of 'Majority's happiness' as advocated by Adhibhautik discipline. Like we said in the 4th chapter, a major flaw in this approach is that it doesn't take into account the relevance of intrinsic pleasure attainable by humans. While this can still be overcome by using the term 'Universal well-being' instead of 'Majority's happiness', there's another key superiority of Adhyātmik approach over Adhibhautik which we shall discuss now. Righteousness of an action can be evaluated by two methods – First, by studying the repercussions of that action on the outside world and second by studying the intent or desire of the doer. First method is the Adhibhautik way. The second method further splits itself into two – Doing a righteous deed requires a pure desirous intellect. For a pure desirous intellect, the professional intellect must also be pure. The approach that considers this pure professional intellect as a separate deity is the Adhidaivik approach. The approach that doesn't consider this pure professional intellect as a separate deity but an internal organ of the soul is the Adhyātmik approach. It considers Ātmā (soul) as the principal factor while deciding the purity of the intellect. Our sages have declared that the Adhyātmik approach is superlative. Kant and Green too, agree with it in their treatises, directly or indirectly. For any action to take place, first there needs to be intent. The righteousness of an action must therefore be decided based on purity of the intent or intellect. If the intent is bad, the action would be bad as well. However, the converse needn't be true, as a bad action may also be a result of ignorance, error or misunderstanding. Such action would not be called ethically wrong. The principle of 'Majority's happiness' only applies to external factors and effects. As there's no yardstick of measuring external happiness or sadness yet, this principle isn't adequate while evaluating righteousness or ethicality. Similarly, even if a person is smart, it doesn't guarantee righteousness so long as their intellect isn't pure; especially in matters where their self-interest is prevalent. Hence, it is declared by our sages that a person's intellect or intent is the essence of deciding ethicality or righteousness and an equanimous intellect is the core of ethics. Gitā declares people with equanimous intellect and without any attachment to the fruits of their action as superior while those who always keep an eye on the fruit of their Karma as inferior (Gitā 2.49). Even in the conclusive 18th Adhyāya, Gitā stresses on the Karma done without attachment and with equanimity as the best or Sāttvic Karma. Similarly, assessing the behavior of a Sthitapradnya lets us see that while they wouldn't do any harm to anyone and work towards universal welfare, it's clear that they don't do it for physical pleasure of everyone but to try and ensure that everyone evolves with respect to their intellect and achieves spiritual progress. The aim of ensuring Adhibhautik happiness is considered ancillary or secondary. Once someone attains this state of equanimity, selflessness becomes second nature and such a person is never likely to commit a sin. Gitā tells us that while one can fake doing charity, one can't fake the awareness of universality of soul and the equanimity and stability of intellect that comes with it. At the same time, Gitā emphasizes that one need not wait until attainment of the ultimate state to act without attachment to the fruit. It asks one to adopt this behavior as much as possible while on the path to achieve the final goal.

Even after proving that knowledge of universality of soul and equanimity of a Sthitapradnya are the epitome of ethics, explanation of real-world behavior is incomplete according to some. This objection is inspired by observing the behavior of a Sanyāsi Sthitapradnya. After doing a little examination we realize that it doesn't apply to a Karmayogi Sthitapradnya. Rather the two principles stated above explain the practical ethics better than any other principle. Let's take the example of philanthropy which has been recognized the world over as one of the key virtues. The Adhyātmik principle of universality of soul explains the rationale behind philanthropy like nothing else. Adhibhautik disciplines, at best, claim that philanthropy is a naturally occurring virtue which is increasing with evolution of humans. This doesn't however explain the rationale of philanthropy. Rather, it leaves room for smart selfishness to prevail when it comes to a conflict between selfishness and philanthropy. On the other hand, there are arguments that if one always engrosses themselves in philanthropy, how would they survive? These arguments are neither new nor inevitable. Bhagwān Shri Krishna has answered this question in Gitā under Bhaktiyog and Adhyātmik principles explain the same as well. One must keep a view of ensuring own survival for achieving welfare of the universe. Rather, when someone recognizes the same soul being omnipresent, the boundary between ensuring own welfare and that of everyone else in the universe vanishes. Only someone who considers themselves separate from everyone else could think of such a predicament. However, an Advaiti for whom this duality doesn't exist doesn't think on these lines. This is a key difference between the Adhibhautik dualistic vision of 'Majority's happiness' and the Adhyātmik monistic goal of 'Universal welfare' which one must remember clearly. Just as Sun doesn't give light thinking of helping life on earth, a Sthitapradnya doesn't help universal welfare by thinking of it in their mind. It becomes their nature. Once we understand this, we can appreciate that for such people there's no question of comparing self-interest and that of the others. For those whose thinking has been built on the notion of seeing the world dualistically, there would always be a likelihood of tilting towards self-interest.

We saw explanation of philanthropy from Adhyātmik point of view. Let's now see the set of guidelines given in our scriptures on how to behave with others. One who's attained knowledge sees themselves in everyone and everyone within themselves. Naturally, they behave with others how they would with themselves. This is said to be the characteristic of a true Karmayogi. Gitā and Mahābhārat emphasize on this quality multiple times. Buddhist scriptures, Christian bible and even Greek philosophers like Aristotle seem to agree with this notion of 'Do unto others as you would have them do unto you' (Mathew 7:12). Even Confucius who was born 200 years before Aristotle has explained this principle through a single word in Chinese which can be roughly translated as 'Reciprocity'. Upanishads have stated this principle centuries before anyone else (Ishāvāsya and Ken Upanishads). Mahābhārat, Gitā and many subsequent scriptures have reiterated this. Adhyātma is the only discipline, however, which has provided a reasoning for following this principle; while no other religion or sect has. Once we see that universality of soul is the only concept which explains the above principle, we see the importance of Adhyātma and Karmayog.

This principle or guideline is so broad and inclusive that one doesn't need to be told other virtues like mercy, compassion, philanthropy etc. They all flow naturally once one realizes the existence of same soul in everyone. Just as everyone instantly recognizes their own interest, so does one, of others. Family is the first extension or application of understanding this principle and one must start ensuring love and care for the family the same way they would love and care for themselves. However, one mustn't stop at family but gradually extend the same to friends, kin, fellow citizens, fellow countrymen, fellow humans and ultimately to every living being in the universe. This is said to be the epitome of awareness or knowledge. Whatever actions help one in achieving this knowledge are naturally the actions recommended in the scriptures as ones to be followed.

Even after listening to this explanation, some argue that upon realizing this principle one loses all other virtues such as patriotism, religious pride, family pride etc. and with these virtues would dissolve many realities of today's world like family, nation etc. Moreover, by the logic of 'not hurting someone because you wouldn't want to hurt yourselves the same way', the sages wouldn't oppose vile people and fall victim to their despicable acts. Almost all religions state that one must not act violently even if the other person is acting so with you. We don't intend to belittle these guidelines or deem them wrong. Rather, we agree that mercy or forgiveness is as good a virtue as truth. In a perfect or model society, this virtue shall undoubtedly prevail. However, when Arjun started thinking on similar lines and thought of shying away from battling his own kith and kin to support this notion, Bhagavad Gitā or Karmayogshāstra was born. Hence, the explanation on this topic is best explained in Gitā. While Buddhism and Christianity accept the notion of non-enmity towards anyone, neither of them explains the difference between the behavior of an ascetic and a Karmayogi. While a Sanyāsi would not care about universal welfare or even protecting themselves; a Karmayogi, despite having same purity of mind, would behave differently. This difference and its explanation are unique to Bhagavad Gitā. Western philosophers are still puzzled about how to combine Jesus Christ's notion of 'Love thy enemy' with the ethical principles of today's world. Our scriptures have been very clear about this. Manu has recommended not getting angry with someone who's angry with you. However, it's not for someone in familial or political life but for someone pursuing asceticism. Many superficial critics mix the separate teachings and criticize our scriptures without taking efforts to understand them first. Karmayogshāstra says – "There are exceptions to the virtue of forgiveness. Till the time other people in the society are not following the virtue of not hurting others, it's no good following this virtue blindly with everyone". The word equality necessitates subjectivity. Thus, killing a vile and cruel person doesn't impact the principle of non-violence. Punishing a criminal doesn't have a bearing on universality of soul. Instead, there's righteousness by the virtue of protecting others from this criminal. If the almighty has taken births to protect the righteous and punish the criminals, we need not debate this any further. Gitā tells us to quit selfish tendencies and to let go of our ego. It doesn't tell us to ignore worthiness of anyone. When it says everyone has the same soul, it doesn't advocate equality but equitability. There's a difference between the two. Even while talking about charity, Gitā says that Sāttvic charity is one done with nation (place), time and eligibility of the receiver in mind. Bhagwān Shri Krishna says – "The way one worships me, I oblige them so with the fruits". A judge, while declaring death sentence for a criminal, isn't considered an enemy of that person as there's no enmity in the judge's mind but simply a sense of judicial duty. If another person is hurt by any action of a Sthitapradnya, it would inevitably be a result of the other person's Karma and not any hatred in the mind of the Sthitapradnya. Thus, 'Tit for Tat' is the equivalent in ethics of the Newton's third law – "If an object exerts a force on another object, the other object must exert a force of equal magnitude and opposite direction back on the first object". People with selfish motives twist this principle to their advantage, duping people into repaying disproportionately to their crimes. Some exert force onto weaker people to feign justice by extorting disproportionately. A selfless, knowledgeable person would instead perform such a task with zero involvement, thus ensuring judicious punishment to the criminal and justice to the innocent. Gitā declares it one's Dharma to ensure balance in the world by punishing the cruel and protecting the weak. Even a war waged for such a noble cause is justified. This is the essence of Gitā. While Gitā agrees with the principle of non-enmity, it doesn't advocate inaction or encourage non-retaliating nature. It only focuses on the intent of the doer. Once a person quits the feeling of enmity, there would still be a strict and judicious action but without any selfish motive. Moreover, as there's no negativity or enmity, there's no residual feeling held about the other person once justice is done. While this is true, one must also remember that whenever one can achieve the goal without retaliation one should do so. One should try to counter wickedness with goodness first. Only when the other person refuses to be reasonable, one should resort to the principle of 'Tit for Tat'. The point is to counter or overcome the wickedness in the world. For that, one should first try peaceful measures and resort to violence as the last resort. As this knowledge of Dharma is very minute, many scholars have faced predicament about their choices of actions. In such instances, one should not resort to the wisdom of pundits whose motives are likely to tilt towards selfishness. One should surrender to the ultimate Sthitapradnya and know what action is advisable. Equanimity trumps intelligence in such cases.

Misconception about sages with non-enmity and peaceful nature is a result of decline of Karmayogshāstra and prevalence of Sanyās among Adhyātmik community. Gitā neither advices nor intends to advocate that. As a Sanyāsi has no interest in the material world, they are indifferent about the fate of themselves as well as that of the universe. However, a Karmayogi would be peaceful, exhibit non-enmity and still continue to perform karma as per the demand of the situation so as to ensure justice. Naturally, Karmayog neatly explains pride towards family, religion, country etc. as these are nothing but increasing levels of achieving universal equanimity. Just as worship of Saguna is required before understanding Nirguna Brahma; pride about family, religion and country are required before one can assume universal identity. Till everyone in the universe assumes this identity, one must handhold others on this path of ascension. Naturally, these sages have to understand the prevalent condition of the society and tailor their tutelage accordingly. Even after reaching on a higher floor the requirement of lower floors doesn't vanish. Similarly, familial, religious and national identity remains relevant for a society till everyone doesn't assume universal identity. From the point of view of entire society, a familial identity achieves what a national identity wouldn't. Similarly, the required result achieved by national identity isn't achieved by assuming a universal identity. When someone assumes national identity as supreme, they may get ready to crush other nations in the name of patriotism. However, it is not the case with a universal identity. It is the teaching of a Sthitapradnya that in case of a conflict between a lower and a higher level of identity, the higher identity should prevail. There's a beautiful quote in Mahābhārat which sums it up – "One must sacrifice a man to save the family, a family to save the village, a village to save humanity and the whole world for one's soul". Here, soul indicates the universal soul. Step by step, the verse tells us to put universal interest before everything else. It also tells us that if someone tries to behave wickedly you must protect your soul first before anything else. However, there's a thin line between when to sacrifice even one's life and when to protect oneself; one that's easy to cross but difficult to identify. For knowing this, intelligence of the highest order isn't enough. One must be of pure and equanimous mind. For such a person, there's never a dearth of familial, religious or national integrity as they've attained universal integrity. They can instantly identify which aspect is relevant in a certain situation and provide the correct advice accordingly.

The clothes we buy for a child are always either fitting or slightly bigger so that the child would grow into it shortly. Similarly, in case of people, they need to be taught and told to achieve an identity equivalent to or just broader than one they're currently identifying themselves with. If we tell them to assume universal identity, it would not be understood. Even if it is, they may not be able to accept or digest it. This is why even Upanishads have recommended slowly ascending forms of worship – From Saguna to Saguna-Nirguna to Nirguna. Sages, while themselves having attained the highest stage, are conscious of the current stage of the society and act accordingly for its betterment. Once we think of this holistically, we begin to appreciate why knowledgeable people should not assume ascetic life. While they should maintain a universal identity themselves, they ought to understand the stage of the prevalent society and act as a role model to improve it slowly but surely on a path of spiritual progress and righteousness. The various known incarnations of the Almighty have been of such nature and similarly Sthitapradnya knowledgeable people should behave and live a pure life without attachment, yet with full enthusiasm and zeal for the betterment of society. This is the essence of Gitā. This is the true Loksangraha or Karmayog. When Shri Krishna explained to Arjun the Vedānta philosophy and the knowledge of Karmayog based on this principle, he became aware and quit his thought of dropping weapons and assuming ascetic life. Not only did he prepare himself for the war with full conviction but he also defeated Kaurav righteously and without any attachment. This universal ideology also trickles down and applies to other virtues such as philanthropy, non-violence, chivalry, justice etc. Explaining each of this would demand writing a separate book. We've tried to explain the essence of it briefly for the reader. We firmly believe that the basis of ethics should never be based on selflessness vs selfishness but it should be based on a broader principle of universality of soul. Once you assume universal identity, the rest falls into place automatically. When the whole world attains this identity, we would have Krut Yug on earth. However, until we have it, we could base the foundation of ethics on such strong fundamentals to guide us in difficult times better than any other path proposed anywhere else in the world. Let us now finish one important aspect of understanding Gitā in the next chapter before proceeding to summarizing it all.

CHAPTER 13

Bhaktimārg

We saw how the knowledge of 'Universality of soul' and Nishkām Buddhi (intellect without attachment) is the source of Moksha (liberation) and how one must continue performing Karma relentlessly with this state of mind. However, the philosophy in Gitā is not over till we cover an important chapter. While it is beyond doubt that Personal soul and Universal soul are the same and there's no other reality that exists, everything that we've seen till now has been about attaining it through intellect. There arises a question as to how should one attain such high level of intelligence and does it mean that a person without such high level of intelligence would lose out on the opportunity to attain Moksha? This question is absolutely valid. Even the most intelligent are silenced when asked to define Parabrahma and all they can say is 'Neti Neti' (Not this, not this either or something that can't be described). Moreover, intelligent people would always be in minority. Isn't there a simpler path for everyone to grasp this knowledge and be liberated? If one advises relying on the knowledge of these intellectuals, even these intellectuals seem to be arguing among themselves all the time. Consequently, one is forced to say that 'relying on belief or faith' is an alternate path to Moksha. To be honest, some faith is needed even for the most scientific theories. Take an example of the principle that Sun rises every morning. While it is proven through observation and through satellites, that rotation of earth around its axis in 24 hours is certain and that it would continue the same way tomorrow, ultimately, we always believe that the setting Sun would come back from the east tomorrow, based on the faith on the motion of earth cyclically. Similarly, in day-to-day life we rely on beliefs more than anything else when it comes to facts and principles learnt in school or being told to us by learned scientists. Every person using that principle or basing their actions on that principle needn't have validated its truthfulness through personal experience. They nevertheless base important decisions by showing faith on the reliability of those principles through others' experience. Just as a bullet requires gunpowder to propel it through, one needs the support of belief and emotion along with knowledge to go all the way. Even after gaining knowledge about something with intellect, one needs to ingrain it in one's being with the help of emotions and bring it into practice. Similarly, after understanding through intellect that the fundamental principle underlying the universe is primordial, eternal, all-pervasive and conscious; one must take the final leap of faith within. It is for this reason that Gitā calls faithful Karmayogi superlative.

If it's arduous to fathom the Nirguna Parabrahma, the difficulty can be overcome by faith or belief. It's achieved by believing in personal experiences of the knowledgeable. These are reliable people who we can depend on. In our day-to-day life we regularly depend on such reliable data points. E.g. Many know the height of Mount Everest as 8,848 m whereas a handful few have actually measured it. All others rely on these handful few for having determined the number accurately. When we use a calculator or a computer to take important business decisions, we rely on the capability of the manufacturer of these instruments for providing reliable data which we use to base our decisions on. Similarly, if someone asks the nature of Brahman, we immediately say it's 'Nirguna'. Even though everyone may not have the intellect to evaluate the true nature of Brahman, faith or belief is something they have through which they can trust the nature of Brahman to be Nirguna. Studying history of Moksha Dharma, we realize that even before the knowledge of the Nirguna Parabrahma humans have worshipped the Almighty in some form through faith or belief. Even in the discipline of Physics, one first experiences something and then explains it theoretically. Similarly, in Adhyātma (spirituality), while one uses intellect to analyze the knowledge earned through experience and find explanation; the experience isn't deemed as an illusion till an explanation is achieved.

Anyway, had it been enough to understand that Brahman is Nirguna, it would be possible through belief as said above. However as mentioned at the end of 9th chapter, simply knowing that Brahman is Nirguna isn't enough for attaining enlightenment or the state of wisdom. Through sustained practice and regular habit, one must inculcate this knowledge in their being and instill universal identity and universality of soul in their practice. To reach this stage, it's imperative to understand Parmeshwar (Almighty) through love and to become one with it. This path is ancient in India and is called the path of devotion or 'Bhakti'. Bhakti is defined in Shandilya sutras as unconditional love for Parmeshwar. When this devotion is from a point of view of demanding something from the almighty, it has got an element of a trade to it. Such Bhakti is Rājas and not complete and doesn't help in attaining Moksha. The Adhyātmik principle of non-attachment is continued even in the Bhakti Mārg (path of Bhakti). The Bhakta (devotee) who, after gaining knowledge of Parmeshwar, worships without any demand but simply as a duty, is considered the greatest.

As we have seen in the 6th chapter, Buddhi (intellect) is an internal organ only concerned with distinguishing between right or wrong, good or bad, dhārmic and adhārmic etc. All other tasks are performed by Man (mind). Naturally, there are two parties – Man and its Upāsya (object of devotion). However, the supreme form of Brahman is Nirguna, Avyakta (unmanifest), infinite and homogenous; thus rendering it impossible to be taken as Upāsya. Once someone experiences it, the dualistic division of Upāsak (devotee) and Upāsya (object of devotion) vanishes. Nevertheless, it is the ultimate goal and not a path. Till we train the mind to become one with Nirguna Brahman, it doesn't realize the same. Naturally, the symbolic object of devotion needs to be separate from the devotee (dualistic) and Saguna (with attributes) even if it is Avyakta (unmanifest). It has been denoted variously in different techniques. Even though it is described as Avyakta, human mind is structured in such a way that it becomes impossible or at least extremely difficult to worship or even focus on something which is unfathomable through senses. As mind is inherently wavering, it fails to focus on something formless. Unless it has something with form to hold on to, it wavers time and again. Just as we draw a small, finite segment with two arrows on both sides to represent the infinite 'line' while studying geometry, we imagine a symbolic object with Nāmroope (name-forms) to represent the almighty, omniscient, all-pervasive and formless Parmeshwar. Call it inherent structure or flawed nature of human mind, it's impossible to imagine formlessness without first seeing some form. Till this nature of human mind is there, one must have a symbol with form for beginning Bhakti. This is why symbolic idols have existed timelessly in human history. This direct approach of attaining knowledge of Parmeshwar is called Bhaktimārg (path of devotion). It's true that an intelligent person may be able to focus their mind on the unmanifest form of Brahman once they establish its true nature with intellect. Still, in this path, attaching their mind onto this unmanifest would still have to be achieved through faith and love, thus making that path indirectly a Bhakti Mārg. However, as the form of Brahman to meditate on is unmanifest and predominantly understood by intellect or knowledge, it's called Adhyātmavichar (Spiritual thought), Avyaktopāsanā (devotion of unmanifest), simply Upāsanā (devotion) or most widely **Dnyānmārg** (path of knowledge). When this Upāsya (symbol or object of devotion) is considered Saguna (with form), Vyakta (manifest) and especially in human form; the path is called **Bhaktimārg** (path of devotion). While there are two paths, both lead to understanding of the same Parmeshwar and attainment of the same universal identity. Just as there may be two separate staircases to reach the same place; even though the above two paths are different, the goal is still the same. First path is via intellect and the second is via faith and love. Any path you take would lead you to the same knowledge of Parmeshwar and ultimately to Moksha. Thus, there is no Moksha without experiential knowledge. Once we firmly understand this, we realize the pointlessness in debating superiority of one path over another. While the paths are different, Gitā deems them equal and terms them both under the same umbrella name – Adhyātma (Gitā 11.1). However, while Dnyān (knowledge) and Bhakti (devotion) may be equal as tools, Bhakti can never be the goal. Only knowledge can be considered as the goal or the ultimate state. This is the principal difference between the two. While both Bhaktimārg and Dnyānmārg can lead to the knowledge of

Parmeshwar, if someone quits all material life and indulges completely in this knowledge, Gitā calls such a person a 'seeker of knowledge', never a 'seeker of devotion'. Devotion is by nature dualistic and thus can't exist in this ultimate stage. Bhakti (devotion) leads to Dnyān (knowledge). Thus, Bhakti is a path and not the goal. Thus, knowledge can first be a tool or path (in case of Avyaktopāsanā) and later be the goal or the ultimate stage. When it's necessary to show this distinction, we use two different words – Dnyānmārg (path) and Dnyānnishthā (state). Similar is the case of Karma. When used within the guidelines of Shāstra (doctrine) for purification of mind, it is the tool or path. This path further leads to knowledge and peace. However, once this is attained, if a person doesn't indulge completely in this knowledge but continues doing all Karma with peace and without attachment; it becomes Karma full of knowledge and becomes the ultimate state which is called Karmanishthā (Gitā 3.3). As Bhakti is not so and can't be the final state, Gitā mentions two Nishthā (states) at the start viz. Dnyān (Sānkhya) and Yog (Karma). Of these, it mentions that for Yog (Karma) Nishthā, there are two paths – Avyaktopāsanā (Dnyānmārg) and Vyaktopāsanā (Bhaktimārg). Between the two, it tells us that while Dnyānmārg is arduous, Bhaktimārg is simpler and more accessible for everyone in general. While ancient Upanishads praise Dnyānmārg, scriptures like Bhāgwat praise Bhaktimārg. However, Gitā is the sole scripture that while illustrating these two as separate paths, seamlessly integrates them with Nishkām Karma (Action without attachment).

The aforementioned analysis shows that for attaining knowledge of the primordial, eternal, indescribable form of Parmeshwar, one must employ devotion as a path. Now, while the all-pervasive, almighty, omniscient and shapeless Parmeshwar is Saguna (with form), it is Avyakta (unmanifest) and Buddhigamya (fathomable through intellect) and thus difficult to devote to. Hence, Bhaktimārg accepts a Saguna, lovable, Vyakta (manifest), articulate form of Parmeshwar who is truthful, merciful, purest, and beautiful who loves its devotees beyond measure. This is evident in almost all religions. This originally unmatched and indescribable entity, later converted to a lucid nature, is termed 'Ishwar' or 'Parmeshwar' in Vedānta. One may ask why this almighty Parmeshwar is described as a symbolic, Saguna, Humanoid entity? It is for a devotee to slowly graduate from. While the ultimate is formless, it's described as this Pratik (symbol) for a reason. The word 'Pratik' is formed by two words Prati (towards) and Ik (turned). It means 'that which is turned towards us'. Just as we see an object from one of its sides first before we understand the true and complete shape or form of it, any dimension of Parmeshwar which we see first can be a Pratik (symbol). Even Bhagwān Shri Krishna has described this path of devotion as 'superlative among all disciplines of knowledge and secret, holy, actually perceivable, righteous, unfailing and happily pursuable' (Gitā 9.2). Many scholars argue against this obvious and straightforward meaning which logically and contextually fits in Gitā and claim that this is said about the path of knowledge (Dnyān Mārg). It is highly improbable as Shri Krishna is unlikely to call the previously described arduous path of knowledge as 'actually perceivable' and 'happily pursuable'. Even the verse appears in the middle of the verses describing Bhakti Mārg. The sweetness or love in Gitā is a result of this path of Bhakti Mārg (path of devotion) mentioned in it. As Bhagwān Shri Krishna gives this knowledge of Parmeshwar by speaking in first person, the audience (Arjun and now each one of us) develops a feeling of having witnessed this Parmeshwar in person. Our belief in knowledge of the soul becomes stronger. Moreover, as Dnyān and Bhakti are beautifully woven into each other, there's no conflict between Buddhi (intellect) and Prem (love). This enables the audience to enjoy both knowledge and essence of Parmeshwar. It activates equanimity and gives a blissful calm to one's mind. No wonder then that many sages have called the knowledge in Gitā to be applicable in this world and beyond!

Our analysis explains what Dnyān Mārg and Bhakti Mārg are and why Bhakti Mārg is called the easier one and why Bhakti is not called a separate Nishthā (state). Still, we must offer a word of caution about a big pothole in this primordial, easy and direct path; lest the follower stumbles and falls. Gitā mentions this pothole and this differentiates it from other texts describing Bhakti Mārg. We discussed how a Saguna Pratik (symbol with form) is necessary to stabilize and concentrate our mind. However, often people argue and fight over what symbol should be taken for worship. Spiritually, there's nothing in this universe without Parmeshwar. Even during Gitā when Arjun asks Shri Krishna which form he should worship, Krishna tells him numerous examples from a plethora of categories. He also goes on to say that he's occupied this whole universe by having his essence in everything. Once we understand that Parmeshwar is all-pervasive (as displayed to Arjun by Shri Krishna in 11th Adhyāya during Vishwaroopdarshan), we can't point out anything without the presence of Parmeshwar. Parmeshwar is far and near, death and dead, pious and ghastly, scared and scary. We can thus take anything in this universe as a symbol to begin with, before realizing the omnipresent nature of Parmeshwar. Someone may worship the Sun, someone else the Moon. Someone may idolize their parents as Parmeshwar while someone else may worship Ganesh, Vishnu, Shiva or any other deity as Parmeshwar. People may keep arguing if Ganesh is the greatest or the Sun is, or if Vishnu is the most supreme or is Shiva the ultimate. All these arguments are baseless and rooted in ignorance about the universality of soul or Parmeshwar. This ignorance makes people carry false pride in considering their symbol as the greatest and fight others who consider some other form of God as supreme. Forget the disagreement between Vedic, Buddhist, Jain, Christian and Muslim religions, there are conflicts leading to massacres within the religion as well; which is evident from the example of St. Bartholomew's Day Massacre of Protestant Christians by Catholics in France in 16th century. These fights are ongoing even today about which God is the ultimate. Is there a way to avoid this religious warfare apparent in Bhakti Mārg? If yes, what is that way? We must see how Gitā answers this question.

While a symbol is recommended right since ancient Upanishads, in Gitā or even in more recent scriptures, it is always reminded that this symbol is nothing but a tool. All-pervasive Parmeshwar can't be contained in or limited to this mere symbol. Gitā mentions this where Shri Krishna says – "While I'm Avyakta (unmanifest), fools consider me Vyakta. However, it's not my true form and my unmanifest version is the true form (Gitā 7.24). After showing the Vishwaroop (universal form) to Nārad, just as was shown to Arjun in Gitā, Shri Krishna tells Nārad – "What you saw was not me but only Māyā. For truly 'knowing' me you must go beyond". Upanishads propose Mind, Word, Sun, Space etc. as Vyakta or Avyakta symbols, yet they say that whatever we can perceive through our senses is not Brahman but it is 'that which can't be thought of, as our thought is included in the thinking ability of Brahman and whatever is worshipped as a symbol is not Brahman'. Even 'Neti, Neti' (Not this, not this) communicates the same. These symbols are nothing but objects chosen depending on individual or collective preference. However lovable they might become for the devotee; it is not equivalent to Parmeshwar or Parabrahma or Brahman. The power of Bhakti Mārg doesn't lie in the animate or inanimate symbol but in developing the emotions within the mind of the devotee. After all, a symbol can never be bigger than what it essentially is – a symbol. The way you feel about the symbol is how Parmeshwar (not the symbol) rewards you. What's the point then, in arguing about the symbols? If one performs Karmas that are detrimental to innocents, no worship of any symbol would reverse their fruits. Even Gitā mentions this – Those who have selfish or professional motives must worship various deities and with this selfish thought they get addicted to them (Gitā 7.20). Whoever you worship with whatever desire, rewarding you with fruits is the doing of Parmeshwar and not the symbols or deities. We see that while Parmeshwar is one, it rewards different devotees differently based on the deity they worship. This is explained by what Shri Krishna says – 'Humans are devotional. Whatever be the symbol, the way one devotes, one becomes' (Gitā 17.3). Other accounts from Gitā communicate a similar meaning – E.g. 'Worshippers of deities go to deities; worshippers of ancestors go to ancestors and worshippers of me come to me' (Gitā 9.25) or 'The way one worships me is how I worship them' (Gitā 4.11). Shaligram is a stone. If you worship Vishnu in its place, you'd go to Vishnulok (place of Vishnu). If you worship Rākshas (Demon), you'd go to Rākshaslok (place of Rākshas). This is the logic behind Prāna Pratishthā (Consecration with your Prāna). You consecrate the idol with the feeling or emotion of that deity whom you intend to worship. Nobody worships it as metal, stone or wood of which it is made. If one does, they would achieve only that, as said in

Bhagavad Gitā. Once you understand and accept this, there remains no reason to fight over the symbol; as the feeling is now towards that one Parmeshwar and no longer towards the symbol.

It is truly unfortunate that humans have gone to the extent of believing that only a certain person born in a certain place at a certain time is the true form of God; when as a matter of fact the Almighty is omnipresent. It's frustrating and saddening to see people being killed in the name of so-called God and religion. While Bhagwān Shri Krishna has said it himself – 'If you want to know my true self, go beyond the visible Māyā'; there have been many more people in India who've tried to teach this knowledge to the world. Yet it's unfortunate to see people still engrossing themselves in the futile debate about the greatness of their deities over another.

Despite understanding this concept, a question arises – It's impossible for most people to imagine the pure emotion about Parmeshwar owing to their innate nature and ignorance. Although devotion replaces knowledge in Bhakti Marg; one simply can't understand the pure form of Parmeshwar through devotion or belief. While emotions are a function of Man (mind), we can't do it without Buddhi (intellect) because intellect decides what to worship and what not to. Devotion or Belief is blind that way. Even if a person is not intelligent, they must have enough intellect to decide what to devote to and what not to; lest they'd fall flat by blind devotion and blind love. On the other hand, if only intellect is at work, it would keep wavering from here to there and would make a person unstable and disturbed. Plus, there's no action with just intellectual knowledge and without love or devotion as discussed at the start of this chapter. Thus, devotion needs to be paired with knowledge and mind with intellect. As both mind and intellect are Trigunātmak (made of three Gunas – Sattva, Raja and Tama) they can be classified as Sāttvic, Rājas and Tāmas. While the two of them are always together, the understanding, nature and behavior of a person varies depending on their purity. Even if either of the two is Rājas or Tāmas, the other is affected and the person doesn't stay on the right path. Generally, for someone born with an impure intellect, their mind is often correspondingly impure and then this naturally makes one believe or devote to the wrong entity. Even if they're preached about the pure form of Parmeshwar, it doesn't stick. Rather, if both intellect and mind are weak or immature, they misinterpret the advice. Different disciples of the same Guru don't have the same impact on them. The same Sun has different impact on different objects – while a plant blossoms into a flower, other burns in the same sunlight. Gitā describes that just as there are 3 types of Buddhi (intellect), there are 3 types of Shraddha (devotion). As one is born with a particular state of intellect, mind and thus Shraddha; naturally Sāttvic devotees tend to worship Dev (celestial deities) while Rājas and Tāmas devotees tend to worship Yaksha-Rākshas and ghosts-spirits respectively. Naturally the next question then arises – 'While one may be born with such tendencies, is it possible to attain Sāttvic intellect and elevate oneself with the help of guidance and devotion as per one's capacity?' The answer in Bhakti Mārg is just like the answer to a similar question about knowledge in the process of Karmavipāk (fruition of Karma). Shri Krishna tells Arjun – 'Concentrate your mind on my purest form. If you're not able to, keep practicing. If you're not able to even practice, keep doing Karmas that purify your mind. If even that is not possible, quit attachment to Karma and attain me through that' (Gitā 12.8). These different paths of ingraining the true form of Parmeshwar in one's mind are specifically for guiding people at different stages to begin with. If one is born with Tāmas nature, the attempt to concentrate their mind on the true form of Parmeshwar may not be possible in a single birth. However, just as in Karmayog, nothing goes waste in Bhaktiyog and once on the right track, one attains the true knowledge of Parabrahma, in this birth or the next to attain Moksha (liberation). Whatever symbol you want to worship, you start by considering it to be the best form of Parmeshwar as per your imagination. For some time Parmeshwar (not the symbol) rewards you as per this imagination of yours. However, gradually without any other tool, this imagination goes on improving and becomes purer and purer. This ultimately culminates into attaining true knowledge of Parmeshwar and the distinction between Upāsak (devotee) and Upāsya (object of devotion) vanishes. Just as one reaches enlightenment once they get on the wheel of Karmayog through curiosity, one attains enlightenment once they begin on the correct path of devotion to Parmeshwar. As the ultimate state attained at the end of either path is the same, the description of a Sthitapradnya (someone firm in wisdom or someone with stoic calm) in 2nd Adhyāya is same as that of a devotee in their ultimate stage mentioned in 12th Adhyāya. Either path one takes to begin with, depending on their capacity or preference, they definitely attain the same Moksha or enlightenment. Dnyān Mārg teaches the same knowledge through intellect right from the start whereas Bhakti Mārg uses devotion to begin with. Yet this difference in the beginning disappears at later stages and one becomes unified with Parabrahma.

Many argue about Bhakti Mārg by questioning how one can attain Advaiti (monistic) knowledge if they start on a Dvaiti (dualistic) base of devotion where Upāsak (devotee) and Upāsya (object of devotion) are different. However, this argument is flawed. It's correct if one argues that Bhakti (devotion) stops once the devotee realizes the true form of Parmeshwar and becomes one with it. This is because the triumvirate of Upāsya (object of devotion), Upāsak (devotee) and Upāsanā (devotion) dissolves in this ultimate stage. However, it's incorrect to claim that attainment of this Advaiti knowledge is impossible with the Bhakti Mārg rooted in Dvaiti logic. Just as unity always begins with diversity, just as rivers flow hundreds of kilometers first to get united with the ocean, this Dvaiti Bhakti Mārg ultimately leads to Advaiti knowledge. In this matter, the experience of great sages and devotees is truly the benchmark. Great Sant (Saint) Tukārām says in his Tukārām Gāthā – 'Just as sweetness is in jaggery (a product of sugarcane), almighty is within everything. Whom to worship now that God is within me and outside?' This verse beautifully describes the evolution of a Bhakta (devotee) into the knowledgeable person who's attained enlightenment. It's noteworthy that Sant Tukārām had never read the Upanishads to have attained the concept of Advaita (monism) through reading anything and yet these verses show him speak the stage of Advaita with a beautiful metaphor. It's clear that the ultimate goal is identical in both Bhakti Mārg and Dnyān Mārg and the notion that 'personal experience of Parmeshwar or Parabrahma leads to Moksha' remains common to both. Gitā retains the concepts of Adhyātma and

Karmavipāk even in Bhakti Mārg. While Gitā includes the path of Bhakti Mārg, it neither entertains nor advocates any blind beliefs. Moreover, while Gitā advocates merging of Adhyātma with Bhakti or that of Devotion with Knowledge, there are some modifications done by Bhagavad Gitā in adopting Adhyātmik notions of Bhakti Mārg. Considering these modifications as inconsistency in Gitā has originated from insufficient understanding of the unification of Adhyātma and Bhakti explained in it. Let us clarify that here. Gitā mentions the Adhyātmik notion of universality of soul in 6th Adhyāya as – 'The same soul which is in me, is in every being of this universe' (Gitā 6.29). It also mentions the same notion in the context of Bhakti Mārg – in 10th Adhyāya – where Shri Krishna describes various incarnations of Parmeshwar; and in 11th where he displays Vishwaroop (his cosmic form) to Arjun to iterate how the whole universe has Parmeshwar in it. Adhyātma mentions that Karma gets extinguished through knowledge while Bhakti Mārg says there's nothing other than Saguna Parmeshwar in this universe. It doesn't indulge in concepts like Sanchit, Prārabdha and Kriyamān and simply says that there's one single Parmeshwar who generates thought of Karma, gives rewards of Karma or reduces Karma. Gitā says that Ishwar stays in everyone's hearts and makes them perform actions like a machine (Gitā 18.61). Adhyātma says soul is free to attain knowledge while Bhakti Mārg mentions that Parmeshwar generates this intellect in one's mind. In summary, whatever we call 'giving up of attachment', 'dedicating Karma to Brahman' or 'Dnyānkarmasamucchay' (combination of knowledge and Karma) in Adhyātma Mārg is called 'Karma dedicated to Parmeshwar' in Bhakti Mārg. A Karmayogi says that whatever Karma they're doing is for welfare of the universe. A Bhakti Yogi would say whatever Karma they're doing is dedicated to Parmeshwar. Today we see many blind interpretations of this true knowledge. Priests ask people to perform rituals and people do them mechanically. Originally, it was about letting go of the attachment to the fruits of Karma. Joking about it only exposes one's ignorance, it doesn't prove our scriptures wrong in any way. As everything is and has Parmeshwar, there's no other logic needed for doing what's righteous. Just as we saw in the last chapter that a knowledgeable person's own welfare is a part of the universal welfare, in Bhakti Mārg Bhagwān promises to ensure the welfare of such great devotees himself. Thus, we see that the same principles of spirituality or Karmavipāk are also prevalent in Bhakti Mārg albeit communicated or explained in a slightly different way. It's evident how a blend of Knowledge and Devotion has been prevalent in our country since ancient times. However, this doesn't indicate that the meaning is altered in any way. For example, while it's said in Karmavipāk that one has to take efforts for increasing their own knowledge; it's not translated in Bhakti Mārg that Parmeshwar would ensure growth of a devotee. Even in Bhakti Mārg it's said that we're our own friends and our own enemies (Gitā 6.5). Philosophy of devotion belonging to any other country or religion doesn't blend complex concepts of philosophy with the natural affinity of humans for a perceptible or manifest form in as beautiful a way as Vedic Dharma does. Many people get so attached to the manifest symbol that they lose track of the ultimate truth and get entangled in vanity about the symbol itself. While the importance of the 4th ashram (Sanyās ashram) or the stage of renunciation is critical in Smārta tradition, it is not relevant in Bhāgwat tradition as its main focus is on devotion. Thus, whoever the person be (from whichever ashram or stage of life), their greatness depends on the extent of their devotion. Despite this, there were a few followers of Bhāgwat tradition who were seen to have adopted the life of a Sanyāsi. However, they were more of an exception than a rule. Later on, when the prevalence of Karmayog explained in Gitā diminished, ideal devotees began to be portrayed as those who have completely ignored Karma and dedicated themselves only to devotion. To clarify this, we must see the true message conveyed in Gitā about devotion and how a devotee should be. As per Bhakti Mārg, the Saguna Parmeshwar is identified as Bhagwān. If Bhagwān had taken birth on the planet from time to time to perform various deeds of great magnitude and effect to ensure welfare of the universe, it is easily inferable that a devotee must walk on a similar path. Hanumān, who was a great devotee of Rām, didn't renounce. Rather, he aided Rām in the war with Rāvan along with his entire army. Bheeshma, who had taken a vow of celibacy, was an ardent devotee of Bhagwān. However, he continued to serve the rulers of the kingdom till his last breath, as per his Dharma. Even in Bhakti Mārg, while it's true that there's nothing more to be attained after the moment of enlightenment or becoming one with the object of devotion; all emotions like love, compassion, duty etc. do not disappear. Rather, they're elevated to their purest form and the person naturally begins to work relentlessly for the welfare of the entire universe in an unbiased way. Moreover, as the whole universe and all its entities have been created by Parmeshwar, it is pretty evident that their actions are intended by the will of that same Parmeshwar. Every person is destined to perform certain actions. If they refuse to perform these actions, they're actually perceived as defying the purpose of their existence. If on the other hand, they imagine these actions to be their own doing and start considering them for selfish motives owing to their ego; they shall be entitled to bear with their respective fruits. On the other hand, if one performs all these actions imagining themselves to be just the means as per the will of Parmeshwar; their dutiful behavior is considered as Sāttvic form of Bhakti according to Gitā. In the 18th Adhyāya, Bhagwān Shri Krishna has summarized all this as follows – "I operate all beings in this universe like a machine by staying in their hearts. So, the feelings of 'quitting' or 'doing' any Karma are illusory. Quit attachment to the fruits and keep doing all Karma with the feeling of dedicating them to Shri Krishna. Even if you decide not to do those Karma, you'd end up doing them as per your nature. Hence, for welfare of the universe, you must give up all selfishness in the name of Parmeshwar, adopt selflessness and detachment and continue to work. I'm doing the same. Look at my example and get inspired to do the same". Some litterateurs ignore this central message of Gitā and claim that Gitā insists on Bhakti and considers Karma trivial. Like Sanyāsi communalists, this claim of devotional fanatics is biased, too. The Bhakti Mārg shown in Gitā is centered on Karma and encourages worship of Parmeshwar not only through flowers and hymns but also through relentless Karma devoted to Parmeshwar. As this particular principle of Bhakti based on Karma is not advocated in any other text, it should be considered the unique characteristic of Bhagavad Gitā.

After witnessing the unification of Dnyān Mārg and Bhakti Mārg rooted in Karma explained thus in Gitā, we shall discuss one last important aspect of Bhakti Mārg before concluding this chapter.

While we discussed how Dnyān Mārg demands sharp intellect as its prerequisite and is thus inaccessible for many, there's one more hurdle in Dnyān Mārg which is overcome in Bhakti Mārg. If you see Mimāmsā (by Jaimini), Upanishads or Vedānta Sutras; it's full of discussion about rituals or unfathomable nature of Parabrahma. It mentions the rights for these rituals or knowledge to be available to the men of first three tiers of society (Brahman-Kshatriya-Vaishya) leaving out men from Shudra tier and women from all tiers. Vedas are also silent about the rights of women or Shudra. Thus, these texts don't discuss how these sections of society shall attain Moksha (liberation). On the contrary, Upanishads have shown women like Gārgi and Maitreyi while Purānas have shown Shudra like Vidur having attained enlightenment. Thus, we can't infer that they are not believed to be eligible for Moksha, either. It is thus imperative to show, what the means of attaining Moksha are for these people. Gitā clears this apparently biased notion in its description of Bhakti Mārg. "Hey Arjun, even women, Vaishya, Shudra or people from the lowest class of society attain enlightenment by devoting to me" (Gitā 9.32). This verse also appears in another Parva of Mahābhārat again. Moreover, Mahābhārat has instances of a butcher (belonging to Shudra tier) teaching knowledge to a Brāhman and a trader (belonging to Vaishya tier) teaching path of Moksha to a Brāhman. Thus, it is decreed that someone whose intellect has become equanimous is great; may they be of any caste, creed or gender. This declaration of Bhakti Mārg opened doors of Moksha to one and all. It's evident from history how this resulted in mass acceptance of this path of devotion by all classes of society in their aspiration to attain enlightenment.

Thus, Gitā beautifully describes Bhakti Mārg (path of devotion) to be the path which anyone can adopt for attaining Moksha. If one is perplexed by looking at the plethora of rituals and paths described in various texts, Bhagwān Shri Krishna tells this perplexed person to 'forget all this and surrender to me alone'. He reassures his devotees that he shall free them of all sins and reward them with enlightenment. Gitā also very clearly mentions the equal status of Bhakti Mārg with all other paths to attain Moksha.

As we conclude this sweet chapter of Bhakti Mārg, we are nearing conclusion of this great scripture which shall be done in the subsequent chapters.

CHAPTER 14

Geetādhyāyasangati (Sequential Account of Gitā)

As we've seen in all chapters till now, Bhagavad Gitā advocates how spiritually or devotionally one should attain Moksha and even after attaining it one should, instead of renunciation, continue to perform all actions dutifully for welfare of the universe. However, the sequence of these chapters in Gitā is different from the ones we've followed. Hence, it's imperative to explain how Gitā is structured in a certain way and why. Any concept can be elucidated via two ways – Scientific and Story-like. Explaining principles of a concept through commonly known facts that follow a logical and sequential arrangement is the scientific method. Geometry is a classic example. From our scriptures, while Nyāya Sutras or Vedānta Sutras employ this scientific method of explanation; Bhagavad Gitā doesn't. Although Bhagavad Gitā is absolutely scientific, it doesn't employ the scientific method of explanation. It uses the beautiful technique of storytelling by weaving the subject in a lucid question-answer format. This is told as a dialogue between Arjun and Shri Krishna which makes it both relatable and enjoyable. While it's impossible to describe in detail all aspects of 'Dharma' in a 700-verse dialogue, it's noteworthy to see how Gitā touches upon almost all subjects albeit briefly or cryptically. It showcases the literary might of the authors of Gitā and shows us how meditatively it's been written. Some topics, knowledge of which Arjun is likely to have possessed; haven't been elucidated in detail. On the other hand, some others have been explained elaborately. Similarly, some concepts have been abbreviated or repeated depending on topical relevance and maintaining the flow of dialogue. Naturally, there are many concepts which are touched upon in Gitā – Shrauta Dharma, Smārta Dharma, Sānkhya Shāstra, Vedānta etc. where one is likely to get confused; in case they're uninitiated in these respective disciplines. Then, because of inability to decipher the logic behind the sequence of such cryptic messages one infers that Gitā is too complicated. On the other hand, some infer that Gitā must've been composed before the scientific method and hence lacks perfection and displays contradictions. Some other give up by saying the knowledge in Gitā is beyond comprehension for them. Ironically, even if someone refers to the critiques of Gitā, they get further confused as they're mostly communalistic and thus often contradict each other. To tackle this, we've explained various topics touched upon in Gitā as per our understanding; in a scientific way till now. Let's now see how those topics are included in the dialogue between Shri Krishna and Arjun in the form of queries and answers. Doing this would lend completion to the whole analysis and we can proceed to summary in the next chapter.

Bhagavad Gitā is a guidance provided by an almighty, brave, successful and reverential warrior to another skilled warrior to make him understand the necessity of the righteous war and his duty in waging it. Any guidance needs a reason and for it to be effective the disciple needs to be eager to receive it. To explain these two things, sage Vyās has described the reason for this guidance of Shri Krishna to Arjun in the **'First Adhyāya'**. On the eve of the Great War, Shri Krishna who was Arjun's charioteer took the chariot in the middle of the battlefield and showed him the armies set to go to war with each other. While the war was pre-planned and had weeks of preparation preceding it, the actual sight of his own kith and kin made Arjun feel perplexed with the thought of having to kill them for the kingdom. This made him think about quitting the war and renouncing to go live away in a forest. He gave up the will and sat down in the chariot, crestfallen. This part is covered in the first Adhyāya which is called Arjun-Vishādyog (Arjun's gloom). While Gitā's central tone is (Karma) Yog Shāstra (Doctrine of Karmayog), each Adhyāya is named after the primary topic conveyed in it and called so. E.g. First Adhyāya which communicates Arjun's gloom over the war is called Arjun-Vishādyog. It's noteworthy to see that if Bhagavad Gitā wanted to promote Sanyās or renunciation, Shri Krishna would've been glad to see Arjun ready to live a life of renunciation willingly. Rather, he'd have congratulated him on this realization and accompanied him to go live an ascetic life. It would've been perfectly possible for Shri Krishna to allow Arjun to assume this ascetic life if he found it acceptable. However, instead of doing anything like this, he says at the start of the **'Second Adhyāya'** – "Where did you get this foolish idea from? This weakness doesn't suit you. This would damage your reputation. So, you better get rid of this thought and ready yourself for war!" However, Arjun still kept at his repentant stance and surrendered to Shri Krishna. He asked him which path he should choose, the one to kill or the one to die. Shri Krishna then understood the perplexity that had clouded Arjun's judgment and started elucidating the knowledge to Arjun. While Arjun showed his intention to behave as a knowledgeable person, he was trying to favor renunciation. This is when Shri Krishna started by showing him the two paths of knowledgeable people – 'Doing Karma' and 'Quitting Karma'. The first message of Shri Krishna to Arjun is that he would be mistaken if he chooses either path. Then Shri Krishna explains the Sānkhya discipline which Arjun was claiming to base his decision of renunciation on. Subsequently, he explains the (Karma) Yog discipline through which he advises Arjun to go to war. We've discussed these two paths in 11th chapter in detail. Shri Krishna tells Arjun that even according to Sānkhya, the soul is immortal and hence the feeling of 'killing' someone is false. He also tells Arjun that if he's contemplating the need for war, it's against his duty to run away from the war he's duty-bound to fight. Then Arjun is asked to quit this thought of him 'killing' or someone 'dying' and to simply go to war as per his duty without any attachment to the Karma. However, the explanation through Sānkhya discipline still advocated both options – One was to go to war (to either win or die trying) while the second was to renounce. This left room to think that if quitting everything or renunciation is the ultimate goal, why not renounce then and there instead of going to war. Thus, it became clear that a definitive decision was not taken using Sānkhya ideology. This is when Shri Krishna started explaining Karmayog (which has then continued till the 18th Adhyāya) with various different illustrations to prove how one must remain action-oriented and how Moksha is attained (rather than being blocked by) continuing to perform Karma. While deciding goodness or badness of a Karma, it is important to note whether the desirous intellect behind the action was pure or impure; rather than just looking at consequences of the Karma. This is the major principle of Karmayog. However, before explaining it, Gitā covers the importance of stabilizing the professional intellect through Samādhi, as this professional intellect eventually decides whether the desire generated in one's mind would be pure or impure. Normally, most people perform various rituals only to achieve some desired goal for themselves and hence their intellect is busy running after one materialistic goal or the other and is thus selfish and unstable. Then Shri Krishna goes on to tell Arjun through arguably the most famous verse of Gitā – 'Karmanyevādhikā Raste, Mā faleshu Kadāchan' (Gitā 2.47) that he must keep his intellect stable and unfazed whatever may be the outcome. He must not perform actions keeping his eye on the fruit but shall work without attachment. He doesn't have any right to choose the fruits of his Karma but only has the right to perform Karma. However, once he attains the state of a Sthitapradnya (someone firm in wisdom or someone with stoic calm), he shall achieve what 'Yog' truly means and would continue to perform all actions without being bound by any of their fruits. Then when Arjun asks, Shri Krishna narrates the characteristics of a true Sthitapradnya towards the end of 2nd Adhyāya. Let us see what questions are raised further.

Arjun asks at the start of the **'Third Adhyāya'**, "If intellect is considered superior even in Karmayog, I better stabilize my intellect like a Sthitapradnya. Why do you ask me to perform ghastly deeds like the war?" The question is why can't one maintain equanimous intellect and assume inaction. It's not that Sanyās is not possible with equanimous intellect. Bhagwān answers this question by telling him that while he told him about the two paths viz. Sānkhya and Yog, it is impossible to 'quit' karma altogether. It's an impossibility. As long as we're within a body, nature would follow its course and force us to perform natural processes. As natural Karma is anyway unavoidable, isn't it better to restrain our senses, stabilize our intellect and continue to perform all Karma with our organs? Parmeshwar has created Karma along with creation of the universe. While it's true that those who've attained knowledge have no more duties for themselves, they still have to continue performing karma for welfare of the universe. Krishna tells Arjun that people like Janak have followed this path and so has he. When Arjun asks why one commits a sin, Krishna answers by telling him that desires compel people to do so; yet one must control their senses and not give in to such urges. This concludes the third Adhyāya.

At the end of the third Adhyāya, Krishna asks Arjun to 'dedicate all karma to me' and provides a hint of Bhaktiyog. He tells Arjun at the start of **'Fourth Adhyaya'** that this preaching is not just to convince Arjun to go to war. The same teaching had been given by him to Vivaswān, through to Manu and to Ikshvāku at the beginning of the era. However, somewhere in the course of time it got lost. This is why he's teaching him that. Krishna also tells him how he incarnates himself time and again for protecting the sages, punishing the sinners and to protect Dharma. Yet, as he does everything without any attachment to it and simply for welfare of the universe, he doesn't get bound by any of it. Just as offerings in Yadnya (ritualistic fire), one must offer their actions to the broader Yadnya (cycle of Universe) without any attachment. While according to Mimāmsaks the karma done in rituals isn't separately binding, it is binding to the fruit of the ritual. Hence, one must perform even the rituals with selfless intent and without attachment so that the ritualistic karma is non-binding. The knowledge that all beings are one with Bhagwān is the knowledge of equanimity. Once this knowledge is acquired, all karma gets extinguished and reduced to ashes, thus rendering their fruits non-binding to the doer. Hence, Arjun is requested to quit ignorance, adopt Karmayog and get ready for war.

While the necessity of Karma and Karmayog is explained in the 3rd and 4th Adhyāyas, Sānkhya is also explained in the 2nd Adhyāya, along with superiority of intellect. Hence, it becomes imperative to decisively tell which path is superior. If both paths are equally potent, one is left with a choice to select whichever path appeals to them.

This same dilemma is expressed by Arjun and he now requests Shri Krishna at the start of **'Fifth Adhyāya'** to decisively tell him which path is better. Shri Krishna clears this dilemma and answers by saying that while both paths are capable of yielding Moksha, Karmayog is especially better. In fact, he tells Arjun that even Sanyās needs the same detachment of intellect as in Karmayog and thus there's no need to treat these paths differently. Even as a Sanyāsi (ascetic), one doesn't quit karma like breathing, walking, sitting, seeing etc. Then what's the point of trying to 'quit' karma. It's better to perform all karma without attachment and still attain Moksha.

'Sixth Adhyāya' continues on with the same topic and explains the efforts needed for attaining the equanimous intellect. Shri Krishna tells in the first verse itself that someone who performs all karma without attachment is a true Yogi or a Sanyāsi, and not someone who remains idle. Then he explains freedom of the soul as the choice to achieve restraint of the senses needed for achieving equanimity of the intellect. The Adhyāya then mainly explains how one can achieve control of their senses through Pātanjalyog. Still, equanimity is reiterated as the key to attain Moksha. When Arjun asks Shri Krishna the possibility of failure to attain this in a single birth and having to start afresh every birth, Shri Krishna explains him how nothing goes waste. He tells him that the evolution that happens in the current birth continues in the next and ultimately one attains Moksha. Thus, there's a definitive message to quit all other paths and to continue being a Karmayogi.

Many believe that this (6th Adhyāya) concludes the explanation of Karmayog while Bhaktiyog and Dnyānyog are explained as other mutually exclusive (equally potent and separate) paths. They claim that 7th to 12th Adhyāyas explain only Bhaktiyog while 13th to 18th Adhyāyas explain only Dnyānyog. Once we do this allotment, all three paths (Karmayog, Bhaktiyog and Dnyānyog) get 6 Adhyāyas each and Gitā is equally divided among them. However, this is incorrect. The main question of Arjun was the choice between quitting the war as per Sānkhya and choosing the war despite its ghastly consequences as per Karmayog. To claim that Shri Krishna answered this question by iterating equal status of Sānkhya and Karmayog while adding a third option is highly unlikely. When Arjun wanted a definitive answer, how and why would omniscient and wise Krishna show him three options and add to his confusion? To be true, Gitā only discusses two Nishthā (states) viz. Sanyās and Karmayog. Bhakti is not shown as a separate state at all. Considering the three Nishthā is a communalist inference having been inspired from Bhāgwat. However, it's important to note that the moral of Gitā and that of Bhāgwat aren't identical. While Bhāgwat assumes Bhakti as an essential component of attaining Moksha and agrees that it requires Dnyān (knowledge) and not just Karma, Gitā only considers Bhakti as one of the simpler tools or paths of attaining Moksha while stating that one may choose the path that agrees with them. It doesn't stress on Bhakti but focuses on whether or not one should continue with Karma post attaining Moksha. Hence, 'doing karma' and 'quitting karma' are shown as two different paths at the beginning of Gitā. The first is not called Bhaktiyog (as called by followers of Bhāgwat) but called Karmanishthā or Karmayog while the second is called Dnyānnishthā or Sānkhya in Gitā. If we accept this terminology of Gitā, Bhakti can't be a third Nishthā as there's no possibility of a third state after seeing the nature of the two as either/or. Bhakti can be a tool or a path but not the state. If one attains Moksha through Bhakti and continues to perform Karma, they would be called Karmanishtha while if they quit Karma, they would be called Sānkhyanishtha. Of these, Karmanishthā is definitively considered superior by Gitā as said in 5th Adhyāya. The main objection of Sānkhyanishthā on Karmayog is that doing Karma acts as a hurdle in attaining knowledge of Parmeshwar which is essential for Moksha. Thus, one must quit Karma to attain Moksha. However, it is shown as incorrect in 5th Adhyāya (Gitā 5.5). Still, as it's not elaborated there, answering this important question of 'how one attains Moksha while doing Karma' is initiated in **'Seventh Adhyāya'**. First shloka mentions Yog (which logically is the Karmayog described in the first 6 Adhyāyas) and yet it is ignored by most critics. There's no mention of Bhaktiyog anywhere. It's amusing to see how some still claim this to be the start of Bhaktiyog. This verse is where Shri Krishna tells Arjun how focusing his mind on Krishna and following (Karma) Yog would yield him knowledge. This is called as Dnyān-Vidnyān in the second verse, and it is then explained in subsequent Adhyāyas, the process that yields this. First 5 Adhyāyas explain the necessity of Karmayog and its superiority over Sānkhya Yog and 6th Adhyāya explains how to achieve restraint of the senses necessary for Karmayog. However, this doesn't complete the description of Karmayog. The restraint is an exercise which achieves control but isn't exhaustive by itself. If one has vile Vāsanā (desire), this restraint would be used for performing evil activities by someone and hence one must achieve purity of desire or intent. The process to achieve this is now explained from 7th Adhyāya. Here, the terms 'while practicing (Karma) Yog' are key and prove that while the subsequent Adhyāyas include practices from other paths to attain knowledge, they're inclusive and not exclusive. Moreover, everywhere through these Adhyāyas, Arjun is asked to perform Karma in the form of war (Gitā 8.7, 11.33, 16.24, 18.6). This proves that all these Adhyāyas are complementary to the Karmayog advocated in the first 6 Adhyāyas. It's thus clear that Bhakti Yog or Sānkhya Yog are not independently advocated there.

Once we've thus seen why Bhakti and Dnyān are explained in Gitā, the sequence of Adhyāyas from 7th to 17th is easily understandable. As we saw earlier, discussion of the knowledge of Parmeshwar needs to be done once through Ksharāksharvichār (discussion of impermanent and permanent) and then through Kshetrakshetradnyavichār (discussion of Body and Soul). This then leads to the principle of universality of soul as explained in the 6th chapter. Once we start discussing the form of Parmeshwar, both Vyakta (perceptible or manifest) and Avyakta (imperceptible or unmanifest) forms are debated. It's also debated which form is superior and how the inferior form is led from the superior. Similarly, many other topics are discussed. It also becomes imperative to see which form should be worshipped for attaining knowledge of Parmeshwar. This invariably takes the discussion to diversity seen in nature as an expression of the unity. It's only understandable that it's taken 11 Adhyāyas (7-17) for explaining all of it. We don't argue that Bhakti and Dnyān are not discussed or explained at all. We simply deny the argument that Gitā denotes three different and equally potent Nishthā (states) and propose that it advocates Karmayog which is infused with Bhakti (devotion) and rooted in Dnyān (knowledge). Everything else has been mentioned to reinforce superiority of Karmayog, not to separately advocate any other path or state.

Let's now see the sequence of the subsequent Adhyāyas with this logic. 7th Adhyāya starts with discussion of universe and Bhagwān Shri Krishna explains how Purush and Prakruti are nothing but his different forms and those who see his form beyond these, achieve equanimity of intellect and attain Moksha. **'Eighth Adhyāya'** begins with discussion of Adhyātmik, Adhiyadnyik, Adhidaivik and Adhibhautik disciplines. It goes on to explain the indestructible and eternal principle of the universe, along with the when and how of 'destruction of the universe'. It briefly opens the topic about the fate of those who attain knowledge of Parmeshwar and those who perform Karma while being attached to their fruits. **'Ninth Adhyāya'** continues this discussion and describes the Vyakta (manifest) form of Parmeshwar through Bhakti (devotion) and how path of Bhakti is the simplest and the most direct. However, Bhagwān Shri Krishna continues to emphasize on importance of Karma (action) through these 3 Adhyāyas (7-9).

'Tenth Adhyāya' describes all great beings of the universe as different Vibhutis (forms) of Shri Krishna (Parmeshwar) while **'Eleventh Adhyāya'** has Bhagwān Shri Krishna displaying his magnificent Vishwaroop (cosmic form) as per Arjun's request, emphasizing how Parmeshwar is present in everything. It goes on to display Arjun how it's Shri Krishna (or Parmeshwar) getting everything done through everyone and asks Arjun to 'quit all indecision and get ready for war' (Gitā 11.33). **'Twelfth Adhyāya'** begins with Arjun's question about which form of Parmeshwar to worship; whether it's the Vyakta form or the Avyakta form. Here, Shri Krishna answers by calling worship of Vyakta (manifest) form as the simpler one and gives the description of the best devotee (which is identical to the description of a Sthitapradnya (someone firm in wisdom or with stoic calm) as given in 2nd Adhyāya).

Some argue that while there may not be a clear distinction between Karma, Bhakti and Dnyān into 6 Adhyāyas each, Adhyāyas 7-18 can be clearly differentiated as Bhakti (7-12) and Dnyān (13-18). A little deeper examination proves this theory wrong as well. We see discussion of Dnyān-Vidnyān in 7th Adhyāya (supposedly a Bhaktiyog Adhyāya) and various accounts of justification of Bhakti in 13th, 14th, 15th and 18th Adhyāyas (supposedly Adhyāyas belonging to Dnyānyog). This, among many other accounts, debunks the myth about the so-called structure of Bhagavad Gitā. Gitā doesn't try to describe Dnyān and Bhakti separately but weaves in both Bhakti and Dnyān-Vidnyān starting from 7th Adhyāya. Other than differentiating the two paths (Bhakti and Dnyān) as easier/simpler and complicated/difficult respectively, Gitā does little in the way of distinguishing between the two. A few instances of one while describing the other are inevitable and should not be taken as accounts of division.

After giving a perceptible view of the universal nature of Parmeshwar in Vishwaroopdarshan (display of cosmic form) earlier, **'Thirteenth Adhyāya'** now explains how the same Parmeshwar lives in a human body in the form of Ātmā (soul) and talks about Kshetrakshetradnyavichār (discussion of body and soul). After describing Parmātmā or Parmeshwar as per the description given in Upanishads, it discusses its link to the Purush-Prakruti discussion of Sānkhya philosophy. It then tells us how someone, who understands the difference between Purush and Prakruti to 'fathom' the truth about Parmātmā, gets truly 'liberated'. Yet it continues to emphasize on non-binding nature of Karma in this state (Karmayog) and also makes a mention of Bhaktiyog. **'Fourteenth Adhyāya'** continues this discussion and portrays how Sattva, Raja and Tama Gunas result in endless diversity (as per Sānkhya philosophy) in the universe. It then says that someone who understands that all these are nothing but manifestations of Prakruti and understands their own independent nature to worship Parmeshwar is the one who's beyond these 3 Gunas are truly independent. **'Fifteenth Adhyāya'** begins with the description of Parmeshwar in its tree-form as found in some scriptures. It then compares it with the whole spread of Prakruti as per Sānkhya philosophy. Then it advises Arjun to know the Purushottam (supreme Purush) beyond Kshar (impermanent) and Akshar (permanent) and to worship it. **'Sixteenth Adhyāya'** explains how there are two types of nature in people viz. Daivi (divine) and Āsuri (demonic), just as there is diversity in the universe due to variations of Prakruti. It then explains what their actions are and consequently what they're destined for. **'Seventeenth Adhyāya'** discusses impact of different combinations of Gunas on Shraddha (belief), Dāna (charity), Yadnya (rituals), Tap (Worship) etc. and how it varies accordingly. Then the gospel of 'Om Tat Sat' is elaborated and it is shown that 'Tat' (meaning 'That') denotes Karma without attachment and 'Sat' denotes good Karma but done with desire. Finally, it's established that Parmeshwar is everywhere, whether you perceive it through knowledge or through senses. Kshetradnya within the body and Akshar within the universe are one and the same. It's shown how one must see the unity in all diversity and understand true nature of Parabrahma either through worship of manifest or that of unmanifest. The essence of these 11 Adhyāyas (7-17) is that one must stabilize their intellect, and with that intellect, which is free of attachment and full of equanimity, they must continue to perform all actions as duty. As we've discussed this elaborately in various chapters, we've gone through them briefly here, only for understanding the sequence.

At the beginning of **'Eighteenth Adhyāya'**, Arjun asks Shri Krishna to explain the secret of Sanyās (renunciation) and Tyāg (sacrifice) and whether Karmayog disagrees with knowledge given in Smrutis which describe four ashrams or stages, eventually culminating in renunciation. To this, Krishna answers by telling Arjun that even in Karmayog there is renunciation of attachment and it is 'Sanyās' in a way. Even if one doesn't beg for alms, the principle of detachment is pursued. Here, there's another argument raised as to whether there's any need to perform worldly actions. To this, Bhagwān answers by saying that these actions purify one's mind and must be continued (albeit without attachment) for welfare of the universe. What follows is an explanation of different types of Dnyān (Knowledge), Karma (action), Karta (doer), Buddhi (intellect), Dhruti (determination or courage) and Sukh (pleasure) depending on inherent nature – Sāttvic, Rājas and Tāmas. Then Gitā explains Chāturvarnya (Four-tier) system and how performing one's duties as per the system with Sāttvic intellect (without attachment) leads to peace and Moksha. It then concludes by asking one to continue with Karma by surrendering everything to

Parmeshwar and to believe that Parmeshwar shall rid them of all sins and liberate them.

Thus, Gitā starts with Karmayog, tells us the ways to attain it through Pātanjalyog, explains in detail how knowledge of Parmeshwar liberates us and finally reiterates supremacy of Karmayog in conclusion. This is when Arjun, who wanted to take the path of renunciation at the beginning; quits that thought with conviction through knowledge of Karmayog and gets ready for war. Gitā begins and concludes with a consistent goal of convincing Arjun for war.

This detailed explanation of Bhagavad Gitā and its sequence explains how it is not a haphazard mixture of Karma, Bhakti and Dnyān Nishthā (states) but a meditatively drafted, thoughtfully sequenced and definitively conclusive gem of a scripture that imbibes knowledge of Karmayog in Arjun and consequently in every reader as well. The beautiful method of storytelling ensures easier absorption and makes it interesting for the reader. Yet it leaves no stone unturned and is exhaustive in tackling all topics. We've now covered an in-depth analysis of Shrimad Bhagavad Gitā through the exhaustive Mimāmsak method as said at the beginning. While it is clear that Gitā propounds Karmayog throughout its narrative, it is noteworthy to see why so many communalistic critics have still derived a conclusion that it advocates renunciation. Let us discuss that before concluding this chapter.

Our scriptures firmly consider that attaining knowledge of fundamental principle of the whole universe and attaining Moksha is the ultimate goal of a human being who's born with a superior intellect and a broad perspective. However, looking at the practical aspect, the scriptures also divide this goal further into four steps viz. Dharma (here as living with righteousness), Artha (obtaining wealth), Kāma (fulfilling desires) and Moksha (attaining liberation). Naturally, one must look at interrelationship among these four, where Gitā agrees with all paths that there's no Moksha without obtaining knowledge of fundamental principle of the universe. Gitā also agrees that Artha and Kāma must be done with Dharma (righteousness). Attaining knowledge and Moksha is a tedious and time-consuming process and till one attains that, it is natural that one must conduct oneself with Dharma and complete their duties while living in this universe. Obviously, before one masters the art of completing their duties, it is meaningless to claim quitting those and take Sanyās (renunciation). This explains why scriptures prescribe the four-fold path while conducting oneself through this. The question is what one must do after completing this arduous task of attaining this knowledge. Proponents of Sanyās claim that a knowledgeable person gets apathetic towards the mundane proceedings of this universe after attaining the precious knowledge of Parmeshwar and spends the remaining life being one with it. Gitā claims that while one must follow Dharma first to purify their mind, later they must follow it to pursue all tasks as duty (without any attachment to them) and achieve welfare of the universe. However, Gitā never condemns or belittles the path of Sanyās or Sānkhya. Just as there are different types of people with different tendencies, it is perfectly natural for some people to feel like assuming renunciation after attaining knowledge. As there have been great beings who've chosen that path in history, it cannot and should not be boycotted. Even if this liberated person chooses to renounce from worldly life, achieving this feat of attaining Moksha through arduous ways is nevertheless commendable and there's definitely respect for the path of Sanyās in Gitā and in general. However, what Gitā argues is that when a person has overcome their natural tendencies and become truly 'free' and liberated; they must use this enormous capability for welfare of this universe. Thus, Gitā maintains that this path of Karmayog is thus superior to the path of Sānkhya or Sanyās.

While we saw the difference between the two paths, we see a clear equation of Karmayog as:

Sānkhya + Nishkām Karma = Karmayog

Naturally, the whole description and analysis of Karmayog in Gitā also covers analysis of Sānkhya path. This gives opportunity to communalistic critics to point out only these bits in Gitā and claim that Sanyās is advocated in it. They claim that the description of Nishkām Karma (action without attachment) mentioned in different verses is nothing but illustrations which are accessory or supplementary to the core idea of Sanyās or Dnyānyog. However, considering Karmayog trivial and Sanyās central to Gitā is like treating hosts of the house as guests in their own abode. We've discussed and proven this in numerous ways throughout our analysis. While Gitā is exhaustive, covers various different topics and explores several different paths; the central essence of Gitā is unique. It shows amalgamation of knowledge with detached action to show us the supreme path of Karmayog. It praises and borrows from different paths – Sānkhya for its explanation of origin of the universe, Bhakti for its simplicity and accessibility and Pātanjalyog for its capability to purify one's mind. Yet, it doesn't indulge in restricting itself to any of these paths. It blends Bhakti and knowledge to advocate Karmayog as we've seen throughout our book. Just as a mighty river takes in currents from different tributaries and yet maintains its own unique identity, Bhagavad Gitā welcomes topics from all paths or philosophies but maintains its central idea of Karmayog and communicates it clearly and definitively throughout. We request proponents of Sanyās path to graciously accept the fact that Karmayog is central to Gitā and indulge themselves in other Vedic texts which accept Sanyās as the core concept. Just as Bhagwān Shri Krishna recognizes the credibility of Sānkhya path in Gitā, members of these sects should appreciate the relevance of Karmayog, as all reincarnations of Parmeshwar have appeared and conducted themselves on this potent and superior path. They should agree that Gitā emphasizes on Karmayog.

CHAPTER 15

Upasanhār (Epilogue)

As we've seen till now, it is clear that the central idea of Bhagavad Gitā is upholding Karmayog enriched with Dnyān (knowledge) and Bhakti (devotion and love). It covers various topics and touches upon numerous topics pertaining to human behavior. It explains that path of attaining Moksha which ensures continuation and welfare of the universe. Endowing this knowledge to Arjun, and along with him to every reader, is the principal purpose behind this scriptural gem.

There are two ways of discussing or explaining ethical or moral conduct. One is to enlist all good or holy deeds – e.g. don't practice violence, don't steal etc. Smrutis and Upanishads depict these gospels about ethical behavior clearly. However, human being is an intelligent animal and is not convinced by such gospels without giving any explanations as to why to follow these codes. Naturally, humans have delved deeper into this topic and deciphered the elementary principles governing it. This task is of Shāstra (loosely to be translated here as philosophy) while the list of moral or ethical codes are simply called Āchārsangrah (Codes of conduct). Yog or Karmayog is the philosophy explained in Gitā and hence the verse at the end of every Adhyāya mentions this by calling the scripture Yog Shāstra (philosophy of (Karma) Yog).

Western intellectuals who deny the transcendental view call this same Karmayogshāstra by different words – Ethics, Moral codes, Principles of ethics etc. Referring to the literature of these people might make someone suspect if Sanskrit literature has no scripture on discussion of the principles of ethics. This couldn't be further from the truth. Reading of Mahābhārat would clear this misconception. However, it's way too big (100,000 shlokas or verses). While Gitā is smaller with 700 shlokas, communalists have made up their mind that it speaks only about knowledge for attaining Moksha. It's surprising how they ignore the fact that Karmayogi have always and would always outnumber Sanyāsi. Almost all great people from history have been living examples of Karmayog. Would it never have occurred to any of them advocating the importance of Karmayog? While there are many other scriptures, the glory of Gitā outshines them all. While we discussed in detail various aspects of this Karmayog in preceding chapters, this book would not be complete unless we do a comparative account of the Adhyātmik principles of Gitā and the ethical principles of Western philosophers. While it also necessitates comparison of spiritual knowledge of both these disciplines, we have not covered it as it's unanimously accepted that the reach of Vedānta philosophy far exceeds that of Western philosophy when it comes to spirituality. Thus, we have decided to do a comparison of the principles of ethics which the Westerners claim that our scriptures have not explained.

Good behavior and Bad behavior or Dharma (here as righteousness) and Adharma (here as villainy or sin) are terms depicted for human behavior. This should make one understand that ethics are not in the actions but in the intent behind these actions. Even if a furious bull or river causes catastrophic damage, we don't file a case on the bull or call the river wicked. Many argue that while it's accepted that this ethical evaluation is only limited to the deeds of humans, why should one not do it looking at the actions alone? Answering this is simple too, as a criminal action committed unknowingly or innocently is not considered a crime. E.g. If a toddler throws a rock on the street which causes an accident and someone is killed, no trial or criminal proceeding is undertaken against the child. Similarly, whenever we're evaluating a good deed, it must be done according to the intention. There's a beautiful story in Mahābhārat about a heavenly Mongoose which interrupted the praise of Yudhisthir when he was undertaking a huge Ashwamedh Yadnya (an elaborate ritual). Mongoose said that even if you feed hundreds of thousands, your feat is trivial when compared to the charity done by a poor Brāhman to a guest who had visited him when his family was about to feed on a meagre meal. That Brāhman and his family fed the guests even though they were hungry themselves. This beats any feast where a mighty king is feeding thousands. This story is a testament to the evaluation of a good deed based on the intent. If one tries to evaluate these two acts based on the Western principle of majority's happiness, the charity of the poor Brāhman would stand no chance against the feast of the king. This would leave no hope for the poor to aim for equal level of ethics or morals as the rich. However, upon little evaluation we understand that, not only was the deed of the poor Brāhman as virtuous as Yudhisthir, his act was even better. There was a possibility of his family starving when he fed the guest with their own food, whereas this was not the case in Yudhisthir's ritual. Even bible has an incident where Jesus Christ declared the act of a widow as most virtuous, who donated both the pennies she had. This proves that even Christ believed in the importance of intent behind an action. Conversely, same act performed under different circumstances with different intent needs to be treated differently. E.g. Killing of someone is different when one is trying to defend themselves against a deadly attack and different when one is trying to loot someone for money. This differing purpose is called Intent, Desire or Buddhi (intellect). While Buddhi is an organ that decides professionally; knowledge, desire and intent are products of this Buddhi and hence included in it. Shri Krishna didn't ask Arjun to get ready for war depending on who or how many would get killed. He asked him to get ready based on his intent. If the intent behind the war was correct and righteous, he would not have to worry about who or how many he killed.

While we conclude that Buddhi is the key behind evaluating any action, we need to define what pure intellect means. As Man (mind) and Buddhi (intellect) are both manifestations of Prakruti, they're Trigunātmak (defined by 3 Gunas namely Sāttvic, Rājas and Tāmas). That intellect which recognizes and understands the soul which underlies everything and takes a decision with that knowledge is considered pure or Sāttvic intellect. This intellect is also called Sāmya (equanimous) intellect. Recognition of this Sāmya Buddhi is done based on behavior. Gitā thus doesn't ask us to ignore the behavior altogether but asks us to go deeper and see both intent and actions. Gitā also says that someone with Sāmya Buddhi would never commit a wrongful action as every action is rooted in intellect. Moreover, such a person is thus said to be free from notions such as virtue and sin.

We clearly see the inadequacy of Adhibhautik sect believing in majority's happiness and Adhidaivik sect relying on the deity called Conscience when we observe the above discussion. Along with Vedic school, even Christian and Buddhist schools consider physical, mental and verbal purity to be essential for righteous behavior. Once someone attains Sāmya Buddhi (equanimous intellect), that person doesn't need to be separately asked to consider concepts like majority's happiness because the state attained is all-encompassing. Moreover, the bliss sought by a Sthitapradnya (someone firm in wisdom or someone with stoic calm) is internal and independent of anyone's sorrow or happiness. Adhibhautik happiness is however purely materialistic and thus needs to be derived by depriving someone else of it. The equanimous intellect of a liberated being is considerate not just of all humans but of all living beings. Thus, it maintains a much broader view of ethics than any other sect or school. Till one develops an awareness of seeing everyone as themselves, they would never be able to evaluate their happiness or sorrow. Hence, truly impartial equanimous intellect sees everyone as themselves and then decides the course of action. This action thus decided is naturally righteous and ethical. Adhibhautik view evaluates everything by its external or apparent consequences and thus risks encouraging development of calculating nature through which someone may cause damage to the society. Thus, Gitā's prescribed method of evaluating a righteous person through purity of intellect is the best criteria of evaluating ethics according to us. It clearly beats the Adhibhautik or Adhidaivik criteria. If we get past the Adhibhautik and Adhidaivik philosophies and look at Adhyātmik view of ethics employed by other Western philosophers, we find striking similarities with the philosophy in Gitā. While they may not be as exhaustive as Gitā, they're still similar to the extent of evaluating on a deeper level of intent or intellect. Professor Deussens who was a follower of Schopenhauer propounds that restraining of desires is essential to eliminate sorrow and even after eliminating sorrow through this, one need not quit action. He reiterates the importance of action without attachment and even mentions a verse from Gitā in his book. This indicates that he must have got inspired about this idea of action without attachment from Bhagavad Gitā. Either way, it is no small feat that centuries before Deussens, Schopenhauer and Aristotle our scriptures had dealt with and definitively conceptualized these principles.

Some people feel that Vedānta is a dry and laborious study of quitting familial life and aiming for Moksha. However, it couldn't be further from the truth. It looks at the universe beyond what we perceive through our senses and goes on to tackle questions like 'Who are we?' 'What is the fundamental principle behind the universe?' 'What's our ultimate goal here?' etc. Practically speaking, all ethics and behavioral science is a subset of this deeper study. Hence, Karmayogshāstra needs to be explained through this Vedānta philosophy. Just as Science can be classified as 'Pure Science' and 'Applied Science', Vedānta can be classified as 'Pure Vedānta' and 'Applied Vedānta'. Kant agrees with Gitā in its practical view of Vedānta and says that evaluating ethics without tackling spiritual questions about Parmātmā (universal soul), Immortality and 'Freedom of soul' is incomplete and involves a risk of encouraging animalistic behavior in humans. While Kant has written two separate treatises called 'Critique of Pure reason' and 'Critique of Practical reason' on these topics, Bhagavad Gitā has discussed both these concepts in detail as per philosophy from Upanishads long ago. Gitā also includes discussion of the path of Bhakti (devotion) and thus has a broader view and a wider acceptance.

As envisaged in our discussion so far, we've established that Sāmya Buddhi is superior; be it for Moksha or for evaluating ethical principles. It's important to see why other schools of ethics would've originated. As put forth aptly by Dr. Carus, an American author – As humans think about the origin and structure of themselves and the universe, their view of ethics gets shaped accordingly. Unless there's a definitive view about it, there's no question of discussing ethics. While someone may naturally behave ethically, this behavior would be exhibited as a somnambulist (sleepwalker) without any fundamental principles. It's more of an innate tendency or nature, rather than ethics. However, once a person or a community starts debating about the mystical questions like origin of universe and purpose of our existence and arrives at a conclusion, naturally the same decision also shapes how people should behave with each other. Yet, it's unlikely that this conclusion would be identical among different communities existing in different parts of the world. Christianity depicts God as Saguna (with attributes) and imagines that God has created the universe and discoursed the codes of ethical behavior for all humans. Thus, Christian intellectuals imagine all ethical philosophy to be based on these codes. Later when these codes were observed to be practically insufficient, concept of conscience was developed. Later when different people's conscience was observed to be operating differently, the concept of Majority's happiness gained roots. All these thoughts consider Saguna, Almighty God as the creator of the universe and revolve around this assumption that God has willed us to behave ethically or morally. When scientific development began to disagree with the religious theories of creation and structure of the universe; a thought began to develop, basing ethical behavior without having any Saguna God at its core. This gave rise to arguments based on the concept of Majority's happiness and humanity. This never explained why a human being should strive for majority's happiness, other than calling it human nature. When selfish nature of many humans was observed, more debates arose contesting this concept. It's not that these explanations of ethics are completely flawed. However, all of them deny the possibility of any invisible, imperceptible, fundamental entity at the base of the universe. Hence, despite the roadblocks they face while providing explanation to ethical principles, they keep attempting to explain them with some or the other Adhibhautik (corporeal) logic. This shows that while everyone is intent on including ethics, they differ widely on its explanation due to difference in their opinions on the structure of the universe. This is why we discussed in detail the key points and differences between three major approaches to ethics (Adhibhautik, Adhidaivik and Adhyātmik) in chapters 3-6.

Even before any discussion of ethics, humans behaved in particular ways based on their intellect, adapting it to their surroundings. Great human beings across history have proposed different codes of righteous behavior as per their capacity. Ethics is nothing but an organized way of representing such codes which also delves into the principles governing these codes. We observe that some codes of ethics have remained common among all sects across the world. E.g. Virtues of non-violence, truthfulness, philanthropy have been advocated in almost all sects and religions. The fundamental difference among these different groups lies mainly in their explanation about the origin and structure of the universe, as said by Dr. Carus.

Adhibhautik philosophy rejects the principle of 'universality of soul' or 'seeing everyone as oneself' and attempts to build the tower of ethics based on majority's happiness or everyone's well-being. Hence for someone who's keen on seeking answers to certain questions, Adhyātma is the only philosophy to turn to. These questions are – 'Who am I', 'Is universe independent or not', 'What's the fundamental principle at the base of the universe', 'Why should one strive for someone else's happiness' etc. Even though Adhibhautiks justify the intent behind great people fighting for future generations as their own happiness or majority's happiness, a little pondering would illustrate that it isn't so. There's definitely more to it than that. Those who've recognized the immortal principle at the base of the universe tell us that 'becoming one with this pure, supreme and eternal principle through knowledge and experience' is the zenith of our duties as a human being. Someone who recognizes this universality of soul naturally gets motivated to strive for welfare of the entire universe, as they've understood this eternal and timeless truth. This state of being is called Moksha in Vedānta. No ethics would be independent of this principle and thus it's important to surrender to this ultimate truth. 'Welfare of the universe' is nothing but a manifest form of the ultimate principle of 'universality of soul'. Saguna Parmeshwar and the visible universe are nothing but manifest Nāmroope (name forms) of this everlasting principle. Going beyond recognition of these manifest forms to become aware of this ultimate principle is the epitome of knowledge. Moreover, fulfilment of one's soul is also impossible without this knowledge. Every form of ethics, Dharma, code or philosophy is ultimately based on this. As Bhaktimārg is also based on this principle, becoming one with the object of devotion is shown as the principle behind good conduct and Moksha. The only objection against Vedānta philosophy is against the notion advocated by some Vedānti to quit all Karma after attaining this knowledge. Hence, Bhagavad Gitā shows that while ultimate knowledge may remove attachment to the Karma and mundane life, it is not against action. Even if one is free from all desires and attachments, they must submit themselves to Parmeshwar and dutifully continue to strive for welfare of the universe. This is the final doctrine of Karmayog explained beautifully in detail in Gitā. While Arjun is contextually asked to go to war, the same message applies to every farmer, carpenter, goldsmith, clerk, trader, manager and every human being. They must continue to work dutifully and strive for welfare of this universe. All actions are equal. It is the intent that is solemn or evil. Those who don't want to base their philosophy of ethics on this principle, may base it on some manifestation of this truth. However, while such approach may appear different, it isn't novel. It's only a question of whether you take efforts to go to the root of everything or you choose to be content with knowledge of the superficial. Ignoring the existence of roots doesn't change the fact about the roots but merely reflects your ignorance of it. Sānkhya who don't follow monistic approach of Vedānta and consider every Purush to be independent, have delved deep in observing the origin and destruction of the universe and assigned properties to three Gunas that govern everything. Of these, they claim that it is the ultimate goal of every human being to enhance Sāttvic Gunas in themselves and achieve a state beyond the three Gunas. Gitā covers this with a slight variation in 17th and 18th Adhyāya. Adhibhautiks have adamantly refused to delve into matters beyond physical and perceptible and forcibly tried to base ethics on inadequate corporeal principles. Bhagavad Gitā has not only explained every aspect of physical and perceptible principles in detail, it has gone beyond these into the realm of the unmanifest, ultimate principle of the universe. It has provided a detailed and fitting explanation and unified Moksha (liberation/enlightenment), ethics and behavior. Those who deny this unification would never understand its significance. However, those who are willing to quit their rigidity are unquestionably bound to find the explanation of Karmayog to be plausible, apt and superior. As no other place on earth had shown development of Adhyātmik (spiritual) discipline as much as Indian subcontinent did, it was impossible for such detailed explanation of Karmayog to flourish elsewhere.

While we've discussed how Gitā proposes Karmayog over Sanyās/Dnyānyog/Sānkhya Yog, we shall now throw some light on the comparative study of Gitā's Karmayog with Western action-oriented path and that of Indian Sanyās (path of renunciation) with Western asceticism. Vedic way of living was centered on actions and rituals before Upanishads and Sānkhya proposed that one must quit all familial life to escape sorrow and binding and attain Moksha (liberation). However, sects other than Vedic Dharma have advocated Sanyās from the beginning. Take example of Buddhism or Jainism, both of which tilt towards renunciation. Even the sermon of Jesus Christ was inclined towards adopting asceticism. Christ clearly said that one must quit home and family in order to achieve immortality which is the ultimate goal of Christianity. There are many accounts of asceticism being proposed or advised by Christ in bible. There's no record of Jesus Christ ever proposing a path like Karmayog where one can continue to live with their families and still attain immortality by living a full life; as long as one doesn't have attachment to any of the fruits of their actions. There's a lot of similarity between the Sanyās path of Moksha and the original Buddhist path to Nirvāna or Christian path to Immortality. The practice of followers of Christianity living a family life is a phenomenon which has come afterwards. Even in Greece, there was always a debate about which path is superior – Dedicating life to philosophical thoughts or entering politics for welfare of people. In summary, the western approach of asceticism and our ancient path of Sanyās are almost identical and so is the justification done in its support. However, the justification of an action-oriented life being superior to the life of asceticism as given by Western philosophers are much different from the rationale given in Bhagavad Gitā.

Happiness of entire humanity or Majority's happiness (which is material happiness, naturally) is predominantly considered as the ultimate goal of humans according to Adhibhautik proponents of action-oriented path. To support this, many argue that happiness dominates sadness in the world. On the contrary, Western asceticism is mostly born out of apathy towards mundane life. This makes us consider those promoting action-oriented life as 'optimists' and those promoting asceticism as 'pessimists'. However, Karmayog and Sānkhya, which are the alternate paths mentioned in Gitā are not comparable to these two paths from Western philosophy; as we've explained in 11th chapter. Gitā says that as quitting Karma altogether is anyway impossible, it's better to move beyond thinking whether this worldly life has more of happiness or sadness. It says that we must consider ourselves blessed enough to have been born as humans and perform our respective duties with dedication. We must play our part in the larger scheme of welfare of the universe without getting frustrated. As Chāturvarnya (four-tiered) system was prevalent in Indian society during the times of Gitā, it advises one to follow their duties as per their place in that system. It must be noted, however, that principles of Gitā are not limited to or dependent on the Chāturvarnya system at all. Gitā doesn't base its philosophy on any particular social system but on a larger foundation of universality of soul. Thus, it is applicable equally across time and space. References to Chāturvarnya system were made simply to make the concept relatable in the erstwhile context. It advocates that whatever system we live in, once we're either born in or choose a particular profession as our duty; we must consider it our Dharma and do it diligently. Naturally, an ideal person according to Gitā performs tasks that happen to be for the welfare of the society they're a part of. Yet, there's no feeling of pride or ego in doing so. It's merely a natural behavior as their Buddhi (intellect) has become Sama (equanimous). Having differentiated between western path advocating action and Karmayog mentioned in Gitā, there are a few exceptions like Schopenhauer who have promoted action-oriented path despite considering the world to be dominated by sorrow. This path is called Meliorism and the followers Meliorists. While this path is similar to the path of Karmayog in Gitā, freeing world of sadness is not what Gitā bases its philosophy on. Gitā gives preference to internal bliss over material pleasure and recommends performing all actions dutifully without any pride; not even about making others' lives better by reducing their sorrows. Thus, Western Meliorism still has a long way to go before it catches up with the philosophy of Gitā. While both follow path of action (Karma), Western Meliorists still have attachment whereas Karmayogi from Gitā are without any attachment. In other words, Western Meliorism is Rājas while Gitā's Karmayog is Sāttvic.

This action-oriented Dharma advocated in Gitā, that follows Karmayog and recommends continuing with familial life and duties without attachment, is also called 'Bhāgwat Dharma'; which is described in Mahābhārat and Manu Smruti. Descriptions of this path given in Samhitā and Brāhmanas of Vedas point out that this path was prevalent in ancient times. All accomplished greats from history across the globe have belonged to this path. Yet, these followers of Karmayog have never displayed or even felt any pride or vanity about their greatness. Bhagwān Shri Krishna was a great proponent of this path. It is clear from evidence that path of Sanyās (renunciation) was equally ancient and a few knowledgeable people were inclined towards this path even back then. While these two paths always existed due to variety of human nature, Karma Mārg of Mimāmsaks dominated the Vedic period and Karmayog of Gitā dominated the Mahābhārat period. How then, one may wonder, did path of Sanyās overtake this action-oriented path of Karmayog which was strongly prevalent in those times? Many assume that this was because of Shrimad Ādya Shankarāchārya. However, a little attention to history proves this assumption wrong. The sect of followers of Shankarāchārya was further divided between two subsects – followers of Māyāvāda and Advaita knowledge (monists accepting the whole universe as Māyā or merely an appearance) and followers of Sanyās Dharma (path of renunciation). While both paths are equally ancient, following one doesn't necessitate following the other. Many knowers of Advaita knowledge like Janak were Karmayogi while others like Yādnyavalkya were followers of Sanyās. While we agree that Shankarāchārya resuscitated this path of Sanyās which had received a debacle during those times, it is impossible to have sustained without an existing inclination towards ascetic tendency. Observing history tells us that no thought process gets adopted without there being conducive circumstances for its acceptance. We believe that prevalence of Buddhism and Jainism prior to Shankarāchārya's time is that key factor for acceptance of Sanyās path and debacle of Karmayog even among followers of Bhāgwat sect. As Buddhism and Jainism had opened up the path of Sanyās to all classes of society, this path took prominence strongly after that. It is noteworthy however, that even ascetic path of Buddhism later improved itself to advocate active striving for the purpose of spreading the religion. This then helped proliferation of Buddhism in Nepal, Tibet, Burma, China, Japan, Sri Lanka and even Europe through Turkey. Centuries of strong presence of Buddhism before the period of Shankarāchārya helped instill respect about Sanyās in the erstwhile Indian society. Ironically, while Shankarāchārya strongly criticized Buddhism and Jainism, he leveraged this respect about Sanyās and modified it to Vedic form and created apostles of Sanyās. Many may have begun criticizing this striking similarity between the ascetic thought process of Buddhism and that of followers of Shankarāchārya. This may have caused Shankarāchārya to vehemently fight Buddhism and Jainism, proving their religion alien to Vedas and reiterating their own path of Sanyās to be Vedic and authentic. Whatever be the case, he ended up creating teams of Sanyāsis who were more active than ascetic and strived to establish Vedic Dharma. Later Muslims began invading the subcontinent and defender class of Kshatriyas began to fall under their marauding armies. It is in this period of Muslim occupation that path of Sanyās began gaining ground among common people, to cope up with the foreign rule. This was never the case in eras before. Truth be told, this state was not even Sanyās in its true sense as they had neither quit all work like a Sanyāsi nor were they performing their familial and national duties like a Karmayogi. They must be categorized as a third kind. Typically, this results in near-extinction of original Dharma, like that of Pārsis after their violent persecution in Iran from where they had to flee. Thankfully in India, Sant (Saint) Dnyāneshwar in Maharashtra and similar sages elsewhere in India kept the Hindu Dharma (in some form or the other) alive by simultaneously educating people about it.

In fact, it even impacted Muslim invaders and produced sages like Saint Kabir and resulted in translation of Hindu texts; like that of Upanishads done by prince Dārā Shikoh who was the elder brother of erstwhile Mughal ruler Aurangzeb. It is seriously doubtful if Hindu Dharma would've survived had it not been founded on strong Adhyātmik principles. Yet, its revival happened during Muslim occupation and that too almost unilaterally as Bhakti Mārg with influence of Sanyās. This created a false interpretation that Karmayog is a subset of Bhakti Mārg, just as it was misinterpreted as a subset of Sanyās during the period of Shankarāchārya whereas actually it's a separate discipline based on action without attachment. Sant Rāmdās was one of the few fortunate exceptions to this who taught this Karmayog to the great warrior king Shivāji Mahārāj who went on to establish an expansive Maratha empire, defeating Mughals. The only point to be made is that despite its ascetic interpretations, Karmayog advocated in Bhagavad Gitā shone through with its emphasis on Karma without attachment.

As we've discussed earlier the word Dharma has two divisions – esoteric as well as practical or liberating and ethical, may it be Vedic, Buddhism or Christianity. Its main focus is making members of the society conduct all their activities in a progressive manner so as to liberate/enlighten all of them. This division of esoteric and practical didn't exist in ancient times as they firmly believed that one must behave righteously for ultimately attaining liberation or enlightenment. Development of Adhibhautik knowledge reduced this belief in Western regions which initiated attempts to base ethics on material principles. Still, they've failed as expected and have indirectly accepted unmanifest principles like humanity, like in the example of French philosopher Comte. Similarly, while German philosopher Nietzsche denied existence of God, he ended up justifying phenomenon of Karmavipāk (fruition of Karma) and reincarnation. He accepted existence of an unmanifest ultimate principle, and saw attaining it as the goal of all humans. This proves that despite denial of any invisible principle by Adhibhautiks, one has to ultimately rely on an imperceptible, unmanifest principle to be pursued as the ultimate goal. Instead of relying on narrower principles like humanity, Adhyātmik discipline is more inclusive and encompasses all living beings while advocating their welfare. While it is beyond debate that progress of science has resulted in unparalleled benefits to humans and empowered human domination, you must turn to Adhyātma when you wish to know the fundamental principle of the universe. While practical applications of this all-pervasive fundamental principle would rely on physical knowledge of everything through Science, Gitā indulges itself with explaining the epitome of being human and how one should approach life and ethics. Gitā is so comprehensive when it comes to matters pertaining to Karma, Neeti (ethics) and Moksha (liberation), founding them on the ultimate universal principle of Parabrahma; that we need not turn to any other text when it comes to these matters. Gitā thus eliminates the contradiction between Dnyān, Bhakti and Karma (Knowledge, Devotion and Action) and unifies them in a comprehensive path of Dnyān-Bhakti yukta Karmayog (Karmayog enriched with knowledge and devotion).

We'd like to conclude our analysis of this magnificent epic Shrimad Bhagavad Gitā with a sincere prayer from Rig Veda –

Samāni Va Ākootih Samānā Hrudayāni Vah

Samānamastu Vo Mano Yatha Vah Susahāsati

Yatha Vah Susahāsati

(May your opinions unite, may your hearts unite, may your minds unite; so that you strengthen yourself through unity)

Appendix Chapter: Geeteche Bahirangpareekshan (Peripheral analysis of Gitā)

We've discussed in detail how Shri Krishna explained the importance of Karmayog and also that of continuing with the righteous war in answer to Arjun's predicament of whether or not to go for it. Once we understand the true essence of Gitā, questions about relevance of Gitā in Mahābhārat are answered. As we can see, while Mahābhārat has a plethora of different chapters where various topics pertaining to ethics are explained in bits, it was essential to collate them all and represent them in a single chapter. This can be found in Bhagavad Gitā. Different anecdotes spread across chapters don't singularly justify whether people should follow in the footsteps of Shri Krishna and Pāndav. Moreover, writing an epic of 100,000 verses by sage Vyās which took 3 years to write, also comes under criticism if one argues that material life is pointless and Sanyās is the ultimate goal. It became necessary to explain somewhere in this epic how behavior of several great characters of Mahābhārat was justifiable from ethical point of view. There was no better place to explain this other than just before the start of the Great War, which constitutes the core part of Mahābhārat. Placing Gitā anywhere else would've risked trivializing it. Even if we forget the traditional view for a minute that Shri Krishna told Gitā to Arjun at the start of the war, its place within Mahābhārat fits contextually in a perfect way. Once we understand its relevance, trivial questions such as debating its context or claiming its introduction in Mahābhārat as an afterthought prove to be insignificant.

Let us now proceed with the peripheral analysis of Gitā as a poem and discuss a few other arguments which have arisen over time considering Gitā and other scriptures – both Indian and foreign. We shall discuss 7 topics – 1. Gitā and Mahābhārat; 2. Gitā and Upanishads; 3. Gitā and Brahma Sutras; 4. Rise of Bhāgwat Dharma and Gitā; 5. Chronology of current Gitā; 6. Gitā and Buddhist texts and 7. Gitā and Christian Bible. We must note that being a peripheral analysis, we shall discuss these strictly on a practical and chronological basis.

Part 1: Gitā and Mahābhārat

While Gitā is widely accepted as comprising of 700 shlokas (verses) (as mentioned by Shrimad Shankarāchārya from 9th century in his commentary on Gitā), there's another edition of Mahābhārat printed in Mumbai where Gitā appears in Bheeshma Parva (chapter) and is cited to be comprising of 745 shlokas. This version notes 620 verses of Shri Krishna against 575 as followed by us commonly, 57 of Arjun against 84, 67 of Sanjay against 40 and 1 of Dhrutarāshtra identical to 1 as considered in common interpretation. It is curious to note that while the total verses of Arjun and Sanjay remain the same at 124, only individual count varies which might be due to misinterpretation of who cited the verses. However, it is important to investigate how Shri Krishna's verses exceed by 45. This contradiction would appear trivial if we compare number of verses in the magnum opus Mahābhārat. While it's widely accepted that it consists of 100,000 verses, investigation shows disparity between different versions regarding total as well as chapter wise verses. As the epic is way too large, the likelihood of modifications in transmitting it is much more. However, it's not the case with Gitā. As it's comparatively smaller at 700 verses, there have always been people who've known it by heart and it has remained consistently at 700 verses in total and even in terms of number of verses belonging to each character. As it's imperative that we consider some version as standard before beginning our book, we've decided to stick to the 700-verse version of Shankarāchārya and the edition of Mahābhārat printed at Kolkata by Babu Pratāpchandra Rai as they're the most widely accepted versions till date.

Once we proceed this way, there are many cross-references within Mahābhārat which point towards Gitā being an integral part of Mahābhārat. E.g. Ādi Parva mentions how later Shri Krishna would clear Arjun's predicament by demonstrating essence of Moksha (Ādi 2.247). There are two more such references in Ādi Parva. Later in Shānti Parva, it is mentioned that 'these rituals of Nārāyan Dharma (another name for Bhāgwat, Sātvat or Aikāntik) have been explained earlier by Shri Krishna to Arjun at the time of war between Kaurav and Pāndav' (Shānti 348.8). There are 2 other similar mentions within Shānti Parva. Later in Ashwamedh Parva after the war, while sitting by the lake before Krishna is about to depart for his kingdom, Arjun asks Shri Krishna to recount the discourse he had given him before the war. Shri Krishna says that while it's unfortunate that Arjun has forgotten the sermon, it's impossible even for him to recreate it exactly. He then goes on to narrate Anugeetā, which is a similar but modified version of Bhagavad Gitā.

Thus, there are 7 references of actual Gitā within Mahābhārat which clarify that Bhagavad Gitā is an integral part of Mahābhārat. However, there's no limit to debate and some still question by claiming there's no proof that these verses were not deliberately introduced later for justifying Gitā's context in Mahābhārat. We shall give more proof to refute these claims. While evaluating whether or not two poetic works have been authored by the same person, analysts check for two parameters – Similarity of vocabulary and Similarity of meaning. Similarity of vocabulary not only covers words used but also the style of language used, verse arrangement etc. Mahābhārat being too vast, there are varying styles used across the 100,000 verses. It is thus difficult to ascertain whether style of Gitā matches that of Mahābhārat. However, the Sanskrit vocabulary, grammar and terminology used in Gitā points clearly that it's from a period preceding great historic Sanskrit poet Kālidās and are similar to those used in Rig Veda. The same is found in Mahābhārat as well. Another substantial and certain proof is the presence of common verses between Gitā and rest of Mahābhārat. It's a herculean task to search through Mahābhārat and point out exact verses. However, while reading through Mahābhārat, we have found numerous verses identical or mostly similar between Mahābhārat and Gitā. In all, there are 27 entire verses exactly reappearing whereas 12 verses partly identical between the two. (I've not mentioned the actual verses but Lokmānya Tilak's Geetārahasya enlists these 27 and 12 incidents of common verses). If one delves deeper, it's possible that we may find more partial or full verses common between the two scriptures. Even if we check the contextual relevance of these verses in either text, they perfectly fit the context and don't appear to have been forcefully added retrospectively. There are also cross-references of previous Parvas of Mahābhārat given in Gitā and vice versa in later chapters of Mahābhārat.

Even when we look for similarity of meaning, we find similar results. Like we saw the similarity between description of Bhāgwat Dharma and that of Karmayog explained in Gitā, there are many more accounts of resemblance substantiating this. The Vedānta philosophy and Adhyātmik (spiritual) knowledge explained in Gitā also agrees completely with other such accounts in Mahābhārat. In addition to the core concepts of Karmayog and Adhyātma, the similarity continues in other supplementary concepts. E.g. Description of army given by Duryodhan in Gitā and in a later chapter of Mahābhārat, description of Arjun's predicament at the start of the war in Gitā and that of Yudhisthir at the start of Shānti Parva, description of Pātanjalyog in 6th Adhyāya of Gitā and that in Shānti Parva and Anugeetā which come later in Mahābhārat etc.

Thus, after considering similarity of vocabulary as well as meaning along with numerous cross-references of Gitā and Mahābhārat in either scripture, it is clear that it's the same author who has drafted current version of Gitā as well as current version of Mahābhārat. There would still be some who would disagree despite seeing so many proofs. However, we consider their opinion as irrational and unacceptable. Rāmāyan is also a famous and unanimously accepted great epic and covers topics such as truthfulness, duty etc. However, as its author Valmiki's intention while drafting it wasn't to create a timeless, multidimensional epic which would act as a guide to all people about ethics, morality and Dharma; Mahābhārat is especially superior in terms of these topics. What better scripture than Mahābhārat to include a scientific and philosophical treatise on ethics and action? We should be grateful that we were blessed with such a great author who created such a masterpiece.

Let's delve a little deeper into the etymology of 'Mahābhārat'. As the epic describes events in the life of kings who were descendants of Bhārat clan, it should be simply called 'Bhārat' on similar lines as Rāmāyan or Bhāgwat. Just the sheer size shouldn't be the reason for calling it Mahābhārat (Maha means Great) as even Rāmāyan is not a small epic by any means. We firmly infer from historical descriptions of Mahābhārat that the adjective 'Mahā' (Mega) before Bhārat has been put to signify its importance and weightage as an epic. As is known, it was originally called 'Jaya' meaning victory which indicates that it was depicting victory of Pāndav over Kaurav. It is natural to infer that current version of Mahābhārat has evolved from original Jaya through subsequent additions and modifications. Āshwalāyanguhyasutras (another scripture) mentions that sage Vyās told this epic to his son Shuka first and then to his other disciples. Further, Shuka, Sumantu, Jaimini, Paila and Vaishampāyan wrote separate treatises or Mahābhārats as mentioned in this scripture. In summary, the current version of Mahābhārat is not the original one. However, even original version is most likely to have included Gitā, along with Vidur Neeti, Shukānuprashna, Anugeetā, Nārāyaneeya Dharma etc. While we can't claim there were no changes made in original Gitā to make the current 700-verse version, it is beyond doubt that current Gitā has always been developed along with the current version of Mahābhārat through this evolution and was always an integral part of the epic. The chronology of current Mahābhārat and Gitā shall be covered in a subsequent chapter. For now, let's conclude by reiterating the integrity of Gitā with Mahābhārat.

Part 2: Gitā and Upanishads

Let's now discuss the interrelationship between Gitā and different Upanishads. There are numerous accounts of general occurrence of various concepts from different Upanishads appearing across Mahābhārat; e.g. Reference of Bruhadāranyak and Chhāndogya

Upanishad while describing the battle against senses; or the famous allegory of a chariot where Buddhi (intellect) is depicted as the charioteer of the five senses (as horses), borrowed from Kathopanishad. Moreover, there are more identical verses borrowed from various Upanishads in Gitā and Mahābhārat. We can go to the extent of saying that the spiritual knowledge given in Mahābhārat is mostly from various Upanishads.

We've covered in 9th and 13th chapters how Gitā borrows from Upanishads in terms of the spiritual knowledge and also while describing Bhakti path. Some Upanishads are in the form of prose while others are as poems. Naturally, Gitā has not borrowed from prose Upanishads word by word as changes have been made for lyrical reasons. E.g. 'Jyotishām Jyotih' (Gitā 13.17) is clearly similar to text from Bruhadāranyak Upanishad or 'Yam Yam Vāpi Smaran Bhāvam' is from Chhāndogya Upanishad. In poetic Upanishads this similarity is even more pronounced. E.g. 'Na Jāyate Mriyate Vā Kadachit…' (Gitā 2.20) is a verse exactly borrowed from Kathopanishad. There are many occurrences of other exact or partial similarities between various verses of Gitā and Upanishads. Thus, it is beyond debate that the Vedānta philosophy advocated in Gitā is borrowed from Upanishads. The key point of discussion is the difference in analysis or interpretation of this philosophy between Gitā and Upanishads. Out of numerous Upanishads, some are clearly more modern than Gitā. We've thus only considered the Mukhya (Key) Upanishads for the scope of our discussion, which have been included in Brahma Sutras. While some Upanishads call the Saguna (with attributes) as Avidyā, some later Upanishads also call it 'Māyā' or 'Adnyān'. Gitā's use of Māyā or Adnyān indicate that Gitā has been drafted post these Upanishads.

If we compare the explanation given in Gitā with that in Upanishads, we notice that there's a considerable significance given to Sānkhya philosophy in Gitā. While some Upanishads don't even mention Sānkhya philosophy or terminology, some only use some terms in Vedānta context. Vedānta Sutras go to the extent of explaining evolution through three principles (as in Chhāndogya Upanishad) instead of five (as in Sānkhya). This is not the case with Gitā. However,

Gitā doesn't borrow Sānkhya concepts as it is, either. While Gitā accepts the concepts about evolution like Prakruti, Nirguna nature of Purush etc., Gitā doesn't identify Prakruti and Purush as independent originals but manifestations of the same Parabrahma. Thus, Gitā maintains its agreement with Advaita (monist) philosophy while borrowing concepts from Sānkhya. This unique amalgamation of Sānkhya with Vedānta is exclusive to Gitā as well as other parts of Mahābhārat. This further substantiates the placement of Gitā within Mahābhārat (as discussed earlier).

Another unique characteristic of Gitā, different from ideas in Upanishads, is Bhaktimārg (path of devotion) or worship of Vyakta (manifest). While both consider ritualistic Karma auxiliary, worship of Parmeshwar in humanoid form is unique to Gitā. Upanishads agree with importance of symbols as it's extremely difficult to infer Avyakta (unmanifest) and Nirguna (without attributes) Parabrahma. However, these symbols are in the form of Sun, Fire, Ritual fire etc. in Upanishads. Although some Upanishads mention names like Rudra, Shiva, Achyut etc. they may not necessarily point to the humanoid forms. While there are some Upanishads where mention of deities in human form is seen, period of these Upanishads isn't certain for proving their existence before Gitā. However, existence of Bhakti in Vedic philosophy can be dated to more ancient times, with Patanjali's Yog Sutras (around 250 B.C.) or even texts written by Pānini (much older expert on Sanskrit Grammar) that mention Bhakti (worship). Even Buddhist scriptures mention Bhakti. We've shown in subsequent chapters how Mahāyān Buddhism may have originated by drawing inspiration from Bhāgwat Dharma. Bhaktimārg was thus well established before Gautam Buddha or more than 6 centuries before Christ. Bhāgwat Dharma has evolved from the symbolic worship of Parabrahma as described in ancient Upanishads. Pātanjalyog also advises adoption of an actual object substantiating Bhaktimārg. Gitā is particularly instrumental in establishing Indian origin of Bhaktimārg and substantiating worship of Vāsudev through knowledge from Upanishads.

However, even more important and unique characteristic of Gitā is the unification of Karmayog with Bhakti and Dnyān. While a few Upanishads advise continuation of action even after purification of mind, most of them promote Sanyās (asceticism). The advocacy of Karmayog as done by Bhagavad Gitā is unparalleled. Rather, the view of Gitā about Karma is pretty different from that of Upanishads as we've seen in Chapter 11. Patanjali's Yog Sutras are considered the final word on Pātanjal Yog described in 6th Adhyāya of Gitā. While Gitā supports use of techniques similar to ones mentioned in Pātanjal Yog to achieve restraint of senses, it doesn't prove Patanjali's period to be before Gitā. Rather, it is well known that Patanjali had compiled knowledge of pre-existing techniques into Pātanjalyog. Gitā can thus be seen to have referred to these techniques from older Upanishads like Shwetāshwatar or Katha. Due to different interpretations of the word Yog, many have incorrectly interpreted that Gitā has borrowed from Pātanjalyog in 6th Adhyāya. However, the fact is that Yog in Gitā follows in the footsteps of Janak, Manu and Ikshvāku in promoting selfless and detached action and not Pātanjalyog.

We've thus seen the commonalities and differences between Gitā and Upanishads. We can hereby conclude that while the knowledge in Gitā is based on Upanishads, Gitā has not limited itself to it but has added Vāsudev Bhakti (worship) from Bhāgwat Dharma and Ksharākshar Dnyān (knowledge of evolution of universe) from Sānkhya to create an unparalleled work about ethics and Karma that is simple for everyone to follow and live by. This is the distinct and valuable significance of Gitā over any other scripture.

Part 3: Gitā and Brahma Sutras

As we've already discussed the similarities and differences between Gitā and Upanishads, discussion of Gitā and Brahma Sutras appears redundant as Brahma Sutras enlist and collate the principles from various Upanishads. However, 13th Adhyāya of Gitā makes a mention of Brahma Sutras right at the beginning of Kshetrakshetradnyavichār (discussion of body and soul) as –

Rushibhirbahudhā Geetam Chhandobhivividhaih Pruthak

Brahmasutrapadaischaiva Hetumadbhivinischitaih

"Many rushi (sages) have independently, intentionally and definitively explained it (Kshetrakshetradnyavichār) in Brahma Sutras"

If we consider these Brahma Sutras and Vedānta Sutras as the same, it would mean that they predate the current Gitā. This goes against the long-standing notion about the ancient nature of Gitā. This is the reason why Shānkarbhāshya interprets the word Brahma Sutra in this verse as 'statements from Upanishads or Shrutis pertaining to Brahman' to clear this doubt. However, other critics like Anandgiri, Rāmānujāchārya, Madhvāchārya etc. interpret this as the same Brahma Sutras written by Bādarāyanāchārya. Thus, we must independently assess the true meaning of this shloka (verse). The term 'chaiva' in second line clearly indicates that two separate descriptors are used – One saying 'In different ways and independently, many sages have expressed Kshetrakshetradnyavichār (in Upanishads)' whereas the other saying 'Brahma Sutras have intentionally and definitively told the same thought'. Here the connotation of the word Hetumad (intentionally) is similar to how it has been used across Mahābhārat on many other occasions – meaning 'explained with logical reasoning'. Thus, we can see that this shloka mentions both texts wherein discussion of body and soul has been dealt with, one in a scattered way across different Upanishads in multiple independent ways whereas second in a definitive way with proper logical reasoning behind every thought. Naturally, it would tend to agree with the latter description more. As the Upanishads are independently drafted by separate sages and are fragmented, it was necessary to mention Vedānta Sutras which collate them all and present them in a cohesive manner.

After interpreting this verse in above way, it becomes clear that Upanishads and Brahma Sutras were older than Gitā. While there's clarity about Upanishads because Gitā contains many verses borrowed from them, there's still ambiguity about Brahma Sutras as there are at least 8 accounts where Brahma Sutras refer to Gitā not directly but with the word Smruti (remembrances). 2 of these 8 are so clear that all critics unanimously agree that the reference is definitely to Gitā. They are – 'Api cha smaryate' (Brahma Sutras 2.3.45) meaning 'Smrutis are also similar' pointing to interpretation of Jeevātmā in Gitā and 'Yoginah

Prati cha Smaryate' (Brahma Sutras 4.2.21) meaning '(absolute periods) are applicable to Yogis in Smrutis' clearly referring to 'Yatra kāle Tvanāvruttim Āvruttim Chaiva Yoginah' meaning 'those periods wherein Karmayogi die not to be reborn' (Gitā 8.23).

Now that we've established both – mention of Brahma Sutras in Gitā and mention of Gitā in Brahma Sutras, there's absurdity by both statements being contradictory to each other. If you consider either one to be correct and try to prove the other as false, you reach an impossibility. How does one solve this paradox? According to us, the only plausible way is to assume that the same person has authored current Brahma Sutras as well as current Gitā and Mahābhārat. Once we consider this premise, there's suddenly no more contradiction. Moreover, sage Vyās is also considered to have authored Brahma Sutras as they're also called 'Vyās Sutras' and sage Jaimini is described as 'disciple of Vyās, the author of Vedānta Sutras' by Anandgiri in Shānkarbhāshya. We already saw earlier how Vyās has authored Mahābhārat and he told the same to his five disciples Paila, Shuka, Sumantu, Jaimini and Vaishampāyan. This proves that the same Bādarāyan Vyās authored both current Mahābhārat as well as current Brahma Sutras. We don't claim he wrote them afresh but simply collated and consolidated them from available fragments and gave them unified forms. This logic thus aptly explains entire correlation between Gitā and Brahma Sutras while logically justifying the cross references in either.

Part 4: Rise of Bhāgwat Dharma and Gitā

Gitā has capably collated and seamlessly amalgamated Brahmadnyān (knowledge of Brahman), Bhakti (devotion), Sānkhya and Nishkām Karma (Action without attachment). However, those with limited understanding of these concepts or a biased view often deny the possibility of Bhagavad Gitā having achieved this feat. These people then naturally find many statements within Gitā to be contradictory to each other. E.g. While once Gitā says 'both enemies and friends are the same to me' (Gitā 9.29), it also says 'knowledgeable and devoted people are my favorite' (Gitā 7.17, 12.19). However, these are not contradictory statements but simply discussion of the same concept once from spiritual point of view and once from devotional point of view. While these statements may appear contradictory as standalone lines, Gitā has combined them in a broader philosophical sense ultimately. There's still an objection to the authenticity of Gitā for including Vedānta and Mimāmsak concepts combined with Bhakti. They claim that original Gitā only combined Sānkhya and Yog with Bhakti while these are improvisations done later by proponents of Vedānta and Mimāmsak paths. While this objection is false and steeped in ignorance about the holistic form of Hindu philosophy, it is a major one and we shall tackle it by explaining origin and tradition of the philosophy of Gitā from historical point of view.

The nature of Vedic Dharma in its most ancient form was not devotion centric, knowledge centric or Yog centric. It was centered on Yadnya or rituals. Veda Samhitā and Brāhmanas mainly describe this ritualistic path as shown by us in the 10th chapter. As Jaimini consolidated this path in Mimāmsā Sutras, this path begun to be called a 'Mimāmsak path'. While this name may be new, the path is ancient. It is thus unanimously accepted that ritualistic path is chronologically the first step of Vedic Dharma. This is called 'Trayi Dharma' in Gitā specifying its origin in 'three Vedas'. When this path was strongly prevalent in the society, a thought gained roots that questioned how one would gain knowledge merely through these elaborate rituals. Some argued that because knowledge or awareness is a psychological state, there couldn't be any knowledge of Parmeshwar without deep thought. When such questions began finding resonance, the knowledge of Upanishads began to be established. This knowledge came to be called Vedānta later. Just like Mimāmsā, the word Vedānta was coined later. However, Dnyān or Brahma Dnyān (knowledge of Brahman) was ancient. Kāpilsānkhya is another branch of philosophy developed based on knowledge, in parallel with Dnyān Mārg (path of knowledge), with different concepts about evolution of the universe. While Upanishads were Advaiti (monistic) in their approach, Sānkhya were Dvaiti (dualistic). However, they both challenged the ritualistic view of Mimāmsak. On the one hand there were Sānkhya and some Upanishads like Bruhadāranyak which insisted that one must quit Karma upon gaining knowledge. On the other there were Upanishads like Ishāvāsya which proposed that one must continue to work post gaining knowledge (albeit without attachment), as it's impossible to truly quit Karma. Ancient Upanishads didn't give importance to Kāpilsānkhya discipline but a few later Upanishads like Maitryupanishad tried to combine the concepts of both disciplines. Overall, there were three paths – 1. Ritualistic path of Mimāmsak 2. Knowledge based path of Dnyān or Sānkhya proposing asceticism and 3. Knowledge based path of Dnyānkarmasamucchay combining knowledge and action. Path of knowledge branched itself into two more disciplines – Yog and Bhakti. The path that emphasized on restraint of mind and senses in order to focus it on attaining knowledge of Brahman, developed into Yog (Pātanjalyog). Devotional path evolved from taking abstract symbols to worshipping humanoid deities culminating into Bhakti Mārg. This path hasn't evolved separately but as an extension of the path of knowledge. Initially it worshipped ritualistic deities, followed by Omkar, then deities like Rudra, Vishnu etc. and finally human deities like Rām, Krishna, Narsimha etc. As these two paths of Yog and Bhakti evolved from the path of knowledge, importance of knowledge of Brahman continued to be the ultimate goal in either path. Thus, while there continued to be newer developments, they maintained agreement with one of the previous thought processes and so has Gitā. Claiming that Gitā developed its philosophy entirely afresh isn't plausible or even likely.

After understanding the history of the five principal branches of Vedic Dharma – Ritualistic Karma Mārg, Knowledge path of Upanishads, Kāpilsānkhya path, Pātanjalyog and Bhakti; we now move on to see how Gitā seamlessly combined these paths. If we see some verses of Gitā from the description of knowledge path, they appear to have been borrowed from Upanishads and so it appears Gitā follows Upanishads. However, if you see the tradition of Gitā, there's no mention of any Upanishads. While the path of Janak that Gitā mentions was a combination of Dnyān and Karma, we must note that the element of devotion was not present in Janak's times. It is mentioned at the start of 4th Adhyāya that knowledge in Gitā was given by Bhagwān at the start of the Yug (eon) to Vivaswān, through to Manu and subsequently to Ikshvāku. However, as it was lost sometime during the tradition, Krishna is compelled to narrate it again to Arjun. These verses are extremely important in tracing the origins of Gitā and yet they are deliberately ignored by a few communalist critics to prevent trivialization of their sect. This tradition given in Gitā perfectly fits the tradition of Bhāgwat sect which proves that Gitā follows this Bhāgwat Dharma. Moreover, Vaishampāyan clearly states in Shānti Parva of Mahābhārat that Gitā advocates Bhāgwat Dharma. Let's now study the origins of this Bhāgwat Dharma (also known as Nārāyaneeya, Sātvat or Pānchrātra Dharma), that forms the foundation of Gitā.

As there are very few Vedic scriptures available from the period post Upanishads and before Buddha, the only texts available on Bhāgwat Dharma are Nārāyaneeyopākhyān (which is a part of Shānti Parva of Mahābhārat), Shandilya Sutras, Bhāgwat Purān, Nārad Panchrātra, Nārad Sutras and commentaries by the likes of Rāmānujāchārya. Of these, the commentaries written in 12th century onwards are too recent and downright communalistic so they can't be taken as a benchmark. While Bhāgwat Purān is older, it makes mentions of Gitā and Mahābhārat. Thus, its period is clearly later than Gitā. Moreover, the language and tone evidently indicate that it was written to promote importance of Bhakti. When someone realized that the Bhāgwat Dharma followed in Mahābhārat and Gitā didn't emphasize too much on Bhakti (devotion), they wrote Bhāgwat Purān as an attempt to glorify it. Similar is the case with Nārad Panchrātra which also dates to a period after Gitā and Mahābhārat. Nārad Sutras and Shandilya Sutras may have been written prior to Nārad Panchrātra. However, both of them mention and borrow from Gitā and Mahābhārat and thus definitely succeed them chronologically. Thus, we are left with only Nārāyaneeyopākhyān as a worthy reference for Bhāgwat Dharma. While Nārad Panchrātra and Bhāgwat Purān both mention Buddha as one of the reincarnations of Vishnu, Nārāyaneeyopākhyān doesn't mention Buddha at all. Rather, while enlisting the reincarnations of Vishnu, it mentions Kalki as the next reincarnation after Shri Krishna, where Kalki is predicted to arrive later in Kali Yug. It says that avatars of Parabrahma – two sages named Nara and Nārāyan created Nārāyaneeya or Bhāgwat Dharma originally. When sage Nārad went to the Shwetadweep (white island), Bhagwān himself gave the sermon of Bhāgwat Dharma to him. This island is supposed to be in Ksheer Samudra (Milky Sea) which lies to the north of Mount Meru. This geographical description is as per the ancient description of the universe. While Indians don't consider this too significant, some Western experts have tried to interpret this as Shwetadweep being out of India and thereby tried to prove that Bhakti Mārg has come to India from outside, mainly from Christianity. However, this claim is nothing short of childishness as it's a proven fact that Buddhism and Jainism existed before Christ and even they've given references of Bhāgwat Dharma or Bhakti from Hinduism in their treatises. Thus, it can be established that devotional Bhāgwat Dharma must be dated post the era of Upanishads and before Buddha.

Gitā mentions that the Bhāgwat Dharma which Shri Krishna is telling Arjun about, got lost earlier. This philosophy calls Parmeshwar as Vāsudev, Jeev (self) as Sankarshan, Man (mind) as Pradyumna and Ahankār (ego) as Aniruddha. Of this, Vāsudev is Shri Krishna's name. Sankarshan is the name of his elder brother Balaram. Pradyumna and Aniruddha are names of Krishna's son and grandson respectively. This Dharma is also called Sātvat Dharma. The Yadav race that Shri Krishna was born in was also called Sātvat. Thus, it can be interpreted that Shri Krishna who was born in this race or caste told this to his friend Arjun. This same Dharma may have existed as Nārāyaneeya or Pānchrātra Dharma earlier but later it was called Sātvat because of Shri Krishna. Later on, considering Bhagwān Shri Krishna and Arjun as reincarnations of sages Nara and Nārāyan, it must have come to be called as Bhāgwat Dharma. This is how we can establish the chronology of Bhāgwat Dharma or sect. This theory must've been established by observing the different developments and stages of evolution the sect must've gone through. Just as Buddhist or Christian religions have gone through various stages and into different branches, Bhāgwat Dharma seems to have proceeded through different stages.

While some object that Mahābhārat and all its characters are fictional, someone with an impartial and objective view would easily disagree by looking at old historical texts. There's no doubt that there's historical evidence for the events described in Mahābhārat. If we try to find out the exact period in history when Shri Krishna existed, the period of Shri Krishna, Yadav, Pāndav and the Mahābhārat War is established as the start of Kali Yug. As per chronology in Purānas, more than 5,000 years have passed since. However, if we follow the generations enlisted right from Pāndav to Shak (78 AD), there's discrepancy. Thus, going by the statement from Bhāgwat or Vishnupurān, the period of Pāndav and the Mahābhārat War can be established to around 1400 BC. Naturally, Shri Krishna must've existed around the same time and this proves that Bhāgwat Dharma must've been established roughly 1400 years before Christ. This makes it around 800 years prior to Buddha. Many argue that the Bhāgwat Dharma must've been established much later after people deified Shri Krishna from being just a man to being a reincarnation of Parabrahma. However, we don't agree with this argument. If you look at the lives of Gautam Buddha or Jesus Christ, they were considered deities and worshipped during their lifetimes. While Shri Krishna was not an ascetic like Buddha or Christ, there's no reason to believe that he was not deified during his own lifetime or at least immediately after that, especially if he had founded the Bhāgwat Dharma.

While it's clear from the above explanation that Shri Krishna's period was around 1400 BC, many Western scholars disagree with it because of another reason. They date period of Rig Veda to be no older than 1500-2000 BC and hence deny the possibility of Bhāgwat Dharma to have been founded around 1400 BC. This, according to them, is because Rig Veda was followed by Yajur Veda and Brāhmanas, then by Upanishads and Sānkhya and then by paths centered on Bhakti. If Rig Veda is assumed to have existed around 1500-2000 BC, there is not enough time for so many schools of thought to have developed and prevailed before Bhāgwat Dharma. This is why they try and claim that Bhāgwat Dharma may have developed much later, after Buddha, to prove their logic of dating Rig Veda as correct. However, this forced chronology claimed is proven wrong in the book 'Orion' (written by Lokmānya Tilak in which he's scientifically proven chronology of a myriad of historical events based on mathematical and astronomical calculations using references of constellations as quoted in the texts). As per our calculations, the period of Vedas cannot be after 4500 BC.

Even logically, if you consider this to be the period of Vedas, there appears to have been enough time for all different philosophies to have developed gradually. As the Brāhmanas subsequent to Rig Veda mention Kruttikā constellation, they must've been from around 2500 BC. If we see Upanishads, they are numerous and while some may be modern, some are very old. E.g. Language wise, Maitryupanishad appears to have been from before Pānini (the famous ancient Sanskrit Grammarian) as some phrases from it had phased out before Pānini consolidated Sanskrit Grammar. It's not one of the oldest Upanishads. It combines Sānkhya and Brahmadnyān (knowledge of Brahman) and also borrows from older Upanishads like Chhāndogya, Bruhadāranyak etc. As per the description of 'Maghā to Shravishthā constellation in the sky during Dakshinayan (Period between summer solstice and winter solstice of northern hemisphere)', the period of Maitryupanishad seems to be roughly between 1880 and 1600 BC. Whatever be the case, it also proves to predate Vedanga Jyotish (Principal text on Astrology based on Vedas) which dates to around 1200 to 1400 BC as per clear indication of constellations in both. As Upanishads like Chhāndogya are even older, we arrive at following approximate chronology – Rig Veda (around 4500 BC), Ritualistic Brāhmanas (around 2500 BC), Chhāndogya and other Upanishads founding Brahmadnyān or knowledge of Brahman (around 1600 BC). If we follow this, Bhāgwat Dharma appears to have plausibly occurred around 1400 BC (period of Shri Krishna and Mahābhārat) agreeing with its references mentioned in Buddhism. This is the period when Vedic influence reduced while that of Sutras and Smrutis began.

As we've seen above, Ritualistic school of Brāhmanas and Knowledge schools of Upanishads and Sānkhya both existed before the birth of Bhāgwat Dharma. It's unlikely for Shri Krishna to have ignored these prevalent schools of philosophies and conceptualized a path centered on devotion, without incorporating action or knowledge. Even if he had, it's lesser likely that it would've found agreement with erstwhile scholars and philosophical authorities. If you look at Jesus Christ, he too based his devotional Christianity building on similar tendencies of Jews. Showing connection with the action-oriented path given in the Old Testament suited him fine. However, in case of Shri Krishna, he had to amalgamate the three major schools of philosophy with Bhakti (devotion) and Yog (Pātanjalyog) to prove the aptitude and relevance of Bhāgwat Dharma. Going through Nārāyaneeyopākhyān reaffirms this hypothesis. As it combines 4 Vedas with Sānkhya-Yog, it is called Pānchrātra Dharma indicating five arms or branches it combines with Bhakti. While Bhāgwat Dharma thus unified all prevalent schools of philosophy with Bhakti, its purpose was not to establish importance of Bhakti among these disciplines. While there may be some who would've followed the path of devotion to take the path of asceticism, Shri Krishna himself, along with other great followers of Bhāgwat Dharma like Bheeshma, Arjun, Satyaki etc., was a great advocate of action-oriented lifestyle. The main intention of Bhāgwat Dharma was thus to achieve knowledge of Parmeshwar through Bhakti (devotion) and then continue to strive hard for welfare of the universe, just like Parmeshwar. While there had been greats like Janak who had advocated the path of selfless action without attachment, the element of Bhakti was not present. Continuing of action post knowledge was considered optional. Bhāgwat Dharma went one step ahead to prove Nishkām Karmayog (action-oriented path without attachment) to be better than Sanyās (ascetic path of inaction) while also marrying Dnyān (knowledge) and Bhakti (devotion). This is the distinctive accomplishment of Bhāgwat Dharma in history different from Smārta Dharma. The original proponents of this path – sages Nara and Nārāyan were advocates of action. Mahābhārat clearly mentions in Shānti Parva that 'Nārāyaneeya or Bhāgwat Dharma is action-oriented'. Sadly, this proactive principle of Bhāgwat Dharma got diluted later and ascetic devotion began to gain ground as seen from Bhāgwat text. Nārad Panchrātra even includes occult in Bhāgwat Dharma. Bhakti overtook action. We saw how some communalist sects have tried to prove Bhagavad Gitā to advocate renunciation while some other have tried to show dualism being promoted in Gitā.

The original form of Bhāgwat Dharma is the path of Gitā as well. Let's now try to pinpoint the chronology of original Gitā. While the period of Shri Krishna and Mahābhārat war was around 1400

BC, the same can't be said about the two principal texts of Bhāgwat Dharma – Original Bhagavad Gitā and the Original Mahābhārat epic. Establishment of any religious text doesn't happen immediately after the event and so is the case with Gitā and Mahābhārat. Current version of Mahābhārat mentions that it was first told by Vaishampāyan to Janamejay (great grandson of Pāndav) and the same was told by Sauti to Shaunak when the text 'Bhārat' took form for the first time. Whatever be the case, we can safely assume that Gitā and Mahābhārat texts were first drafted within 500 years of the actual events. If you observe Buddhist texts, they've appeared much sooner after Buddha's death. As with any epic, it's not sufficient to only describe the glory of the lead character. It's also important to cover the ethical or moral angle of any actions performed by them or others. Moreover, religion and ethics didn't exist separately back then and hence it was almost imperative that a critical evaluation of various deeds was included in this epic. Most prevalent Vedic texts were promoting asceticism to some or great extent and thus it was also necessary to justify the brave actions of the lead characters of the story. The part that covers this ethical justification of their actions is the original Gitā. This dates Gitā to have first surfaced around 900 BC. It became essential that the Karmayog advocated in it finds agreement with and unifies the prevalent scriptures of Dharma – Ritualistic Vedas, Knowledge-centric Upanishads, Kāpilsānkhya, Yog and Bhakti. The argument that – Vedānta and Mimāmsā (disciplines that have developed later) have been introduced in Gitā afterwards – is false. While these organized disciplines were established later, the concepts in them have been ancient; and these concepts have been mentioned in Gitā. We agree that there could have been some modifications in the original version of Gitā to keep up with the ongoing developments in the philosophies. In fact, this is how we have concluded in an earlier part that current Gitā and Brahma Sutras have cross references. However, as Gitā has always been considered a pillar of ancient scriptures from a long time, these changes couldn't have been made to the fundamentals. Had this been the case, the status of Gitā as one of the three pillars of Prasthānatrayi (three texts to go through) would've been jeopardized. That is not the case. Thus, we conclude that while there may have been minor changes, those changes must have been to supplement, rather than modify the essence of original Gitā.

Part 5: Chronology of Current Gitā

After establishing the period of original Gitā to be around 900 BC (some 500 years after the origin of Bhāgwat Dharma), we saw how this Bhāgwat Dharma changed from originally being action-oriented to later being Bhakti (devotion) oriented. There's not much information available about the original Mahābhārat and Gitā other than what we discussed. Similar was the case with Current form of Gitā and Mahābhārat but many great historians took a lot of efforts to establish concrete facts about them. We've briefly discussed these here, wherein we've discussed the proofs pointing to both Mahābhārat as well as Gitā separately; lest someone finds those about Mahābhārat a bit ambiguous.

Chronology of Mahābhārat: Mahābhārat is a voluminous scripture described to be composed of 100,000 verses. The current versions of Mahābhārat derived from original Bhārat have slightly more/lesser number of verses but not too far from the said number. Let's see the documentary evidences helping us date the current epic Mahābhārat composed of 18 Parvas (books):

1. The 18-book epic and Harivansha (a book describing the life and ancestry of Krishna) had been taken to the islands of Java and Bali (modern day Indonesia) before 5th or 6th century A.D. where they've been translated in the local language Kavi. This translated epic made up of 8 Parvas borrows a few Sanskrit verses. Looking at this, we can assume that the current version of Mahābhārat must have originated around 2 centuries before that or at least before 3rd or 4th century A.D.
2. A rock inscription from the period of Gupta dynasty from 445 A.D. has been discovered which clearly mentions the Mahābhārat text made up of 100,000 verses. Thus, we can safely say that it existed before this period.
3. Renowned ancient Sanskrit poet Bhās is chronicled to predate Kālidās and Chānakya. Thus, he couldn't have been more modern

than 2nd or 3rd century A.D. His works are based on Mahābhārat and Harivansha thus pointing to the fact that these scriptures were written before his time.

4. Buddhist texts have established that a renowned Buddhist poet Ashwaghosh existed around 78 A.D. Both his Sanskrit epics named 'Buddhacharit' and 'Saundarānand' mention stories from Mahābhārat. Moreover, Vajrasoochikopanishad, an Upanishad credited to him, borrows a few verses from Harivansha as well as Mahābhārat. This points that Mahābhārat was prevalent before 78 A.D.
5. Āshwalāyanguhyasutras mention Bhārat and Mahābhārat separately. Baudhāyan Dharma Sutras also have one verse borrowed from Yayāti Upākhyān of Mahābhārat. Baudhāyan also mentions Vishnusahasranam (1000 names of Vishnu) and a verse from Gitā. Baudhāyan is dated to around 400 B.C. thus pointing out that Mahābhārat and Gitā must've existed before that.
6. Mahābhārat mentions the 10 avatars (reincarnations) of Vishnu which doesn't include Buddha and mentions Hans (swan) as the 1st avatar and directly Kalki as the 10th avatar who is predicted to come in future. However, in description of Kali Yug in future, it's mentioned that there would be 'Edook' instead of temples. Edook is a monument which was erected by burying a body part of Buddha such as his hair, tooth etc. Sri Lanka and Myanmar (Burma) have such monuments. This indicates that current Mahābhārat may have originated after Buddha but before he was included as 9th avatar of Vishnu. While Mahābhārat mentions the word Buddha and Prati Buddha, those are not used for depicting Gautam Buddha but to denote an enlightened being (meaning of Buddha is 'an enlightened being' which later came to be used to denote Gautam Buddha colloquially).
7. The mention of constellations is an important clue for determining the period of Mahābhārat. As Mahābhārat has no mention of constellations from Aries and Taurus signs (which were introduced to India by Greeks due to Alexander), it can be dated to a period before Alexander. Even more significant is a conclusion drawn from

astronomic reference given in Anugeetā which mathematically points current Mahābhārat to have been written in 5th century BC.

8. Mr. Rāvbahādur Vaidya has mentioned in his book that Megasthenes, a Greek lawyer who was a member of the retinue of King Chandragupta Maurya (320 B.C.), was aware of stories from Mahābhārat. Translation of his stories in German and English language mention Heracles who appears to be none other than Shri Krishna. He was worshipped by Shaurseni people from Mathura. Heracles was cited to be 15th in line from the primordial ancestor Dionysus, similar to how Shri Krishna is described as 15th in line from Daksha Prajāpati in Mahābhārat. Many other descriptions – like that of a few mystics and of ants that could dig out gold – are taken exactly from Mahābhārat. This proves that not only was Mahābhārat prevalent but also that devotion of Shri Krishna was prevalent during the time of Megasthenes.

The above evidences are mutually exclusive which undoubtedly prove that current Mahābhārat was existent in 5th century B.C. There may have been additions or deletions but the core epic existed then and current Gitā was an inherent part of it. Original Gitā may be older as seen in Part 4 of this chapter. Let us now see separate evidences that help in dating current Gitā.

1. Among the critiques and commentaries on Gitā available today, Shānkarbhāshya is the oldest. Writings of Shankarāchārya indicate that Mahābhārat and Gitā were considered gospel during his time. His birth year is established as 788 A.D. as per a communalist verse. However, our opinion is that this period should be 100 years earlier at 688 A.D. as another account of his life mentions that he attained Guhā Pravesh or Samādhi in 720 A.D. at the age of 32. He's also mentioned and criticized many commentaries on Gitā before him which indicates that Gitā was prevalent at least 3-4 centuries before him.
2. Mr. Telang has proved that Gitā was known to Kālidās and Bānabhatta and their works also show inspiration from a few styles used in Gitā. Both have been dated at least before 550 A.D. thus indicating that Gitā has been around at least from before that.

3. Mahābhārat from Java islands mentions verses from Gitā in Bheeshma Parva with word-by-word Sanskrit verses from current Gitā. This makes current Gitā to have existed at least a couple of centuries before 5th century A.D.
4. Vishnu Purān, Padma Purān etc. contain other versions of Gitā inspired from the original. Most ancient of these Purānas were not later than 2nd century A.D. For these to imitate Gitā, it must have existed a couple of centuries before them. Thus, Gitā must've been around in 1st century A.D.
5. Poet Bhās predated Kālidās and Bānabhatta and he has borrowed a verse from Gitā in his work. This puts Gitā before him i.e. before 1st – 2nd century B.C.
6. Mr. Tryambak Gurunāth Kale has proved with evidence that Gitā not only existed before 2nd century BC, but before Baudhāyangruhyashesha Sutras as they refer to verses in Gitā. They also show ways of worshipping Vasudev (Krishna). Baudhāyan appears to belong to 4th century B.C. while current Mahābhārat and current Gitā seem to belong to 5th century B.C.
7. The references we've seen till now have been from Vedic tradition. However, there are other references of Gitā in Buddhist texts. While it's been proven by Indian and European authors that Bhāgwat Dharma existed before Buddha, it doesn't necessarily prove that Gitā existed before Buddha. Ancient Buddhist texts have a clear mention that Four Vedas, Vedanga, Vyākaran (grammar), Jyotish (astrology), Itihās (history), Nighantu etc. existed before Gautam Buddha. Thus, it's clear that Vedic Dharma predated Buddha. The path initiated by Buddha, although didn't believe in existence of a soul, was based on the Sanyās path from Upanishads. During the reign of emperor Ashok (3rd century BC), Buddhist monks had transformed from being forest dwellers like a rhino (as described in primal Buddhist texts Suttanipāta and Mahāvagga) to travel as missionaries to China, Alexandria and Greece. The question is how and when did the followers of Buddhism transform from being completely ascetic as advised by Gautama Buddha (authentic Buddhism known as Theravāda or 'Buddhism of the old') to being active, charitable and missionary (Mahāyān Buddhism as followed

by the newer generations). Ashwaghosh (a famous Buddhist poet) has written an epic Saundarānand wherein Buddha tells Nand after he achieves enlightenment – "Your work is accomplished. Now you have no duty for yourself. Hence, you should now work for charity with stoic calm". Buddha's teaching of adopting complete ascetic life as found in ancient Buddhist texts and this advice credited to him by Ashwaghosh are in stark contrast. Moreover, this advice bears strong resemblance (textual and contextual) with Shri Krishna's advice to Arjun in Gitā – "Now you have nothing left for yourself. Hence, you should perform your duties without attachment" (Gitā 3.17,19). This shows that Ashwaghosh has borrowed this verse from Bhagavad Gitā as we've established earlier that Mahābhārat also existed before him. Additionally, a Tibetan Buddhist text called Tāraknāth mentions that Shri Krishna & Ganesh were the inspiration that made Rāhulbhadra, the Guru of Nāgārjun (founder of Mahāyān Buddhism), to improve upon ascetic path of Buddhism into action-oriented path of Mahāyān. This shows that Bhagavad Gitā was the reason behind conversion of ascetic way of Buddhism into action-oriented way and this has been substantiated by Buddhist poets. Nāgārjun is dated to roughly 100 B.C. and it's safe to assume that Mahāyān Buddhism must've been founded during Emperor Ashok's reign. Thus, current Bhagavad Gitā must've been written before Ashok or Mahāyān Buddhism i.e. at least before 3rd century B.C.

Considering all the above stated independent pieces of evidence, current Bhagavad Gitā can be dated roughly to 5th century B.C. Original Gitā would have been originated a few centuries earlier as discussed previously.

Part 6: Gitā and Buddhist Texts

While we gave references of Buddhist texts in the earlier part to establish the period of current Gitā; it is essential to do a comparative account with similarities and differences between Gitā and Buddhist texts, in order to understand the significance of the evidence. It's true that action-oriented nature of a knowledgeable person is unique to Gitā. However, if we keep this characteristic aside for a bit, all the other qualities of a Sthitapradnya (someone firm in wisdom or someone with stoic calm) in Gitā have striking resemblance to the description of an Arhat (enlightened Buddhist monk). Both are described as calm, free of attachments, free of ego and stoic. There are many textual similarities between Gitā and various texts of Buddhism as well. While earlier there was no tool to find the reason behind this similarity or to establish whether these thoughts are original to Buddhism or to Gitā, new evidence has clarified this. Let's now see what it tells us.

It is a well-known and established fact that Jainism and Buddhism have branched out from Vedic Dharma for philosophical differences. While there's a lot of debate about the actual year of death of Gautam Buddha, it is conclusively fixed at 483 B.C. when he was 80 years old. Whichever date we take, it's clear that Vedic Dharma had attained its completion well before this period. Many Buddhist texts depict that Buddha entered into many a philosophical debate with erstwhile Vedic Brāhman scholars, defeating them and initiating many of them into Buddhism. Just like Gitā and a few Upanishads like Kathopanishad, Buddha also deemed ritualistic path as inferior. It is thus clear, that Buddhism evolved after firm establishment of Karmakānd (ritual centric) and Dnyānkānd (knowledge centric) as separate paths, in order to achieve improvements. As with any improvement, some of the old ways are retained while some are changed. Let's see this with the context of Buddhism. As Buddhist way is predominantly ascetic, we shall first consider Sanyās path vis-à-vis Buddhism and then the Familial path.

If we see Vedic Sanyās Dharma, it mainly believes that all transactions in the materialistic world are born of desire and hence a cause of sorrow. Hence, to escape this and to escape the cycle of death and rebirth one must renounce familial life and focus one's mind on the eternal Brahman which lies within us in the form of Ātman (soul). While Buddha agreed with most of the concepts of Vedic Dharma, he clearly denied existence of an eternal Parabrahma or any entity of that sort at the base of the universe. He claimed that Ātmā (soul) or Brahman (absolute) is nothing but an illusion and hence no one should waste time indulging in its pursuits. If these are considered unreal, the whole concept of Dharma should ideally collapse as there wouldn't exist any eternal principle, thus rendering everything transient. Shankarāchārya contested this very point to defeat Buddhist thoughts. However, we shall not delve into that and only focus on what Buddha explained in his philosophy. He agreed with two things – (1) Due to effects of Karma, body (as Nāmroope or name forms and not soul) has to be reborn in the universe of material world and (2) This cycle of death and rebirth is immersed in sorrow and one must escape this to achieve permanent calm or happiness called Nirvāna. Once the existence of sorrow and the need to escape it are accepted, the important question from Vedic Dharma about how to attain absolute happiness remains to be answered. As Brahman is considered an illusion by Buddha, knowledge of Brahman as a path to attain eternal happiness is out of question. Buddha provides an answer to this question as follows: Just as a doctor cures an illness by finding out the root cause of the illness and eliminating it, this sorrow of familial life can be eliminated by (3) Understanding the cause of sorrow and (4) Assuming a path that would eliminate the root cause of sorrow. Once we delve into the cause of sorrow, we observe that desire is the root cause and this desire is the residue left after the death of an individual that leads to rebirth of new bodies. The only path to escape this cycle of rebirth is to completely eliminate desire through restraint of the senses, meditation and renunciation to assume the life of an ascetic or a monk. Buddha has declared that this ascetic life of detachment is the only way to attain permanent calm and happiness. In conclusion, instead of indulging in rituals or knowledge of Brahman, one must identify and understand four Ārya Satya (noble truths) namely: Dukkha (sorrow and its existence), Samuday (its cause or origin), Nirodh (necessity to eliminate the sorrow) and Mārg (the ascetic path of eliminating it). While Buddhism is based on these 4 pillars instead of the Ātmadnyān (knowledge of the self) from Upanishads, the fourth truth or the path of eliminating sorrow is identical to the path of Sanyās given in Upanishads. While Upanishads call the state of mind as Ātmanishtha that involves merging of one's soul with the absolute; Buddha calls it simply Nirvāna meaning end or extinguishing of desires. As there's no soul or the absolute, who or what would one merge with? As there's no possibility of rebirth after this, Nirvāna can't be equated to death but is called death of deaths. Description of this in Buddhist texts is directly borrowed from Upanishads like Bruhadāranyak. Thus, in conclusion, while denying the existence of soul or absolute, Buddha accepted everything else from the path of Sanyās from Vedic Dharma. Needless to say, as Vedic Dharma preceded Buddha, these thoughts are originally from Vedic Dharma.

Let's now see what Gautam Buddha said about familial life. One must remember that Buddhism is not predominantly action oriented even though it is based on aspects like existence of sorrow in material life. The essence of Buddha's teaching is that one can never attain permanent happiness or enlightenment while leading a familial life. However, it's not that it doesn't discuss household life. He called those who surrendered to Buddha, his Dharma and his Sangha (congregation) without becoming a monk as 'Upāsak' (worshippers). Buddha didn't believe in traditional rituals or Chāturvarnya (four tiered) social system. He advised that everyone should follow Panchmahāyadnya (five rituals) and must also observe Non-violence, no lying, non-stealing, no adultery and no intoxicants which are called Panchsheel (Five precepts) as moral code. It's evident that Buddha borrowed these from Vedic texts and he also praised old Brāhmanas in his writings. He has compared monkhood and familial life saying that familial life would at best lead to radiant divine afterlife. However, it would never result in an escape from the cycle of death and rebirth. He stated that, to achieve it one must quit being a householder and take up ascetic life of monkhood.

Mahāveer was another contemporary and the last of the Tirthankara of Jainism who achieved enlightenment before Buddha. His sermon was similar to that of Buddha. However, he did believe in the existence of soul and suggested stricter observances such as giving up clothes, following strict non-violence etc. While Jainism observes strict vegetarianism, Buddha allowed eating meat of already dead animals as long as they were not killed for consumption. He also banned nudity calling it a crime while some sects of Jainism follow nudity. In essence, while Buddha definitively advised asceticism and monkhood, he was against severe bodily practices.

Other than the concept of Brahman (absolute) and Ātman (soul), all other concepts and practices of Buddhism thus appear identical to Vedic path of Sanyās. In addition to this, Buddhism also borrowed many Jātaka tales (stories related to previous births, mainly of Gautam Buddha) similar to tales in Hinduism. There are many other such anecdotes and examples where Buddhist and Jain texts have literally taken sentences, verses or even paragraphs from ancient Vedic texts and Mahābhārat as well. However, unlike Upanishads, Brahma Sutras and Manu Smriti which are clearly older than Buddha, period of Mahābhārat can't be definitively placed before him as there is a mention of Buddhist 'Edook' (monument which was erected by burying a body part of Buddha such as his hair, tooth etc.) in current Mahābhārat. Naturally, the same follows for Gitā as it's a part of Mahābhārat. Thus, we shall find out if there's any way to explain the similarity between Gitā or Mahābhārat and Buddhist texts.

The original version of Buddhism that didn't believe in existence of a soul and that insisted on ascetic lifestyle didn't persist for long. There was a lot of philosophical debate within the Sangha (congregations) and they got divided into various sub sects after the death of Gautam Buddha. Many have today begun to believe that Buddha only denied existence of soul to ensure that his followers don't indulge in empty debates about the soul and instead focus on making themselves detached while achieving self-control. There's a plethora of different thought processes and opinions that developed within Buddhism supporting or contrasting these which we need not delve into. What we shall focus on is the story of the rise of Mahāyān Buddhism.

As long as Buddha was alive, there was no question of following the path of Bhakti (devotion) to achieve unity with Parmeshwar (almighty); firstly, as its existence was denied by Buddha and secondly because Buddha's presence was so empowering that no one considered the need to seek a supreme authority other than him. However, later it became necessary to find out an alternate path to ascetic monkhood that would be accessible to common people. Alternatively, common followers of Buddhism may have used Vedic path of Bhakti to worship Gautam Buddha. Subsequent to Gautam Buddha's Nirvāna, many started to regard him as truly immortal and advised worshipping him in any form as a way to attain enlightenment. Another belief said that even if someone has spent their lives doing good deeds, they must surrender to Buddha for earning a place in heaven. A scripture states that Buddha mercifully formulated this alternate path knowing that everyone has different nature, capacity and knowledge. While these thoughts were being developed, it was also not possible to completely deny the adoption of monkhood that was suggested by Buddha himself as necessary to attain Nirvāna. Hence, a line of thought developed that advocated that monks need not 'live alone in forests like a rhinoceros' (as written in Suttanipāta) but must perform missionary and charitable activities with abstinence of desire. This further took the form of Mahāyān sect which says that it's not impossible to attain Nirvāna while leading a householder's life. Close inspection of this would easily show that these thoughts are contradictory to Buddha's original sermon of following asceticism. However, this new thought began getting wider acceptance. In fact, the widespread prevalence of Buddhism in China, Tibet, Japan etc. is thanks to this alternative path of Mahāyān sect. According to Dr. Kern, the rise of Mahāyān Buddhism must've occurred towards the second half of 3rd century B.C. However, we feel that this must've been even earlier; as a rock inscription from 230 B.C. (during the reign of Emperor Ashok) very briefly describes the ascetic path of Buddhist monkhood but elaborately shows the action-oriented path of Buddhism. Naturally, we feel this path must've already become prevalent before this and Nāgārjun was not the founder but a leading propagator of Mahāyān Buddhism.

Studying this sequence of events in detail makes it clear that this conversion from the original atheist, ascetic path to the action oriented, devotional path has some strong reason outside of Buddhism as it doesn't logically follow from it. The search to find out the reason inevitably leads us to Bhagavad Gitā. From the erstwhile prevalent paths, Jainism and the path of Upanishads were purely ascetic. While Pashupat or Shaiva sects were based in devotion, there was no institution other than Gitā where there was a combination of devotion and action as we've explained in the 11th chapter. In Bhagavad Gitā, Bhagwān Shri Krishna calls himself the father of everyone (Gitā 9.17). He's also said that he appears on earth whenever the world needs him to protect Dharma (Gitā 4.6-8). These statements are a few among many others almost identical to the ones credited to Buddha in various Buddhist texts. We saw a couple of them in a preceding paragraph of this part. Thus, it can be concluded that just as original Buddhism was based on erstwhile path of Sanyās from Upanishads except the belief in existence of soul; this new path of Mahāyān Buddhism was based on the action-oriented path proposed in Gitā. However, this conclusion is not only based on interpretation. As we saw briefly earlier, a book written by Tāraknāth, a Tibetan Buddhist mentions that Rāhulbhadra (Guru of Nāgārjun, one of the key proponents of Mahāyān Buddhism) got inspired from the ideas of knowledgeable greats Krishna and Ganesh. While this book is not very ancient, it's based on evidence of ancient times. Moreover, no Buddhist follower or author would falsely credit someone outside their sect while writing about principles of their own sect. As Bhagavad Gitā was the only text ascribed to Bhagwān Shri Krishna that advocates action-oriented path, it's pretty clear that Gitā was prevalent before the rise of Mahāyān sect. From all the discussion we've had in this part, following points can be clearly observed:

1. Improbability of action oriented and devotional Mahāyān sect to naturally develop from original Buddhist thoughts that didn't believe in existence of Brahman or Ātman and strongly advocated ascetic life
2. Clear mention of Shri Krishna by authors of Mahāyān Buddhism regarding development of their sect
3. Striking resemblance between principles of Mahāyān Buddhism and devotional, action-oriented principles from Bhagavad Gitā
4. Absence of action-oriented nature in Buddhist, Jain or other contemporary Vedic sects

These conclusively establish that Bhāgwat Dharma existed before origin of Mahāyān Buddhism and Gitā was almost unanimously accepted in the society. Mahāyān sect thus seems to have been inspired mainly from Gitā than from traditional Buddhist thoughts. It also agrees perfectly with the dating we showed of current Mahābhārat and Gitā in earlier parts.

Part 7: Gitā and Christian Bible

After tracing and establishing origin of Bhāgwat Dharma to 14th century B.C. and showing evidence of Gitā to have inspired the rise of action oriented Mahāyān Buddhism (which originated before 3rd century B.C.), it should ideally refute all claims about Gitā having been inspired from Christian Bible. In fact, all the efforts taken by these speculators about establishing similarity between Gitā and Bible hit them back as a boomerang once we clearly establish the period of Gitā well before Christ. However, even today some write-ups still argue about Gitā having been inspired from Bible. To settle this doubt, let's discuss a few research findings on this topic.

The New Testament of Christianity was founded in order to make amendments in the Yehudi (Jewish) Bible or The Old Testament. The word God is translated as 'Eloah' in Yehudi language ('Ilah' in Arabic). However, as per the guidelines set by Moses, the main deity worshipped is 'Jehovah'. The word Jehovah is not originally Yehudi but adopted from the Hebrew word Yahweh, which in turn is derived from Sanskrit 'Yahvah', a word used in Rig Veda for denoting the fire god. This is conclusively proven by Western scholars. Jewish people do not follow any idol worship but rather perform offerings in the sacrificial fire, much like the ritualistic action-oriented path of Karmakānd from Vedic religions. On the contrary, Christianity was originally ascetic and strongly advocated a life of renunciation. The rise of Christianity from Judaism is like the evolution of Dnyānkānd (knowledge centric path) from Karmakānd (ritual centric path). However, unlike Dnyānkānd which evolved over a period of many centuries slowly and sequentially from Karmakānd, Christianity evolved suddenly. Sometime in 2nd century B.C., a small sect of people called Essene suddenly appeared in Jewish history. These people were against the ritualistic practices of Judaism and spent their time meditating and leading an ascetic life. Jesus Christ was a follower of this Essene sect which is evident from their mention in The New Testament, although this is debated among historians. The main monastery of these Essenes was near the Dead

Sea. Whether Jesus was a follower of the Essene sect or not, the original guidelines given by him bear strong resemblance with the philosophy of Essenes. The sudden appearance of this sect on the Jewish landscape is a mystery, as it can't be seen as derived from Jewish ideology. In social sciences, appearance of any new concept happens gradually from the old philosophy. If a completely new philosophy is suddenly found in an existing society, it's generally concluded that it's inspired from some ideology belonging to a foreign territory. When old Christians faced this question, they thought the Essenes to have evolved from Greek Pythagorean philosophy. Modern scientific research proves this wrong and links it strongly with Buddhist philosophy.

If we compare Buddhist texts and the New Testament of Bible, we find remarkable resemblance in many anecdotes. Bible mentions that when Jesus Christ was tempted by Satan, he fasted consecutively for 40 days before attaining enlightenment. Similarly, Gautam Buddha was tempted by the demon Mara when he fasted consecutively for 49 days (7 weeks) before overcoming him and being enlightened. Many other accounts like walking on water, glowing like the sun and liberating thieves and prostitutes are common to both Christian and Buddhist texts. If we delve deeper, there are hundreds of such similar anecdotes, big and small. There are two books written by Mr. Arthur Lily called 'Buddhism in Christendom' and 'Buddha and Buddhism' which talk about these connections in detail. There are only two possibilities that arise – 1. Both philosophies arose in separate geographies independently and 2. Jesus Christ got inspired from followers of Buddhism. From these two possibilities, the first possibility is dismissed easily by a few observations. Any new concept arises gradually from existing traditions and we can trace its path of evolution showing relevant milestones. E.g. we can show how Vedic ritualistic path gradually led to Upanishads and how this further developed into Bhakti path (devotion), Pātanjalyog and finally Buddhism. The rise of Christianity in Judaism is so sudden that no such gradual development could be traced. Moreover, the resemblance between Christianity and Buddhism is so uncanny that it's difficult to imagine two such similar traditions and practices developing independently. Even then, we could still accept this possibility if erstwhile population had no access to Buddhist practices. However, since the time of Alexander and later during the reign of Emperor Ashok (around 250 B.C.) Buddhist monks have been reported to have spread Buddhism to as far West as Alexandria and Greece. Inscriptions from the era of Emperor Ashok mention that he had made a truce with the Yehudi people and Greek king Antiochus. The Bible also states that a few Eastern scholars had visited Jerusalem at the time of Jesus Christ's birth. All these evidences show that Buddhism had entered the land of Yehudi people in around 2nd century B.C. This easily leads us to understand how it must've inspired the Essenes and subsequently Jesus Christ to develop Christianity. This explains the evolution of ascetic path of Christianity in the land of Judaism which centered on ritualistic practices with Buddhism being the missing link. There's another anecdote that supports this. Bible has no record of how Jesus Christ spent his life between the age 12 and 30. It's natural to assume that he must've spent these years of youth in gaining knowledge, meditation and travel. It's quite likely that he may have encountered Buddhist monks who had travelled to those parts of the world. A Nepalese monastery has a clear account of Jesus having visited them to gain knowledge of Buddhism during the same period. Even if some of these evidences turn out to be false or manufactured, numerous such historical records point to the fact that Jesus Christ or Christianity had access to Buddhist philosophy and practices and it's unlikely that their ascetic, devotional path developed independently in Jewish land without any connection to Buddhism.

In conclusion, we could chronicle the turn of events as follows. Karma Mārg (ritualistic) of Mimāmsak, Naishkarmya (Action oriented path of knowledge with detachment) practiced by the likes of Janak, Dnyān Nishthā and Sanyās (Knowledge path and Asceticism) from Upanishads, Pātanjalyog involving restraint of senses and Pānchrātra, Bhāgwat Dharma or Bhakti Mārg (path of devotion) are all part of the Vedic tradition or philosophy. From this, Buddha developed his path of renunciation by being inspired from Pātanjalyog and Sanyās, rejecting Knowledge of Brahman, path of Bhakti and path of Action. Future generations of Buddhist followers included Nishkām Karma (Action without attachment) and Bhakti (devotion) in it and developed Mahāyān Buddhism and spread it to distant geographies. This introduced the ascetic principles in the ritual-centric path of Judaism in the West. This path coupled with his idea of devotion made Jesus Christ give birth to Christianity. Once we observe this, it's clear that not only did Bhagavad Gitā not borrow anything from Christianity, but Christianity seems to have borrowed the concepts like seeing everyone as oneself, devotion, non-enmity and renunciation directly from Buddhism and in turn from Vedic Dharma. Hinduism never needed to look elsewhere for these concepts which were original to their Vedic tradition.

With this, we conclude our Appendix chapter of peripheral analysis of Bhagavad Gitā.

Author Background

Sarang Tilak, an active spiritual seeker, is also a Management graduate from Jamnalal Bajaj Institute of Management Studies, Mumbai. Having over 15 years of experience in the corporate field, his area of expertise is Sales, Marketing & Strategy. He has a Black belt in Keimoudo®, a Martial Arts system that helps in physical, mental and spiritual growth of an individual. In his spare time, he loves writing, driving, riding, traveling & living life to the fullest. He lives in Thane, Mumbai.

He can be reached on tilak.sarang@gmail.com